Imagine if, every Thursday, your shoes exploded if you tied them the usual way. This happens to us all the time with computers, and nobody thinks of complaining.

Jef Raskin

Claude Roeltgen

Everything you always wanted to know about
Information Technology.

A look behind the scenes.

IT's hidden face

Table of contents

Dr. Andreas Resch
Managing Partner Modalis (Germany)
Former CIO Bayer AG
Member of US CIO Hall of Fame (2008)

Foreword by Dr. Andreas Resch

Where can you experience something like this? On the one hand, having an enormous impact on almost all areas of daily life, a strong pervasion of free time and the job—and on the other hand, fundamental misunderstandings about interdependencies, totally contradicting expectations and many misapprehensions. Information Technology offers this every day, again and again. The big things are present everywhere—in aerospace and navigation, at wars, and in hospital operating theatres. But it's also indispensable with the small things—music, TV, telephones, storing appointments, and writing letters. And at the same time, full of surprises, unexpected events, difficulties to evaluate costs, and timeframes.

When engineers began to build machines that were designed to abate the work from our brains, they bequeathed a special challenge to us: do we sufficiently understand the technology that processes the information, the material of understanding? As far as machines have taken over the movement of arms and legs, we could get an intuitive understanding of interdependencies. Of course, there remains a certain astonishment as to why heavy planes can remain in the air, but the basics of lift and the effect of engines are understandable. We basically understand motors, saws, and power stations. With IT, this is all still somewhat different. There, the predictable computer creates a quintessentially unpredictable world.

Books which contribute to a better understanding of IT should, in fact, be available en masse. I'm not talking about user guides that help reduce the number of application errors. I'm talking about the effort to develop a public understanding for the interdependencies in the background. At the very least, we should cultivate a rudimentary reliable intuition to support what IT can deliver, what preconditions must be fulfilled, and how a thing roughly works. But there is hardly any reading material about technology's inner life, from the engine room of IT, this foreign yet so proximal world.

This is what makes this book so precious. It elucidates many of the reasons why things are not as they were expected, why things still don't work the way they were announced. But it also explains how it can be better understood and, therefore, be better managed. The book builds bridges; it connects worlds and, therefore, prevents small incidents at the frontier between technology and applications, as well as hard confrontations between huge expectations and complex projects.

In other industrial sectors, the maturity level of technology and the penetration of application areas were linked closely together. The generator has made its way into every bicycle as a dynamo at the moment when technology was mature and didn't have any major surprises. Cars and washing machines have spread over the globe in the same way as their technology became mature and manageable. To some respect, this has happened differently in IT. Information Technology is, at the same time, a very young industry with permanently changing standards, unexpected innovation, and surprising mistakes. At the same time, it has already diversified very strongly and has nested in the most diverse areas of life. It is very immature and, at the same time, very widespread. A problematic mix.

Claude Roeltgen has made an important contribution about how the disparities can be managed better. The one who has read his book will be wondering much less, will understand more and judge better, will be better prepared, and will be able to react in a wiser way. The one who has read his book will be less a fascinated victim of technology and more an up-to-date epicure of technology, which is supposed to be a favor to our brains.

Mike O'Dell
CIO at Pacific Coast Building Products
www.paccoast.com
Chairperson ASUG (Americas' SAP
Users' Group)

Foreword by Mike O'Dell

As a CIO (Chief Information Officer) with years of experience as a business manager, I'm in the unique position to personally understand the vicious cycle caused by technology and the business not understanding each other. Claude Roeltgen tells us why we find ourselves in this cycle, and notes that the stakes are high—IT projects can often be over budget or time, and/or haven't solved the actual problems they were trying to address.

When I was a plant engineer, and later an operational manager, I experienced the frustration of technology being implemented for technology's sake. Technologists didn't understand the negative impact their decisions were having on the business. Conversely, some on the business side didn't understand how one little change requested by the business could affect the entire IT ecosystem.

While it's generally accepted that IT professionals need to understand the business they're serving, Claude Roeltgen tells us that, in order to together create relevant solutions, it's now time for the reverse to be true.

To end the cycle of business demanding too much too soon, which results in poor-quality IT solutions and/or failed projects that cost "too much" and take "too long", IT needs to learn to educate the business about what's truly involved in any IT solution. Too often, the business's expectations have been set by "plug-n-play" product marketing, while the reality of implementation, maintenance and support processes tell a different story.

Conversely, IT departments by and large are interested in technology, not business. But at Pacific Coast Building Products (PCBP), our number one rule in IT is "Never forget; we are in the Building Materials Business". We use technology as a tool to help the business. We never use it "just because we can". And while educating business people about IT is a worthy goal, we've gone even further by pulling business people into IT roles.

As Claude tells us, because life in an IT department is about solving problems quickly, communication and quality often suffer. At PCBP, we follow his advice by concentrating on the communication piece. For instance, rather than working with the business, then going away to solve the problem in isolation, only to discover three months later that the implemented solution isn't what the business wanted, we shorten the cycle and bridge communication by: working with the business, creating a rough working model, then gathering feedback from the business in this early stage.

This communication process breaks the problem down into nibbles. As Claude postulates, fixing the communication can assuage the quality and time issues. Because over time, the new cycle of learning about each other becomes pervasive, shortening future project times.

This all starts with IT educating the business about what IT does, as well as understanding the business. If you are a business manager who needs to work successfully with IT, or if you are an IT professional who needs to be able to explain why something can indeed be installed in 10 minutes but that success demands many more steps before and after that, this book is for you.

Everything you always wanted to know about IT

All around us, there is an unknown, hidden world; it is so proximal, it keeps millions of people busy, but from the outside, it is totally mysterious. This world is the engine rooms of Information Technology and of IT departments in companies. Surprisingly, this extraordinarily exciting world hasn't issued any reports about its inner workings. Until now.

This book is a translation of the second edition of "Eine Million oder ein Jahr," originally published with large success in German language. It was well-received by the press. As IT moves extremely fast, things change quickly; therefore, the book that you hold in your hands right now is not a one-to-one translation. There is a time gap of more than one year between the writing of the second German edition and its translation into English.

To make things clear, this is not a guide about how to utilize a computer. It is a snapshot of the state of IT and the challenges of an IT department prepared for laymen readers. So far, it is the first and only book with such an approach.

One reader of the first edition wrote at amazon.de: *"The book closes an important gap in the communication between users and providers in the professional*

IT environment." The German management portal ephorie remarked, *"This book should be handed out to every new PC user together with the Support-Hotline."* One CIO colleague of mine called the first edition *"a really excellent description of the real challenges of IT"* and said this about the second one: *"This book is, to my knowledge, the only one that documents the practical challenges for an IT manager in a very structured manner. There are plenty of 'Success Stories' of some IT managers in pertinent books and magazines, but most of the time it can be perceived that they have been written by consultants (or managers, who would prefer to be consultants) who are not in charge of the daily business. There is always the impression that there is a lot of wishful thinking instead of reality."* I received a lot of feedback of this kind, and the book was even presented in a TV talk show.

Let's begin

Again, a program has crashed. Again, the PC is frozen; not even the mouse moves. "What on earth did I do wrong?" you are asking yourself, slowly but surely becoming frustrated. The only correct answer to that question would be "Nothing," but there is no one to tell you this. Computers should work in all circumstances, but they don't, and this is almost never the user's fault. The only way to avoid this situation would be to constantly have an IT expert available to you.

The Information Technology (IT) is an impenetrable and ever-growing jungle for a layman. The computer systems that are used in the business need to be compared to a fragile ecosystem. The common man looks at an IT expert with a mix of respect and compassion.

Most people think the world of computers is treacherous. Everything is so complicated, inscrutable, and—for some people—even menacing. Since the computer has become a massive part of our daily life, renouncing it would be neither possible nor desirable, so taking a discerning look behind the scenes is worth it. It's profitable to understand why this world is so imperfect.

After growing wildly for years, the field of computing appears to be reaching its infancy.

John Pierce

A gap the size of the Grand Canyon exists between the computer user's expectations and that what an IT department can effectively do. Business computer users lack basic knowledge about the specificities of the IT world. Electronics and computers are everywhere around us, but to talk about a high maturity grade of that industry is simply nonsense. Later in the book, I will describe the situation as "storm-and-stress" behavior. A renowned colleague of mine goes even further and describes the situation as an "infantile stadium."

It is important to me to close the massive gap between the understanding of laymen and the expertise of IT professionals. It is obvious that IT experts need to master their own universe and understand the business in the company they work for. On the other hand, users should endeavor to understand the specificities of the IT world. That they don't is one of the main reasons for the comprehension problems that we face.

Too often, we hear from our users in the business that a task should be done at the *"push of a button."* Many misunderstandings between IT experts and users are based on this misjudgment. The tendency of IT experts (who are of a rather calm nature) is to not talk a lot about their world. They are doing far too little (or none at all) marketing for their own sake. It is about time to change this.

This is not a complicated reference book. You don't need any computer know-how; it is enough if you use a PC from time to time. This book will open a door to a closed world, and it will explain in a no-frills style why things are the way they are. It has deliberately been written in an entertaining form to keep it easily readable. There are already too many complicated reference books around.

This book will tell you about things that you cannot know. (For instance, the requirements for security are totally different for a professional environment than for a private PC.) Further interesting topics are: disaster recovery planning, supervision by auditors, job interviews, and problems generated by users developing their own software.
Most of the time, the chapters and subjects are illustrated with examples. Names and places have occasionally been falsified in order to protect some people. The described situations, however, have happened as described.

If you are an IT expert, once in a while I'm sure you had to explain what you were doing all day. If you are not an expert, you might have asked yourself what your colleagues in the IT department do all day and why there are so many of them. Well, this book answers those questions.

In 2009, IT remains an organized jungle. When you work in a company, you know that projects sometimes have been cancelled, have taken too long, or were massively over budget. There are good reasons for this, and this book allocates a lot of room to them. Systems are increasingly unavailable because they get more and more complicated, due to an increasing innovation pace which is difficult to control. When a project wasn't running the way it was intended, one of my previous bosses would say, "That's IT." This hits the point precisely. IT is about unexpected surprises—every day.

But why is everything so complicated? Aren't computers the most logical thing in the world? Information is nothing more than a collection of zeroes and ones, right? Something as straightforward as that should be a piece of cake. But it is not. IT is complex, no doubt about that. When I talk about IT to people who are basic PC users, they usually mention the word "complicated." Someone who is not working in a bank could just as well assume that the logic of debit and credit matches very well with the logic of zeroes and ones. New bank employees learn quickly about the complexity of the banking business, which goes far beyond debit and credit. This is quite comparable to IT.

You will learn that IT is also about being passionate; it is about learning and experiencing something new every day, not knowing how the day in the office will run, and sometimes having to organize some night work. Even after 27 years in the job, this is unchanged. It's an exciting feeling to have a very special task, to exercise a particularly exciting job, and to be in the centre of what is going on. No important things happen in a company without IT playing a central role. It is, indeed, a fantastic job in spite of stress, system breakdowns, ever repeating weekend work, and nightshifts. It is, indeed, a fantastic job in spite of the daily fights with users who have no knowledge about the specificities of the IT world and its providers who, again and again, deliver late and in bad quality. It is possibly the most exciting office job in the world. Boredom is unknown.

A compulsory reading?

The German edition of CIO magazine wrote this about the book:
" 'Why is everything so complicated for us? All this can be done in an easier way.'

Phone calls like these from the CEO are no longer to be expected after having read 'Eine Million oder ein Jahr'."

A compulsory reading then, as written by Luxembourg's Prime Minister, Mr. Jean-Claude Juncker, in his foreword to the first edition? I sincerely believe so, because it will surely increase mutual understanding, and this is always good and right. So, who should read this book?

- IT students, because I think they get a wrong picture of what IT really means. The student's expectations are to work later in some kind of "Silicon Valley" lab as shown in the movies. Reality strikes them hard.

- IT managers, because it is possibly the only truthful description of their world.

- IT staff, basically for the same reasons as the IT managers.

- Staff in companies and administrations (when the text in the book refers to "companies," it of course includes administrations) who have asked themselves at least one of these questions: Why do projects take so long, why do they sometimes fail, and why do they go over budget all the time? What are these IT guys doing the whole day long? Why does my PC crash so often?

- People working with PCs who wonder if it is their fault when things don't work as expected.

If you do not want to read the entire book, read at least chapters 3, 5, and 7. Chapters 9, 11, 13, and 14 are extending the subject. The remaining ones are not unnecessary, but they simply have less weight when you apply the criteria of "compulsory reading," or they might take too much of your time if you are a stressed manager. Anyway, I would recommend reading the chapters in the same order as in the book.

A little hint before we start: to keep it simple, I always use the terminology "IT", even when the text refers to a time when this term was not yet used. The same applies to CEO (Chief Executive Officer = Managing Director) and CIO (Chief Information Officer = Head IT or Head EDP).

The very first business lunch

A never-ending task that has always existed is reviewing and evaluating new systems, either to replace something existing or to introduce something new. Choosing a software system is a long-term commitment. It should be compared to a marriage (from which you may get out, but I guess I don't need to tell you about all the complications you may expect). The choice for a system should be well thought out. When dealing with really large, important systems, a later decision to replace them is more like a heart transplant than a divorce. You should allocate a lot of time to the decision-making process.

The process of choosing a software system has changed fundamentally over time. In the '80s, IBM had such a dominant industry position in the areas of hardware and software that there were almost no serious alternatives, let alone the difficulty to integrate non-IBM products; you either chose to buy IBM or not at all. Microsoft today can only dream about the kind of dominance IBM had at that time. In the early '90s, PCs were introduced to company IT departments, and the choices for software systems grew. IBM's dominance diminished and, today, IBM's role is far from what it used to be. The company has almost vanished from the public consciousness.

Twenty years ago, it was difficult to get a complete and objective overview of the products offered in the market. Only with the success of the Internet did it become easier to peruse the available technology. Not more than 10 years ago, there was an obligation to visit every trade fair and to contact every vendor; today, it is easy to get the complete picture without getting out of your office chair.

In times when notebooks or laptops were rare or non-existent (the youngest among us cannot imagine that such a time ever existed) and in which the spontaneous build-up of a telecommunication line was impossible, it was necessary to personally visit providers in order to get a presentation of their systems. Today, salespeople visit you, open their notebooks, do a PowerPoint presentation, and, if required, give you a demo of the program directly on the notebook. If you don't like the product, you have the possibility to end the presentation with a tactical argument ("My boss needs to see me urgently" or "We have a system crash in our core application") while holding your Blackberry in the air. In the past, you were at the mercy of the provider, as you were on his grounds and escape was not an option. PowerPoint's triumphal procession had not yet begun; therefore, you had received a glossy brochure days before the demo, and you began immediately with the concrete presentation of the program.

In those days, the term "cheatware" (as a reference to hardware and software) was created, because many times we believed that the software being presented was only a façade, a specially-created program for the purpose of that presentation. Although we no longer use the term, the phenomenon of "cheatware" still exists, but in a substantially more refined way.

Who cares how it works, just as long as it gives the right answer?

Jeff Scholnik

For example, a renowned European bank (before the financial crisis) chose a product that had been initially developed in the mid '70s but had missed the path to modern technology. However, in order to sell the product, a GUI (Graphical User Interface) was added to hide the mess in the background and make it look like a modern PC product. (Sort of like putting an art-deco facade on a shanty town.) Well, Senior Management was impressed and bought the product for all of their subsidiaries. Multi-million Euros sale. During execution of the project, the cheating was discovered, and now both companies only talk to each other through their lawyers.

The fact is that this kind of scenario happens quite often, although maybe in less dramatic terms than the example I gave. The reason is that Senior Management has all the power, but the IT department has all the expertise. If the latter are not part of the process, then "cheatware" can still achieve success.

In former times, a product demo could last a whole day, and, in order to provide an enjoyable atmosphere and influence the decision-making process, it was common practice to be invited to an excellent restaurant. More than 20 years ago, I and a colleague from the Finance department were asked to evaluate a specific software system in order to prepare a decision memo for Senior Management. Even though we wouldn't make the final decision, the two salesmen wanted to impress us. So, they invited us to the best restaurant in town.

"I guess you do eat lobster?" asked one of them while we were studying the menu.

With a slight panic in our eyes, we looked at each other. Neither of us had ever eaten lobster before. As we didn't want to lose face, however, we behaved as if this was nothing exceptional and agreed. Later, when the meal was served, we realized we had no idea *how* to eat lobster, so we tried to improvise. Pretty fast, we were at our wits' end. We must have looked pathetic as we messed around with the lobster cutlery.

"Oh! You youngsters, you have no clue about dining culture," one of the salesmen said derisively from the other side of the table. "We will show you how to do this correctly."

The guy opposite me asked me to give him my plate.

"Now watch carefully," he said. He broke off one lobster claw and locked it in the cutlery. Due to a hearty squeeze, the lobster claw flew several meters and landed in the middle of a table where an elderly couple was dining.

The rest of us at our table (as well as several other guests in the restaurant) burst out laughing.

The elderly man at the neighboring table nonchalantly picked up the lobster claw with his thumb and forefinger, got up, brought it back to our table, and said, "I believe this is yours."

Whether we bought the system in the end, I can no longer recall.

One million or one year

The reasons why IT projects take so long, are so complicated, and are so expensive

Trying to understand why and how many IT projects fail, get delayed, and run over budget is a frequent object of market research studies. All these studies come to similar results: roughly 50% of all IT projects and initiatives fail. Of course, those figures need to be looked at with more depth, and the applied criteria need to be checked, but I think that the general result is correct. These studies show that, the bigger a company and the larger the project team, target, and budget, the higher the probability of failure becomes. Those figures seem hard to believe, as most people imagine that computers and software are based on pure logic, an area where there shouldn't be any surprises. When taking the results of these studies as a basis, success could already be measured if more than half of the projects and initiatives come to a positive end. We will see in this chapter where the reasons for these flaws can be found.

Even if a project is successful, it is—in most cases—an expensive and laborious endeavor.

A running joke about the IT industry is this: if you ask your IT department for a software change or the installation of a new system, you either get one of two answers—"It will cost one million," or "It will take one year." Sometimes, if not all the time, you get *both* answers.

Maybe the title of this chapter should contain an "and" instead of an "or."

We should be careful not to blame people in IT departments around the world for this, as they surely are not lazy people. You can assume that they want to help to the best of their abilities, and they definitely want to run successful projects. However, these two answers are most of the time correct, but seldom explained.

For the answer "It will take one year," or alternatively "this would take 500 person days to realize it," a plausible explanation could be that there are just too many projects running already and there is simply no time left. But this explanation would still fall short.

To understand the current situation, a short look back will help. Until the end of the '80s, IT was, from a technical point of view, rather straightforward. A big machine (mainframe) did everything, knew everything, and there were no complicated networks as there are today. In addition, there were no PCs and only a quite minimal and relatively theoretical threat from hackers. In the '90s, things became confusing and complicated, and the term "IT landscapes" was created in order to describe the collection of many different components that are part of IT. The word "landscape" has something appeasing, comforting. It reminds you of green meadows, grazing cows, and chirping birds. Everyone likes this. Everyone thinks it's great. If "landscape" was rightfully used 15 years ago, however, it is no longer accurate as things have gone out of control. At the end of the first decade in the 21st century, IT is described more accurately as an ecosystem, a biotope. It is fragile and complicated; the number of components in it is very often not even known, let alone fully controlled. There are interdependencies of unknown nature, and, most of all, no one is able to predict its behavior when you make changes to it. It is, therefore, much more accurate to say IT "ecosystem" or IT "biotope" rather than IT "landscape."

To understand what can go wrong during the execution of an IT project, we have to take a look at the different tasks and the risks related to these tasks. As we talk about an ecosystem, the risks are comparable to what can happen when a new animal or plant is introduced. It is quite hard to know in advance if it will work, if any added value will be created, or if—worst case—the fragile balance will be broken. The computer industry doesn't have the methods or processes in place yet to have this information; quite opposite to the automobile industry, which is highly mature. To illustrate things, I will quite often compare the computer industry with the automobile industry, where standardization and industrialization have produced a high maturity grade and, therefore, highly-reliable products. The computer industry is light-years away from this.

The tasks that need to be completed when introducing new software can be compared to the building of a new house. A software upgrade can be compared to refurbishing a house. Every action creates its own difficulties and needs to be planned in advance. For a house, you need to calculate the structural engineering, request permits, plan carefully, arrange for the utilities, buy a security system, and so forth. In a software development project, the individual steps need to be repeated every time, and they do create their own difficulties. Now, I can hear already some IT experts standing up and protesting, saying that this problem is about to become history as a new method, SOA (*Service Oriented Architecture*) will fix these problems. Well, to be very frank: this is just (another) new hype which will not solve anything.

Until further notice, it will remain a fact that most IT projects fail. Let's now look at the individual steps, their specific problems, and how they can be managed.

Computers are fantastic: in a few minutes, they can produce such a big error, for which humans would need many months.

Merle Meacham

Selection

Let's start with the selection of software systems. From now on, I will use the term *functional software*, as opposed to software used by the large public. Other words that are frequently used in the business for functional software are *Business Intelligence (BI) systems* or *Enterprise Resource Planning* (ERP). By this, we understand software that is used to organize a company's main activities, be it accounting, order management, payments, or invoices.

A lot of time should be allocated to selecting such software. As already said earlier, such a decision can be compared to marriage, and we all know how complex a divorce can be. A colleague of mine told me once that he had a discussion with his CEO, who did not understand why everything in his company was so complicated when it came to IT matters. He argued that his son usually bought his software in supermarkets and could install it on his PC within minutes. By contrast, in the office, the introduction of new software was something of a drama or even a tragedy. Danger of black ice!

My colleague argued that, if you were going to compare software experiences, why not finances? While the CEO's son was surely able to manage his pocket money all by himself, what was the necessity of the large Finance department in the company? Whether this answer helped him in his career is not certain.

I do have the hope that after having read this chapter, company decision makers will understand why IT takes so long, is so expensive, and, in many cases, even fails.

The process

The days in the '80s and '90s when IT departments made mostly unaided decisions about projects are definitely over. The final "go" for projects are made today by the business. IT departments function as service providers who have the mission to transform the business goals into IT systems and processes. At least there should be a consensus that this is the right way of doing.

Ideally, the selection process is a common process between IT and the business departments. Unfortunately, we do see examples of some business departments who want to execute the selection process by themselves. And here we have the very first reason why projects fail. Business departments don't understand what the impact of a new system can be to the IT ecosystem—it is even quite hard for the IT experts themselves—and cannot evaluate the feasibility. A joint effort between all involved parties is, therefore, key. Usually, this process is not done frequently by a specific business department but is a regular task of any IT department.

Another issue is the expectation by management that this process is comparable to the purchase of a new car, where a limited number of criteria are evaluated in order to make the choice. The thinking goes somewhat like this: "My budget is X. I need a SUV. The color should be grey metallic, and a navigation system and leather seats would be great." With comparable specifications ("The software shouldn't be expensive, all accounting movement types should be handled, and state-of-the-art customer confirmations should be produced"), the selection process is started. Of course, more is needed: first of all, a very explicit project request must be formulated, something which can already overstrain a business department. Based on the project request, an analysis is to be carried out which leads to requirements specifications. And here we have the first source of misunderstandings that brings a project to its knees later on. IT and business departments do not speak the same language. In the same way as IT experts have their own gobbledygook, business departments speak their very own language. Of course, it is mandatory for IT experts to understand the business language, which, often enough, is very difficult. Strangely, the opposite request—namely that business people should understand IT terminology—is never heard of. Sure, it is not realistic to have everyone be an IT expert, but some basics should be expected. I think that a lot of misunderstandings which lead to failures come from this situation. I plead for IT awareness in business, and this book is the effort to achieve this.

What makes things worse is that the complexity in business has also continuously increased in the last years. This phenomenon is not a prerogative of IT. Therefore, the previously mentioned analysis is even more important. As said, this is the attempt to fully understand what is needed. The people in charge of this are called business analysts and IT analysts. They don't only analyze new requirements, but with each introduction of something new, they need to evaluate what this means for the business and for the IT systems. If, for example, a new regulatory requirement comes along, the company needs those experts to make sure that the right decisions are made. Large companies have their own staff for this; smaller ones need to hire external consultants. And already, we have created the first delay and increased cost. (External consultants like to "oversell" the number of days needed for this task. To defend them, it needs to be said that they have to learn first about the existing ecosystem.) It's not like taking a catalogue and marking the items you want with an X. Business users must articulate themselves.

As soon as the requirements specifications are done, detailed discussions with providers can start.

(In order to simplify this chapter, I take the case where external companies will be charged with the delivery of the solution. Of course, an internal IT department may develop the solution as well, but when the requirements are very complicated, it is more common not to do one's own developments anymore. Of course, there are many exceptions to this rule, especially if a company already has its own internally-developed system and doesn't want to abandon it. However, as a general rule, it can be said that software development has become a highly-specialized area which most companies don't want to do by themselves anymore.)

Suppose now that there isn't a list of preferred suppliers with whom umbrella contracts exist and with whom projects are carried out on a regular basis. A "long list" of possible providers is established and those are requested to produce an offer, based on the company's request for proposal.

(An alternative approach could be that a number of systems are pre-evaluated before requirements specifications are done, and then those systems are taken as a basis to define the requirements. This process is perfectly feasible and can make sense. The project problems it may create are similar to the other process described here; therefore, I do not go into further detail for it.)

After having received the offers, a first selection is done, and the "long list" becomes a "short list" with maybe two or three possible candidates. To get there, we may ask those companies to present themselves—we call this a "beauty contest." As a next step, numbers of workshops, discussion meetings, and reference visits at existing customers are done. As opposed to software for the general public—where there are Internet forums to find out how satisfied or frustrated the customers are or if there are special problems that require special attention—there are no forums for functional software. Until the final choice is made, a large number of planning rounds, budget preparation, and steering committees have to be done. A lot of time can pass before everyone is convinced that the right provider has been chosen. Quite interestingly, there are fundamental cultural differences in this process. Some Europeans, such as the Germans or the Swiss, tend to take a lot of time for this—significantly more than our colleagues from the United States.

All requirements covered?

The next difficulty: Does the selected system really match our requirements? Can we be sure that we haven't forgotten something major and that the provider has really understood what we want? Or did we fall for the provider who made the nicest promises and the most beautiful presentation ("cheatware", maybe?), but who has a gap between the reality and the glossy brochures? Or did we possibly not fully understand the implications of the new system? Understanding a new system during the selection process is a "mission impossible." Consider that a system like SAP has 58,000 different functions with more than 100,000 data elements; it is not realistic to expect having understood what this all means for the upcoming implementation. The picture gets only clearer during the execution of the project when large amounts of money have already been spent. Because of the massive complexity of today's IT systems, it can be very difficult for business departments to decide precisely if a to-be-introduced system matches the requirements. At the end of the day, a choice represents a risk with uncertain outcome. Even the recognition of small deviations is hard to identify. In fact, nearly endless time would have to be invested to be sure that this point will not fail—but who has endless time? And on top of that, business departments have usually very little experience in this exercise. But IT departments need to rely on the business decision, as the business experts are not within IT. At the end of the day, it is the business that pays and has the final say.

As a general rule, it can be said that presentations from providers are always perfect! But did we ask the right questions at our reference visits, and most of all, did we get the right and honest answers? Feedback from other customers (even if there is a good relationship with them) is to be taken with prudence, as their saying is strictly related to their biotope. The risk here is that a decision maker will say: "Well, it works for them, so you should be able to get it up and running as well!"

Providers usually don't facilitate things as they tend to underestimate (severely!) the impact of an implementation. The worst I ever heard from a provider in a presentation was that a totally new accounting software could be installed in just ten minutes. You imagine the difficulty of explaining to the business that the project would take at least three months. The really exasperating thing with providers in this question is that they look exclusively at their product and have no clue about, no interest in, and no regards to the customer's ecosystem. Software-as-a-Service (SaaS) is a new trend for using software, and it is a new attempt by service providers to convince the business about how easy software installations are. Basically, it means that a system is no longer installed at the customer's premises, but is offered as a service by remote access; due to this, the IT department would be no longer needed! At first glance, this is an idea that has some charm, but it creates manifold other problems, of which these providers don't inform the business. SaaS providers prefer to talk directly to the business people rather than the CIO. Every CIO comes across their marketing statements, such as: "If you use our SaaS, you will be live in 90 days. And we will integrate it with your core system for just 25,000 Euros." If the business decides to go that way without involving the CIO, it is time to check for open positions elsewhere.

We will see now that the implementation of software takes more than flippant marketing statements suggest.

Implementation

Impact analysis

In order to understand how long the implementation will take (ten minutes, three months, one year?), an impact analysis may be carried out. According to the specific project situation, this can happen before or after the decision for a system is made. Both approaches can make sense.

As we have seen earlier, the longer a project runs, the higher the probability of failure. When I discussed this with an old friend of mine, he said that there were similar experiences in the company that he works for, and for this reason, they had decided not to authorize any project which would run more than one year.

It begins with a theoretical examination to understand how that new system can be integrated into the ecosystem. It might become necessary to make adaptations in other systems (cf. interfaces further down in the text) or in the new system. There is a risk that the chosen technology is not compatible with the already-used one or that there is no in-house expertise because it introduces a totally new technology.

How will it be fed (with data), meaning how will it communicate with the existing elements from the biotope? It is not difficult to understand that this task is very demanding and generates a lot of costs. On top of that, there are no guarantees that the outcome will be positive, and the conclusion may be that further investments (in technology or interfaces, for example) are necessary.

Someone might say now that it could be an idea to ask the providers of computer solutions to give a compatibility guarantee. The idea behind that would be a "plug-and-play" approach. While this exists for very simple things, like compatibility to the current Windows version or a device that is connected via USB, it does not exist for the important elements in the ecosystem. There isn't a chance of finding anything even close to this in the case of functional software. And there's a very good reason for this: there are no two identical IT ecosystems in the world! There are excellent chances that the ways the elements in the ecosystem are linked together are totally unique. There are potentially hundreds of other systems that our new system needs to work with. And every biotope is composed of a vast diversity of hardware components from all different kind of providers, which have hundreds of communication components of their own, as well as various control software. The hardware part alone fills libraries full of books. Technology is a jungle; the IT landscape is a biotope. For each component, there are different versions, which have either (or not) been brought by the IT department to the latest release level (Windows XP, Windows 2000, Windows Vista). To make all this work together, there are bridges between all these components called "interfaces." It is just as unlikely to find two people with the same genes as two IT ecosystems with absolutely identical components and configurations. With this in mind, how could a provider give any kind of guarantee? It would be commercial suicide.

I would like to illustrate with a small example the problems that can be encountered in the technical integration which can bring a project into severe difficulties. In Europe, numbers are separated for each unit of thousand by a point (1.000.000 represents one million), and the decimal positions are separated by a comma (for example, 1.200,50). In the US, it is the other way around. As some American companies don't seem to know that computers are being used in the rest of the world as well and don't imagine that there are also different ways of doing things, we regularly encounter incompatibilities of this kind.

The management of decimal points (and many other settings) is defined in the biotope at a central point, and all programs are kindly requested to follow these rules. When you have bought software that doesn't follow these rules and does as it likes, then a value of, let's say, 1000 becomes a value of 1, and you can imagine how nothing works anymore. When you are dealing with a professional provider, you get this kind of problem fixed, although it may take weeks or months until it is done. If the provider is not prepared to change his program, then the project has already failed at this point. This example is simple, but surely realistic. More complex problems of that nature are regularly encountered in software projects.

Proof-of-concept

In the previous step, the theoretical validation of what it means to integrate a new system has been described. But in fact, we have only bought a promise that everything we have seen on those glossy brochures and user handbooks will really work as described. In reality, there are quite often substantial differences between theory and practice. "According to the user guide, this stuff should work. I do not understand why it crashes" is something you hear all the time. To avoid bad surprises, a POC *(Proof-of-concept)* can be done, in which those parts of the future solution (for which the biggest risks and doubts exist) are installed in a POC-test environment. The mission here is to validate whether all those wonderful things work together as expected. Should you compare an IT project to the purchase of an automobile (which, as already said, is what the business users expect), it would be like testing your Bridgestone tires to ensure they work with your BMW.

When you are the first customer to implement a specific solution, you should definitely carry out a POC. As every ecosystem is different, it is easily understandable that POCs need to be carried out often.

Let's take a business example: a bank intends to open a new branch in, let's say, the Czech Republic, and decides to use the same systems as for all the other branches; the only difference will be an adaptation to the local specificities of that country. Very quickly, you will discover that this country has special alphabetic characters, somewhat similar to French or German. It is obvious that your systems need to be able to handle this end-to-end in all applications—the Czech customers would not accept a permanent misspelling of their names on the account statements. There is some faith in the providers' statements that the systems should be able to handle this, but no one in the world has ever tried this with the systems you are using. During the execution of the POC, then, it will be found out which systems will not be able to handle this, and it will surprise nobody that the promises given by the providers aren't kept. If you are unlucky, there will be places in the processing chain which cannot be changed (the specific provider refuses to make a modification, the costs for it would kill the project, or any other very good reason) or will at least slow down the project substantially. In many cases, the POC hurdle is either not taken successfully or it generates a massive need for adaptation. I haven't come across any statistics on the frequency of this happening, but my guess would be that it is very often.

Integration

After these hurdles are overcome, the integration of the whole solution is started; we have seen that a POC usually only validates a part of the total solution, namely the one which is in doubt. Weeks or months must be calculated for the actual integration. A test biotope is created in order to make a complete validation of everything that has been identified. And very often, new problems come up, or it shows that the results of the previous analysis steps were wrong because not all elements have been validated correctly.

Integration work is extremely expensive because you need highly-skilled staff for it. Daily rates of USD 1,500 are not excessive. On a general note, most problems in a project show up in this phase and consume huge amounts of money. An example: a Customer Relationship Management tool must be integrated with an archiving system that contains scanned customer documents (such as passport copies). Technically speaking, this is no problem at all, as it has been done successfully many times at other customer sites. But the problems can come at a lower level of detail: the archiving tool uses an index of its own (maybe customer alias name) which is unknown by the Customer Relationship Management tool. Of course, this is not an insurmountable hurdle—it's just unexpected and, therefore, calls for more time and money. Frequently, you go from one embarrassment to the next, and every time, you have to explain to the business manager that new difficulties have arisen. As soon as the sum of the difficulties reaches a critical level, the project may be stopped.

How could such a scenario be avoided? Well, more time (and money) could be invested upfront in the analysis steps. Or, better yet, there could be communication at the start of every project that these situations are likely to come up and that time and budgetary reserve should be granted. But where are the Financial Controllers willing to follow that route?

Security concept

It makes a lot of sense to look at security aspects right at the beginning of a project. The questions that need to be answered here are described in the chapter 13: *IT Security*. When drafting such a security concept, vulnerabilities will be documented. No new system can know about and respect all possible internal security rules. The integration of a new system into the biotope creates questions which are asked for the first time: remember, there are no two identical biotopes. Additionally, new questions come up if the IT department needs to develop interfaces for that new system. It might be possible that the security guidelines require an encryption of sensitive data, but the system under consideration doesn't do that. Or the user access rights management possibilities do not correspond to the internal standards. These kinds of questions can create substantial project delays and new costs, as there might be necessary software changes. As a last resort, the security officer can stop a project completely if the security guidelines cannot be respected. As I said, ideally, those questions should be checked in the beginning to avoid bad surprises, but too often, it isn't considered a top priority and only gets attention when it is too late.

Installation parameters

This is a very important point and decisively underestimated, especially in terms of time needed and risks it represents. All software, from the smallest possible tool to full-fledged core business applications, has (installation) parameters that need to be setup. These parameters configure what the software should do, how it will be used, and how it is adapted to the internal rules and processes of the company. Unnecessary functions can be disabled at this point. For products designed for the general public, this question is not so relevant, as they usually come pre-defined and, in most cases, match the user's expectations; only customer-specific things (such as an email address, for instance) need to be configured. Take a look at Word under *Options*, and you will see that are really many, but you can use Word without worrying about them.

When it comes to professional business software, this is totally different. For systems which run the core business (like an accounting system), those parameters are undefined. (I know that there are some very rare exceptions, but also in these cases, it is necessary to review them all.) The most impressive example I ever saw was a core banking software package that had 25,000 such parameters. Before any of those can be defined, they have to be understood. Then, the implications they will have on the existing processes must be determined. It's a piece of cake to make fundamental mistakes in this step, and these mistakes will only get visible once that the system has gone into production; usually, those errors are every hard to correct later on. Special care must be taken that only a restricted number of people get modification rights to these parameters.

Recently, software that complicates this subject even further has surfaced: when a parameter is a value that you define in a table, then the situation is as described. But what I saw recently is a system offering the possibility to dynamically change these parameters: the customer has to develop a program for each parameter, and these programs can change the value of the parameter according to the situation that the software is currently in. Sounds intricate, and it is intricate. Imagine the complexity of testing software with 25,000 parameters when they are static, and now imagine testing this when they can all be dynamic. Phew! I cannot deny the fact that this is creating a lot of possibilities for the business. Now, as the chance to modify them dynamically is given, the business will insist on using this new flexibility—at the expense of chaos and the need for a big team of IT experts.

Other project dependencies

To keep things complicated, relevant elements can change during the implementation phase. It can happen that another project decided for a migration to the next Windows version, and, due to this, some small sub-component in our project becomes incompatible in the biotope. Ok, the provider will possibly respond that the new (compatible) version will be delivered in "six months." According to the strategic commercial relevance that you have for this provider, it might be possible to accelerate things, but this is rather unlikely. With such themes, you may play merry-go-round for a long time without ever making real progress.

It gets really nasty when there are two distinct projects running with different business backgrounds within the same specific software system. Let's take the introduction of the new IFRS accounting rules as an example. Since critical programs will have to be modified, the business department may suggest changing the algorithm for the calculation of customer fees at the same time. From a pure IT point of view, it would be advisable to close the first project first and then attack the fees. But business defines both as "top priority," and therefore, it is decided to kill two birds with one stone. It is absolutely necessary to close both projects at the same time because you cannot go live with the new accounting rules if the part dealing with the fees is not working properly. As we have already learned that IT projects never run as expected, this sort of situation represents a major risk and is the trigger for many crisis meetings.

Change of priorities

The appetite grows while eating. It is common that business departments are inclined to change priorities during a running project. (Either loudly: "If we add this, we will be able to increase our profit." Or more quietly: "There's something we have forgotten to mention.") The best planning is then spotty, at best, and the pressure on the provider to develop additional functionality in a very short time frame becomes immense; as a result, quality will suffer. It may also happen that completely new projects get more attention and that key people are re-allocated to those new projects.

In more general terms, the definition of priorities for the business departments is far from being straightforward. Every business area has a focus on its own interests and does not care much about those of the others; every request is defined as "top priority". The collection of all these requests is done within IT. As not everything can be done immediately, steering committees are established, and they define the global priorities for the company. Smaller requests, which do not get the status of a project, also get a "priority one" label. Every business department knows that it doesn't make sense to make a "priority two" request, because it is clear from the start that nothing will be done for at least the next ten years. But when everything is declared "priority one," there isn't any sense in priorities anymore. So what happens? Quietly, the IT classifies those requests internally as "priority 1a, 1b, 1c" and so on, but will never admit it officially…

Sudden changes in priorities due to legal or regulatory requirements are also very unpopular. This aspect of our work has strongly increased in the last years and will further grow and make the realization of projects even more complicated in the future (cf. chapter 14: *Worst Case*).

Processes

The introduction of a new software solution always also means the necessity to review existing internal processes and create new ones. In the past, software used to be dictatorial, in order to impose its inherent processes and workflows on the customer. This has now changed. We see an increasing number of systems today with integrated workflow management capabilities, and this desirable evolution has led to immensely complex and expensive systems. We have indeed gone from one extreme to the other. Voices can be heard these days asking for less flexibility in systems, thus obliging a customer to adapt to the system's predefined workflows. The positive outcome of this approach would lower costs in terms of software licenses and necessary implementation efforts. Sometimes enlightened dictatorship makes things easier because you don't have to think so much yourself. If a system offers this kind of flexibility, you need to think carefully about the processes that you want to implement. For this task, experts are needed, and if the company doesn't have any, then this know-how must be purchased outside. This task requires money and time—a lot of it. Especially when you have external consultants for this task, they want to design the "perfect" world because they want, first of all, to sell a large number of consultancy days. Applying the 80/20 rule (the target is considered as being reached when 80% of the initial requirements are implemented; the remaining 20% are postponed to a later phase or are even cancelled) is in many cases a very wise approach.

Badly-designed processes or a simple omission of important processes are (together with the already-mentioned problems) a large stumbling block on the way to a successful project.

The providers

It is much more complicated than you might think to explain to a provider the goals you want to achieve with a project. The customer uses his own terminology and might have been discussing the project internally for weeks and months before he tries to find a provider for his project. Some projects are so big that several providers will be needed. Frequently, a specific provider doesn't know the full picture or cannot understand what importance it has. There are parts that are invisible to him, but which will nevertheless play a crucial role during the implementation.

It's a fact of life that each provider does everything possible to get the deal and will tell you anything to get it, even at the risk of running into trouble afterwards. Well, the final risk always stays with the customer.

Even if everything has been fine so far, there's another danger: your provider may decide to change his strategy (or worse, go bankrupt), and you have built your own IT strategy on his. Of course, lawyers are smart in handling the financial implications of such a situation, but that doesn't help the project. Anyhow, it happens that providers change important things in spite of valid contracts, and you are left out in the rain when this happens. It does not help to receive compensation if you run into a situation where you will not have a solution for the business requirements for an unforeseeable time period. I was unlucky enough to experience a fundamental strategy change by a key provider twice during my career, and on both occasions, it had severe consequences for the business.

IT is about having the right people with the right skills; while this is generally true, it probably applies even more to software companies. Sometimes the departure of a key person at the provider's side is enough to run into trouble in a project. Believe me, this happens very often, and there is very little remedy against it. Building up know-how in a software system is a long and tedious task, and you don't replace key people easily.

Or your external provider signs a bigger deal with another client and allocates his key people to that client. Here you have a wonderful occasion to train your management skills by fighting with your provider, but the fact remains that the project has already started to suffer.

Or the external provider is so successful in selling his product that it is oversold—comparable to an overbooking on a flight. Again, this is very frequent.

Project management

There are more reasons for project failures. As a general rule, you can have an internal project manager and one on the provider's side. All strings get coordinated here. It's here where the project risks are monitored and countermeasures are developed. To see the project's status at a glance, the system of "traffic lights" is used: "red" means the project crashed or is about to crash, "yellow" means high management attention required, and "green" means everything is okay. The danger here is that it is the project manager who decides the color, and, according to his level of maturity and his relationship with the company's decision–makers, he might be scared to have too many non-greens in his report.

Most projects have sub-projects which have their own set of colors; these then need to be consolidated into one global color for the main project. It is easy to lose focus about potential risks with this approach.

I have observed an unhealthy trend in recent years, namely the fact that more and more very young people get assigned the role of project managers. While they may have received an excellent education, they don't have the necessary maturity for this function. What I find extremely difficult to explain to these young people is that it is quite okay when one minor project item is not completed on time. Not all project items have the same importance, but this is something that a project plan doesn't show. Sometimes the agreed dates are only an orientation mark and not a dogma; in other cases, it is extremely important that the dates are respected. This difference between important and unimportant is not quickly understood. Each project plan shows how much of the work has been accomplished as a percentage. The worst project manager I ever experienced averaged those percentages and, when the total from the previous team meeting had increased from let's say 68 to 72 percent, he concluded that everything was fine—end of discussion. No joke.

Project management is also about coordinating the resources of all participants. Absence management is part of that job. An unplanned absence can shake the whole project build-up, as it can take some time until the needed persons for a specific task are all in office at the same time again. Probably not so much in the US, but definitely in Europe, holidays are an issue that may endanger the successful execution of a project. If you have a cross-country project with different main school holiday periods in the year, there is only a limited number of days in the year when everybody is on board. In a project team with members from different countries, there are not more than roughly 120 common working days in a year. If you then consider that the Spanish won't start working before 10 a.m., the Germans are reluctant for meetings after 5 p.m., and you have colleagues from other time zones to bring in on conference calls, a day is really short. If you have contractors from foreign countries in your project, you must consider that they possibly need a work permit. When the project gets delayed, there is a risk that the work permit will expire before the project is finished, and you may run into serious trouble. This aspect of time management is frequently neglected in project management.

Good project management is a talent in itself. For IT projects, these people need to understand the business, and they need to understand IT. This demands a lot, and therefore I would advise to only hire very experienced staff for this task. Trying to keep costs low by using young people is a detour, and a very expensive detour at the end. How many projects fail because of bad project management? I don't know any figures, but experience tells me that it is a major reason for failed IT projects.

Bad software quality

If the automobile had followed the same development cycle as the computer, a Rolls-Royce would today cost $100, get a million miles per gallon, and explode once a year, killing everyone inside.

Robert X. Cringely

Some software providers operate in an extremely competitive market—others have a more monopolistic position. The picture is very uneven in this industry. What connects them is that they have to deliver new products as quickly as possible because the market is very hungry for new functionality. This is true for software for the general public and, surely, even truer for business software. This extreme pressure is not conducive to a high quality product. (Bad software quality is a central theme in this book, and chapter 7: *Unexpected error encountered* is allocated to it.) The impact on project risks due to bad software quality is extreme, and almost every day, we hear news in the press about real cases of crashed projects due to this. The bad news is that you can never (never!) know in advance what quality you'll get, and you can never evaluate what it means for the timing of your project. I am not afraid to state that all providers of functional software systems apply the "banana" principle: the product matures at the customer.

Let's also highlight here what bad software quality means in terms of money. To take precautions against bad software quality, the client of a business software provider is obliged (yes, obliged—it is not a choice) to sign a maintenance contract and pay around twenty percent of the purchase price to the provider to get the errors fixed that the latter has created. A sensational business model! In rare cases, this percentage is below twenty, but some providers are now testing this psychological barrier—more about this in chapter 7. Of course, a part of this money is used to adapt the software to external changes that will be applied in all ecosystems, like the next Windows version, for instance. But the lion's share goes to the correction of errors, which we call "bugs." Some providers are even cleverer and add an automatic yearly increase for a possible inflation adaptation; after five years, you will already pay twenty-five percent. There are also examples where a software provider limits in time the usage of the purchased license. After the termination of the period (ten years, for example), the full initial amount is to be paid again. And believe me, business software is never cheap. We invest millions of dollar in no time.

Adhesion contracts, in which the customer commits to pay a certain (but certainly not small) amount of money when the provider delivers a new version of his software, are also very popular. In an honest world, a new version would give you something fundamentally new, but sadly, most of the time, it is just a new label for the same stuff—the only difference being some minor cosmetics. Would it be an option not to sign the contract nor install the new version? Not at all. The business model foresees that, at some time in the future, the version that you use will run out of maintenance; that date is unilaterally decided by the provider. You may now decide to throw that system out (maybe you remember what I wrote about divorce and heart transplant?) or just give up and purchase the new version in order to get maintenance services again. Of course, new functionality and compatibility with the next Windows will only be implemented in the very last version. At this point, you realize that you are in a very weak negotiating position. And when the decision is finally made to order the very last version, guess what? You risk having to pay for all the intermediary versions that you skipped.

In the '80s, maintenance fees were only ten percent, but they have now doubled. This is surely an indication that software can do more, but has also becomes less stable. So, the more errors in it, the higher the maintenance fees the customer has to pay. And one thing is sure (as will be explained in chapter 7): every new version of a program brings new errors.

Interfaces

Writing the first 90 percent of a computer program takes 90 percent of the time.
The remaining 10 percent also takes 90 percent of the time
and the final touches also take 90 percent of the time.

Neil J. Rubenking

In the area of functional software, the more complex the needed functionality, the more it is true that no one product does it all. Every choice is then either for a system which is very broad (doing a lot, but nothing deeply), or for one which focuses very deeply into one specialized subject (but omits other parts). In all cases, more than one system will be needed to cover the functional requirements, and the development of interfaces between systems becomes necessary. This is a massive difficulty in projects. Interfaces are bridges between the different systems, and in most cases, they are developed by the IT department, or at least on their direct demand. Figuratively speaking, the writing of interfaces is like translating a text from Russian into Chinese, whereas you master neither language.

As you know by now that there aren't two identical IT biotopes, the chance is low that you can buy such an interface turn-key on the market. In most cases, it needs to be developed specifically for your own use, which creates a new project risk. The development of interfaces is very unpopular within IT departments, because it is one of IT's most complex and risky tasks, and there is always a striking misconception between the business departments and IT about this subject. Lapidary statements like, "Then our IT will write an interface," are heard frequently. Every time I hear this, I get some more grey hair.

The nice thing about standards is that
there are so many of them to choose from.

Andrew Tannenbaum

In fact, writing interfaces is a totally wrong way of doing things. Systems should be able to communicate with other systems without making a big deal out of it, even then when they don't have any knowledge about what the other system is. In order to get there, we would need standards on how software communicates, stores its data, and is developed. But the industry is as far away from that point as our earth is from the next solar system. The purely *physical* data transport is no longer a problem today and can be compared to a highway (via Internet, leased lines or internal network), but the *logical* data transport, meaning the definition of what is transported on the highway, is totally undefined. There have been attempts in the past, but none of them has been successful.

Every provider documents more or less accurately how the data it manages can be exported from or imported into it. So-called *APIs* (Application Programming Interface) for the automatic feeding have brought a lot of progress compared with ten years ago, but it is, at the end, only a very small step in the right direction. Other industries are much more developed here: in the banking industry, for example, the *Swift* standard is used—a publicly-documented standard that is easy to follow. When a bank executes a money transfer to another bank, it doesn't matter what system that other bank uses. It suffices to send a standardized *Swift* message over a commonly used network. But when data is transported from one system to the next, it is necessary to reinvent the wheel each time. Business departments tend to believe that the writing of interfaces is straightforward and without risk. I believe that IT experts have not succeeded (have they tried?) to explain to the business departments that interfaces are complicated, represent a life-long maintenance effort, and are the wrong way to do things (even if it is the only way today). It might be that the ulterior motive here is to become indispensable—something that might especially be true for software companies. Interfaces are one of the main reasons why the number of employees in IT departments has grown so enormously and why the costs are so high.

To make this clearer, I want to illustrate it with a simple example: software systems store their data in databases. Usually these databases are *black-boxes* to the IT department when the systems are purchased. Documentation about the contents of the database is intentionally left very poor, but over time, the IT experts get an understanding of how it works. The interface has the mission to transfer data from one *black-box* to the next. System A (for example, an order management application) has its customer number defined as a ten-digit number. This information needs to be sent to system B (for example, an invoice generation system) where the database limits the customer number to eight digits. How should this work, if you have customer numbers higher than 99999999? Impossible. Of course, this example is extremely simple, but it illustrates the type of problems you can face. If you have to write an interface where a highly-complex and structured financial product that has been inserted in a trading system needs to be sent to a general ledger application for accounting purposes (which has no clue about this financial product), the limit of what is feasible is easily reached. A solution to these problems can be found, but it might take a lot of time and generate a lot of difficulties in the project.

These already-significant difficulties can be further increased if the interface needs to be written for a system which is not run by the internal IT department, but by an insourcer or at one of the company's customers. Along with the purely legal aspects like liability, availability, connection into a different time zone, and many more, there is a need to create a secure communication channel that overcomes all security barriers (like firewalls). Topics like: "What needs to happen if the counterpart does not (correctly) react?" become important. As long as the interfaces work internally, it is always achievable to manage it, but as soon as external partners join the scenario, then you get imponderabilities.

You might have followed the year-long quarrel between the EU and Microsoft. The core of the fight is that Microsoft does not want to fully publish the description of its interfaces into and out of Windows. "So what?" could be your question. But this question is of great importance, because other software developers, including competitors, are not able to develop new and innovative solutions. They have a need to communicate with Windows functions directly for their applications, and, because of this situation, many projects cannot be realized. One of my colleagues, an IT manager at an Internet bank with customers communicating with the bank exclusively over Internet and email, wanted to develop a system which would allow an automatic reply to thousands of incoming emails per day. This system was supposed to analyze the contents of the emails according to a very complex algorithm and generate the reply automatically. This project was too specific for any software available on the market, as it required very tight integration with Microsoft Exchange. But as the necessary interface descriptions are not available, the project cannot be organized as efficiently as intended. By the way: when you send an email to a company, you will very often receive an automated reply. It is not a person answering you, but a computer program. It's easy to notice anyhow…

Reconciliation

A running interface has specific requirements towards its supervision. A so-called *reconciliation* must be implemented. It is in charge of ensuring that systems A and B are on the same level of information. No data should be lost, and no data injection should fail—otherwise the reconciliation needs to generate an alarm. The development of such a function is nearly as complex as the interface itself, and it generates a need for additional time in the project. Such a piece of software cannot really be tested before the interface tests are completed successfully.

Tests

Slowly but surely, we come to the point where IT has completed its work and the tests in the business departments can begin. We are again facing a complex subject: the biotopes are so large and complex that a business user can't be expected to understand all the implications, especially if even the IT experts can't. Should you have exceptional employees like that in your company, then you are really lucky. At the same time, the specialization in the business departments increases from year to year. This doesn't match, and it increases the complexity. With this as a background, any tests carried out can only be partially meaningful. Staff with a broad IT understanding and business know-how is required. To find such people is not easy. To ease things a bit, it is possible to use specialized software that is able to document all possible interdependencies and test scenarios in order to replay them in the future. By principle, a good thing; however, because of time, costs, and unavailable know-how, it is not often done. And the implementation of such software is a project of its own.

Problems in the execution of testing activities are the main reason for project delays. In this process, the test-users continuously find new errors; detecting a total of several thousand errors during the runtime of a big project is not unusual. When a blocking error is found, it halts all further testing activities. Then the testing activities must be stopped until the provider brings an error correction. This can take an unforeseeable period of time. And, as you might imagine, when you have one error corrected, you tumble into the next one, and the game starts over again. A reliable timeframe, in terms of project planning, is impossible.

Test concept

Before the actual tests can start, it is necessary to create a test concept. The introduction of a new system, or even only a new functionality, creates new business and technical processes that need to be validated before they can go live. Test cases are created accordingly. This represents data that must be fed into the system, and it documents the expected results. As described above, specialized software can be used for this.

A question that is asked again and again is whether the business departments or IT should do these tests. Well, the answer is quite obvious: the business expertise lies in the business departments, and only those people can do a final validation. If the test cases are correctly documented, it does not matter who makes the test inputs—any person off the street could do the job. However, if these test cases are not documented, then the business departments need to repeat this exercise every time a change happens in the system. Testing is so massively important because of the generalized bad level of software quality. This means that testing activities need to be repeated again and again until things finally work—a situation that is highly frustrating for millions of people every day everywhere in the world. In general, it can therefore be said that testing activities are extremely unpopular. And testing is a major risk for project failure. Simply overlooking an important test or a false "ok" to one executed test can make a whole project fail.

Can this be avoided? Yes it can, but surely not with reasonable means. Would any budget be allocated to a cross-check of all executed tests? There might be industries where this is the case (nuclear reactors or space technology, perhaps), but surely not in any business where it's not about life and death.

Regression tests

What I wrote in the previous section is related to new tests and to changes that get implemented. But we also need to check if everything that worked *before* still works now. This is a frustrating statement, however a very clear one: everything needs to be tested. We call this *regression* tests.

A complex system that does not work is invariably found to have evolved from a simpler system that worked just fine.

(Murphy's Laws of Computing)

A source of endless frustration is the fact that new versions of an already-used system regularly (nearly always) bring up old and previously-corrected errors! Can you believe this? Do we need more proof of the immaturity of the software industry? While writing this down, I could boil with rage.

It can get worse than that. Functionality that worked fine and never caused any problem before can be faulty with a new version. I'd like the software vendors to explain this to me someday. Do I exaggerate, and is this frequent? No, I don't exaggerate, and yes, it happens at each delivery of a new version, and it is true for each and every software vendor.

It can still get worse. Functionality that existed in the current version can have disappeared in the new one. It is hard to believe, but IT experts are so used to this, they don't make a fuss about it anymore. So, the conclusion is that to avoid the inherent risks of these scenarios, it is necessary to do full-fledged regression tests. All existing and working functionality now has to be tested again in a test biotope. It is extremely hard to explain to the business that this needs to be done every time, and that the company runs a severe risk if regression tests are omitted. It is easy to imagine how many resources these tests swallow up, and because of the sheer impossibility to test everything every time, this problem is a lot about risk management. At some point in the project, it needs to be decided what parts of all existing test cases will be left out in the regression tests. Making a mistake in this decision is as easy as drinking a glass of water. You will only find out that you made a mistake once you go live.

Regression tests are a mandatory exercise, especially in the area of functional software. In the area of publicly-used software, the situation isn't that bad. New releases usually don't cause the same kind of problems. New operating system releases (like a new Windows version) are somewhat borderline, where it is highly recommended to make large tests.

Just one very small example to illustrate what I wrote: A specialized software for the management of bank safes had "forgotten" all functionality related to access restrictions in a new version. While these rights could still be defined, they were pretty useless, as every user had total access. Imagine the potential risk related to such a situation. The provider's *Release Notes* did not mention anything about a change in the access rights management program, and, therefore, it had been decided not to test this part. Which brings us to a core statement: the provider creates the problem, IT takes the responsibility, and users bear the consequences.

End-to-end

We aren't through yet. As a next step, an *end-to-end* test needs to be carried out. In this step, a complete check of the entire processing chain will be done. Working individual components don't necessarily work well in connection with other components. To illustrate that, it could be that a program answers a question from another program with *Y* or *N*. But this other program expects a *1* or a *0*. While a human being could handle that, a computer cannot—it will refuse the answer as impossible, and that will be the first problem in the *end-to-end* test.

To summarize, the importance of testing activities grows from year to year along with the ever-increasing complexity in IT ecosystems. In many cases, it is the most important task in the business departments when it comes to IT-related work. Sufficient resources should be planned by every business department. Making the situation worse, the unsolved problem of bad software quality makes precise planning impossible. Testing is about frustration and a decisive reason for project failure. The situation will not improve in the near future.

Stress tests

There is an additional, albeit optional, step that needs to be completed before the introduction of a new system: a so-called *stress test*. The target here is to simulate big volumes of data being put in by users or injected by other systems. So far, we have only done unit tests and, once this is validated, it might be necessary to see how the system reacts under stress. This step is optional, because big data volumes are not always handled by a system.

Who hasn't heard stories in the media that systems have become slow and unstable when all users started to work with them? As reality (which is unknown) needs to be simulated here, it is very difficult to organize such tests, and very often, they are not successful. The requirements of software that handle big data volumes are unique. If the software design doesn't consider this from the start, it will be extremely hard and expensive to make appropriate changes later.

Software projects do fail because of this. One example was documented in the German magazine *Computerwoche* 38/2007: "*A school management software that was developed with costs of 20 million Euros is exasperating the users. Already since the last school year, around 2,000 schools were trying to work with the new and immature school management software* LUSD. *The software was developed by CSC. The concept and development started on June 1, 2006. The implementation in the schools began in October 2006. Since then, the complaints from users have grown. Sufferers are mainly the school secretaries. More than 300 complaints have reached the Ministry. 'So much coffee you have to drink while you wait endlessly; the* LUSD-*usage is very bad for the health,' was written in one of the protest emails...The situation escalated at the beginning of the new school year, because at this point in time eminently many accesses were requested to the database.*" The servers were not capable of handling such large data input.

Training

This subject has a chapter all its own. I will just say here that training measures need to be organized for the users as well as the IT experts. Of course, the training needs to be held as closely as possible to the planned go-live date. If this date is postponed many times, the users will have forgotten most of what they learned before they can use it.

Reciprocal influence

All steps listed so far are usually executed in that order. Usually. In reality, this is not necessarily the case, and something may happen in one step which influences the others. For example, a difficulty with the definition of an installation parameter can mean that the interface needs to be changed. Or the other way round: an unsolvable problem in the interface development can lead to a necessary change in the installation parameters. This kind of reciprocal influence needs to be monitored at all times, and it is the responsibility of the project manager to make sure that all involved parties stay aware about what happens in other areas of the project; therefore, regular project team meetings where all difficulties are discussed must be held. If the encountered difficulty is severe enough, it may lead to a full repetition of one or more steps. This reciprocal influence is one reason projects get delayed.

Migrations

What has been said so far applies to the introduction of totally new solutions or functionality. But there is another category of projects which are unpopular with project participants and have a set of unique problems. We are talking about migrations of an existing solution to a new one. Two categories may be distinguished here: technical and functional migration.

Technical migrations

With technical migrations (for example, from Windows XP to Windows Vista), there is no obvious added value for the business users, only highly-visible disagreeableness. Namely, the learning of a new software which ideally does exactly the same thing as the old one, including unpredictable malfunctions—not to mention the necessary testing of all systems that communicate with this migrated system (for Windows Vista, this would basically mean all programs used). For IT departments, the technical necessity is obvious as you cannot allow falling behind in technology, added to the difficulty of convincing the business to allocate the necessary budgets and staff for such projects.

Technical migrations can become necessary for other reasons than just moving to the next release of a software product. Sometimes products are just abandoned by the providers, and the existing solution must be migrated to something new. While this happens, it is nevertheless infrequent. What we see much more often is a situation where two companies merge, and the product of the company being swallowed is withdrawn from the market. As it is not possible to plan in advance for anything like that, the new company will communicate a timeframe (usually one to two years) until all customers must have migrated. This generates profitable new business, as all customers are coerced to plan for a migration project and to buy an expensive migration package. Added value for the company cannot be found in such technical migration projects.

With technical migrations, any IT department comes quickly to the end of the business' willingness to cooperate. The latter are usually very reluctant to waste their resources without getting any added value. In the end, the necessary tests are executed reluctantly, which has an impact on the quality of the test results. As soon as the new Windows version will go-live, you can expect problems, because the tests have not been done properly. Technical migration projects usually don't get any attention from Senior Management, and when you are unlucky, post go-live problems may be escalated to them. You must be prepared to hear something like: "Again, one of those typical and useless IT things in which the business departments have not been integrated properly." Well, that's part of the job, and you get used to it. You can manage this by activating your ears' firewall.

Functional migrations

Then there are functional migrations, where, let's say, an accounting system is replaced by a new one. Sometimes there is an obligation to replace a working system with a new one against everybody's will. If, for instance, the provider announces the cessation of all maintenance support for a certain date in the future (because the product line will be closed), if he goes bankrupt, if he changes his strategy, or if a higher authority (maybe at headquarters) decides to throw everything overboard and reinvent the wheel, then there is no choice. Especially for banks, such projects can take, according to the size of the biotope, many months, if not years, and generate many problems:

- The data from the old system must be transferred to the new one. Large systems have thousands of data files, of which the significance is not always known. This is true for the old system and even truer for the new one. Special programs need to be developed for this one-time exercise, but finding such programs on the market is almost impossible. There's a kind of guarantee of mistakes with this exercise; mistakes that sometimes show up very late after going live, especially in cases where some data elements are only needed at a later stage (for an end-of-year processing, for example).

- The user acceptance of that new system can differ, as not all users will perceive advantages with the new system. Elder colleagues especially can be very intractable.

- The required testing effort can break all boundaries (thousands of person days are no rarity). In very long projects, the moment will arrive when the zest, the *momentum*, will get lost. Vacation is banned towards the end of the project, and weekend work becomes regular. If, on top of that, the new software has a lot of errors (every software has errors), then it gets very critical for the whole project.

- During the migration phase to a new system, it is clear that there won't be any new changes done in the old system. This means a period of standstill for the company, which can have disastrous consequences.

- The old know-how is thrown away, and a new start is taken with a system, which is neither sufficiently mastered by the IT, nor by the business users. A migration is like a move to a new home: some things will get broken or lost. It is wise to hire people who have already this required know-how, provided you are able to find such people and get the budget for it. The full mastering of a large and complicated system (like a banking core application) takes years. You may compare it to learning a new language. Quickly, you may be able to learn and say a few words, but to talk, read, and write fluently is a question of years. Occasionally, I am surprised when I see how flippantly some companies decide to swap their core applications and naively wonder much later why they ran into massive problems. There isn't one perfect system around: replacing one with another is often like swapping black death with cholera.

- A big risk related to migrations consists in not fully understanding what is running in the old system. A software system is also a kind of biotope in itself, and—especially when it has grown over many years—there is nobody around who has the full picture. The same applies to the users of such systems: they also don't know the full picture. Therefore a lengthy (and expensive) feasibility analysis is required before the project can start.

- There's no limitation to the possible complexity of a migration project. The most challenging I came across in my career was the request to organize a migration for another entity in our group from an unknown system A to another unknown system B— without knowing the processes or the people of that other entity and without having a profound understanding of their business activity.

Workarounds

No system is error-free or covers all needs and requirements. No project runs without difficulties. During the execution of the project, the team usually discovers gaps that cannot be closed and which require a decision. A very popular way of handling these gaps is by creating *workarounds*. There are many types of them:

- A request for the provider to create a temporary solution (we call that *quick and dirty*) to circumnavigate the problem until a final solution is found.

- The IT department is asked to develop this *quick and dirty*. This may mean that a program will be written containing instructions like: *If customer = Smith, then apply 10% discount on the charged fees*. Such *quick and dirties* are downright detested because we all know that nothing lasts longer than the temporary. Auditors hate this even more, but luckily, they don't notice such things very often...

- Someone in the business department is asked to carry out a task fully manually. Naturally, this has an impact on the available resources in the business, and it is rarely popular. Not to mention the risk inherent to manual interventions.

- It can be decided to do nothing and go-live with the missing functionality. Possibly some day in the future, the gap will be closed or another solution will be found.

In extreme cases, the identified gaps can lead to putting the project "on hold" or stopping it completely.

An internal IT joke before we close the remarks about the *workarounds*: a *STP* (Straight-Through-Processing) can easily become a Straight-Through-*Printer*...

Go-live: finally!

We have come a long way, and after going through all these steps, difficulties, and risks, the decision is made to start with the new system in production.

Sign-off

The final "go" for the move into production is taken together with the business, at least when it comes to functional projects. The business departments are asked to accept the project, to give their *sign-off*. This might sometimes be difficult to get, because there is something "official" about it and could be used as an argument for finger-pointing later on: "you have signed, so you cannot come with new requests." Making such a decision is very often the result of a fight between those who have a deadline to respect and those who are testing the system. In many cases, the risks of putting the system into production while it still has well-known problems needs to be evaluated.

Backup scenarios

Before day X is there, it is necessary to discuss backup scenarios. The questions to answer are: "What do we do if the system does not behave as expected?" or "What do we do if we have to postpone the go-live at the last minute?" The answers to these questions depend strongly on the available options:

- If it is possible to operate in parallel with the old and new systems for some time, this might be a solution. This means that the business departments will have their work doubled for some time. As this has an impact on resources, it is clear that this option must be limited in time; is not easy to organize, and it is not very popular. Furthermore, mechanisms need to be created to check whether both systems work correctly; possibly, the IT department will have to write a quick-and-dirty reconciliation program. A deadline for making the final decision for a "go" or "stop" of the new system must be agreed upon by all parties.

- Sometimes parallel operations are not possible. This can be the case with the introduction of new regulatory changes or the application of a new law on a precise date. There wouldn't have been a possibility to run an old system that could not handle the new European currency, the Euro, on the day of its introduction. In these cases, there is no choice: Day X means *Big Bang,* and a backup scenario cannot be implemented. The night before day X sees a lot of sleepless IT and business experts.

- Sometimes an emergency stop of the new system (after it has gone into production) must be made if the problems are so huge that no workarounds and no backup scenarios can handle it. However, this should be a last resort, as it documents the failure of all participants in a way that is visible to everyone. Such emergency stops happen regularly to the point that the media sometimes report them.

- It is surely a wise idea to make sure that sufficient resources are available for the first days after the go-live. We call this the stabilization phase. Concretely, this can mean that an already-existing vacation ban is extended, and the employees are kindly requested to do longer hours and not plan anything for the weekend.

Pilot

To minimize the risks of failure on day X, it can be decided to start on a smaller scale, to have a so-called *pilot*. In this case, the volumes are kept low, and not all functionality of the system is made available. If there are no more problems, volumes and functionality are slowly increased. Such a decision is not always possible. A working example could be the introduction of a new technology for the company's subsidiaries: one small subsidiary is declared as *pilot*, and the global rollout will happen in different phases.

Post go-live

During the execution of the project, the project team might have come to the conclusion to break it into different phases; this is especially useful in complex and time-critical projects. This means that after day X, the project will continue with topics of minor importance—which is somewhat of a problem, because the project participants might be tired of that project and would like to do something else, like taking their holidays! Typically, the writing of the documentation (such as the technical interface descriptions or user guides) is postponed. While this is surely not a good idea, it nevertheless happens frequently. A more appropriate example is the implementation of minor functions, such as the automation of processes which does not take a lot of resources or which increases the user's comfort only slightly.

Problems in production

Even with the greatest possible diligence taken, you can always expect problems after the go-live. The systems do not behave in the way they did during the tests. The first days after day X are usually a nightmare with rebelling users: a more-or-less extended stabilization phase is to be foreseen. Studies tell us that error-free new applications are the exception, not the rule.

How is this possible? Well, the move from a test biotope to the production biotope is a process which is not fully automatable. There is a lot of software around that can partially handle this process, like programs that have to be moved into the live environment. But crucial parts remain fully manual. There are a multitude of installation parameters, which require that you design a way to install them. Especially in the case of a software upgrade, by which new installation parameters are introduced, it will be difficult to separate old and new parameters; in fact, they are mixed in one place in the database. So, great care must be taken when changing them. Also, there might be parameters in satellite systems connected to our system that need to be changed. For this, no software will help; this is a totally manual process. And who wouldn't understand that manual processes, especially if they are executed only one time, are prone to creating problems?

Another major reason for the arising problems after go-live is the fact that the test ecosystem is never totally comparable to the live ecosystem. You simply cannot copy/paste this. What makes this even more difficult is that the test ecosystem has been copied from the live ecosystem at some point far away in the past when the project started. The production ecosystem has evolved with the normal day-to-day business. Moving, then, an old test ecosystem to the live ecosystem is a reliable source of problems. Can this be managed? Yes, of course, but not without having dedicated staff around to take care of this question. And now introduce me to a Financial Controller who would be willing to hire more people for these kinds of problems!

Psychology

And then there is the psychological element which can lead to the failure of projects. The professional magazines are full with examples. When key people are not convinced about the necessity of a change (*The old system still works* / *I have always done it like that* / *Why should I suddenly change it after so many years?* / *This is one of these IT things that nobody needs*), the project has many chances to fail at this stage. The involvement of all participants is of major importance, but in too many cases, it is not done, or it is not possible. Without this, however, even the best system in the world (which does not exist!) would have difficulties getting off the ground. Sometimes, some of the participants have tried at the beginning of the project to get another solution than the one that has been finally chosen. After they have lost the battle, they hide their denial and will boycott the chosen solution as soon as the first major difficulties show up. (*You see? I told you!*) Initially, you are powerless against that.

Lessons learned

We finally made it, and the system is running in production. Before the project is closed, it is nice to do a *lessons learned* exercise. You live and learn. It is important that all project participants communicate about the difficulties they have encountered with the view of doing better next time. The role of the external partners should be evaluated to see if it would be a good idea to ask them again for a future project. If this step is done regularly, then just before retirement, every participant will be almost perfect.

Success story!

If the project is of a certain size—and very shortly after the start of the production, if not the same day!—the external provider will ask his customer (in the most friendly words) if he can add the company's name to his reference list and if he would be allowed to present to the market a small flyer with the "success story" of this project. Please, please? The CIO is then happily allowed to give a statement about the system, under the condition that he finds nothing but warm words about the provider. The contents of these flyers are always more-or-less the same and contain phrases like: "With this software we increased our productivity by x percent," or "We were surprised how quickly our requirements were translated into a stable solution," or "With the introduction of this software, we have done a quantum leap." Those flyers don't have much value, as the reader of such a flyer has no clue about how the productivity was before the system was introduced, what the customer defines as "quick," and how ramshackle his situation was. The best is to talk directly to other existing customers, but as we have seen earlier in this chapter, what they say only applies to their biotope.

After some time...

... with the new system, things which are of minor importance begin to surface: how easy or complicated is the daily usage of that system, and how easily can it be adapted to changing needs? If the answers to these questions are negative, a delayed rejection of the system may happen. It is a mistake to neglect these factors in the selection phase.

Mergers

Ah, mergers! Who likes mergers? Mergers arrive as a natural catastrophe to everyone, perhaps with the exception of shareholders and CEOs. IT experts absolutely abhor mergers between two companies. IT is never the trigger for a migration, and it is even extremely unusual that IT questions get addressed during merger discussions. IT-related activities only start once that the merger decision has been taken.

Along with the known general problems of a merger (low motivation among the staff, fears of job loss, and cultural differences), there is an additional IT-related difficulty. In such a situation, two existing biotopes have to compete against each other. A target biotope needs to be defined. It may be that one biotope will be completely abandoned or that the new biotope is a mix of the existing ones. The possible project difficulties that we have seen so far in this chapter explode in such a scenario. Every single piece needs to be reviewed, changed, upgraded, migrated, or removed.

Projects like these are monsters and push the people working in such projects to their limits. Participating in such projects is an extremely intense adventure that no one will forget quickly. Because it is so intense, it may be good to experience it once in a career. But once is surely enough for a lifetime.

Million

Any given program costs more and takes longer.

From "Laws of Computer Programming"

Why does it cost a million, or more? In our analysis of IT projects thus far, it must have become clear that many experts with various skills are required to run a project and, quite obviously, they need to be paid. At many points, external resources are needed—several hundreds or thousands of person days need to be budgeted. A million adds up really fast.

But there are other costs as well: software licenses are very expensive and are normally paid on the basis of the number of software users. Also, twenty percent of the license price should be budgeted for future maintenance cost. Then we need staff to take care of all systems. It's not like a car, where you get maintenance once a year. No, every system needs daily care and monitoring by a skilled team. At the time the decision for a new system is made, calculations (or, most of the time, only estimations) are done in order to understand how many IT experts will be needed to administrate the system once it is up and running. Providers either tend not to give you this information or to keep the figure low since they don't know in advance what functionality you will use in which way and, of course, because they don't know your existing biotope. Sometimes, a ratio—such as a percentage of the number of employees served by the software—can be used for this calculation. The biggest I came across so far was three percent! For a staff of a thousand employees, this would mean that you need to hire thirty IT administrators. Most of the time, this calculation is not done at all, and only the pure software license costs are considered, which is a big mistake and a reason for future participants' frustration. It's a platitude to say that IT staff isn't the least expensive in a company.

I would like to write for a moment about *Open Source*. Not all software must be paid for, and you can find a lot of software for free; this kind of software is developed by a world-wide community of people and companies who bundle their efforts to make software available free-of-charge. Software companies that develop competitive products don't like this at all, and there's a constant discussion about whether it is better to have companies developing software in order to gain money or if the *Open Source* approach is the better one. This, however, isn't the point I want to talk about.

Since software licenses are very expensive, you might think that *Open Source* software could at least fix this problem. Unfortunately, this is not the case, because *Open Source* is limited to software used by the general public. There is no major functional software available nowadays. If you need, for example, an accounting system for a bank, you have no choice but to buy from a professional provider.

Open Source has huge merits, and without it, the Internet would never have become such a massive success in such a short time. It offers the possibility to design sophisticated websites without having to buy expensive software. You can find operating systems, browsers, databases, programming languages, web-servers, office suites, and much more. Open Source is growing fast, but it remains limited to the more technical and peripheral parts of an IT biotope. Today, there are many companies who use *Open Source* programs to a very large extent, but in the area of functional software, this is impossible. I don't think we will see trends in that direction. Therefore, it is true to say that *Open Source* reduces costs, but it is limited to a specific area. Knowing that the biggest IT costs in a company are generated from functional software, the impact of *Open Source* on global IT budgets remains small.

Then we have to add hardware costs. More than one machine is required to implement a software solution—something which is quite different to private situations, where a single PC is normally all you have. Not so in a company: you need a production machine, a disaster recovery machine (cf. chapter 11: *Damage in the millions*), a testing environment, and possibly even a development machine. In the financial industry, there is a ratio of about 3:1 between the number of employees and the number of servers (another name for computers); in other industries, this figure may vary. In any case, a massive and expensive collection of machines is necessary. Not included in that tally is the necessary desktop hardware, such as PCs, printers, and so on. And, every expansion of the computer center requires more electricity (including uninterrupted power supply) or air-conditioning system enhancement.

When we look at the total costs, we should not forget the possible costs related to IT security. When a software system is purchased, real costs cannot be measured by the license costs alone. It is normally two, five, or even ten times the license amount. This is applicable both for the implementation project and future running costs. But who calculates like that? Ideally, a profitability analysis is done together with the business before the final choice for a system is made. But it is rather exceptional that all elements are known or considered correctly. The result of such an analysis still wouldn't give the full picture of all related costs.

Profitability analyses, or business case calculations, are done differently for new systems and upgrades. For a new system, the immediate costs are known, but the real running costs for the life cycle of that system are completely ignored most of the time. While costs might somehow be accurately evaluated (though this doesn't happen frequently), it is much more difficult to calculate the return on the investment for the business. Usually, it is only possible to make assumptions or educated guesses. Once the project is decided and the system is running, nobody checks to see if the assumed return on the investment was really reached. Consequently, after some time, the opinion grows that IT systems are too expensive.

When it comes to upgrades of an existing system, it is even worse. Most of the time, upgrades are mandatory—the current version is no longer supported by the provider—and they need very high budgets; business cases are, therefore, very rarely calculated, and the decision makers qualify such projects as "necessary and expensive evils" that don't bring value to the business.

Now that we have an understanding of the difficulties in IT projects, I want to close with something humorous which, nevertheless, relates closely to the IT world, although it may be a bit far-fetched for the counterpart in private life.

Your bathroom water tap is dripping. You analyze the cause, and you find out that the waterproofing is broken. You go to the nearest do-it-yourself store to get a new one, but the salesperson tells you that this size has been recently taken off the market. He says you can have one specially made, but because of the costs and the long waiting time, he doesn't recommend it. His recommendation is to buy a new water tap, so you do.	Your accounting software produces an error which only happens in a specific condition with one of your customers. You contact the software provider's Service-Desk who tells you that this problem can't be permanently fixed in the old version that you run, but if you insist, they would temporarily fix the problem on a time-and-materials basis. The best solution, however, would be to pay the upgrade fees to the next version. You follow his recommendation.
Back at home, you try to install the new water tap, but you notice quickly that it is a different size, and it does not fit on your sink. You return to the DIY and want to return the water tap. The salesperson tells you that there is no better option, so you keep the water tap.	During the tests of the new version, you suddenly notice that the interests on account are calculated with a different formula, which is of no use to you. The provider tells you that this formula is documented in the product description. Of course, he didn't tell you this before.
After deliberation, you conclude that the sink is old anyhow and a more modern design would improve the whole bathroom. Meanwhile the water tap continues to drip.	You ask an expensive external consultant to analyze the situation. He advises you to buy an expensive additional module in the software. This would solve the new problem, and he says the company could very well take advantage of the new features in the new module. The customer accounts continue to be incorrect.
You order the new sink, wait for it to arrive, and try to install it yourself. During the installation, some wall tiles break off. There's nothing to do now but put new tiling in the bathroom. Meanwhile, you shower at your neighbor's place or when it rains.	During the tests of this new module, you realize that the interface to the ordering system has become incompatible. You have no choice but to start the development of an upgrade of your interface. Meanwhile, you help your customers by having accounting staff perform manual corrections.
You have hardly finished tiling your bathroom when you notice that the bathroom door doesn't close anymore because the new tiles are thicker than the old ones. You decide to leave the door open in future. Over time, you will get used to it.	Your programmers tell you that they need to have the firewall rules changed because the new module obliges the interface to collect data from behind it. Your security officer declines this request with a hint to the company's security rules. You install a temporary bypass solution which

	somehow works, but makes no one happy. There's a good chance that this "temporary" solution will run forever.
Everything is finished now, and you try your new water tap. It works fine—for the first two days—until you notice that the wall behind the tap is wet. You call the plumber to come and see what the reason for this could be. "This is normal," he says. The water tap you bought is not designed for the water pressure you have on your conduit.	Day X has arrived, and you start production with all the changes you have done. Everything works fine— for the first two days—until you get a customer complaint about the fact that you have delivered wrong data for the past two days. A quick analysis shows that the programmer has fixed the initial problem, but has introduced a new one.
Your partner is now really tired with the ongoing construction and proposes to sell the house and buy a new one to have all these problems fixed in one go.	The accounting department loses patience and reports the problem to Senior Management—accompanied with a proposal to replace the old, damned software by something more state-of-the-art, cheaper, faster, more flexible, and more reliable. That would fix all problems in one go.

The first business trip

Business trips are part of the job. There's nothing wrong about that, because visiting trade fairs, networking with peers, or talking to customers and providers is very helpful. Invitations to all possible events are abundant. Theoretically, if all invitations were accepted, a CIO would be traveling all the time and would surely meet himself at some airport. Of course such events are not organized in Chandler, AZ, or Henderson, NV, but rather in New York, Berlin, or London. Especially towards the end of the year, when salespeople haven't yet reached their sales targets, they allure customers with special offers and combine them from time to time with an invitation to a magic event. Last-minute spending finds quite a fertile ground because, like everywhere else, the budget needs to be fully spent; otherwise, you risk a budgetary cut for the upcoming year.

But where is the border between a necessary business trip and a fun trip? I experienced this dilemma right at the start of my career.

My boss sent me on my first business trip. I was supposed to go to the SICOB trade fair in Paris, the French equivalent of the SIBOS. Paris is always nice to visit, but I wasn't quite sure what my objective was. I was asked to get a "picture" of the current software offerings and see if there was anything that would be of interest to us. The Internet did not exist in those days, and there was no other way to get a general overview of available software.

Well, I spent an interesting day at the fair in *La Défense* (at that time a futuristic area outside of Paris).
About two weeks after my return, my boss asked me to see him in his office:

"Where's your report?" he asked.

I thought about it for a second, and said, "Ehm, I didn't know that I was supposed to write a report and—"

"Mister Roeltgen," he interrupted me, "we are not here to finance fun trips. When we send someone somewhere, then— " I braced myself for one of his irascible outbursts. Luckily, the phone rang at that moment.

He answered it. Of course, I couldn't hear what the caller said, but it was not difficult to imagine the missing parts.

"Oh, good morning, Mister Kind, yes we can go through the program together once more...Departure Monday morning, arrival early afternoon in New York, rest of the day at our own disposal...Tuesday 11 a.m. appointment, lunch in Park Avenue, in the afternoon golf tournament...Wednesday morning city sightseeing, afternoon management briefing, evening gala dinner...Thursday visit of their production plant followed by lunch with the Research Directors...Yes, Friday morning a short common debriefing, lunch with management...Friday afternoon flight home. Yes, great!"

After a short break he added: "By the way, will you take your camera with you? Yes? Right, I will take mine as well then. See you at the airport."

Then he realized that I was still there. The enthusiasm about his upcoming trip had made him forget about me completely.
He looked at me and asked: "Where were we?"

I answered, audaciously, maybe a bit cheekily: "You said that I was supposed to write a report about the SICOB and that we are not here to finance fun trips."

"Ehm, yes. Yes...fun trips. Go and write this report. Anything else up?"

*A professor handed out the documents for the final examination
and created some bewilderment among his students.
One of them jumped up and called agitatedly:
"But, Sir, these are the same questions that you asked
us at the previous class exercise!"
"Correct," he said, "but the answers have changed."*

(Unknown author)

Change is the only constant

What are the tasks of an IT department? What do they do all day?

"How would you explain the mission of an IT department in a single phrase?"

A short and simple question, but only at first glance. The CIO of a very big, reputable, and internationally-operating corporate group was once asked this question by a journalist. He started to splutter and had difficulties producing a clever answer. He finally muttered something about "change management." Quite a lame reply, but to be fair, it must be said that this question is, indeed, hard to answer. Answering this question can easily fill a whole book. And the chapter related to the "management of change" would, no doubt, fill a large part of that book.

Change brings instability—this is an all-time correct statement. As change is permanent in IT, so instability is also permanent. It can be summarized by the simple rule that IT is always mentioned alongside the words "problems" and "difficulties." Mr. Resch, until the end of 2008 CIO of the German company Bayer, gave a remarkable interview in the magazine *Computerwoche* 29/2007 (cf. Appendix 3), where he stated that, being a CIO, you are always on the defensive.

It is permanently necessary to solve problems that others have created. IT is like working in an open pit: new channels need to be dug—old ones risk collapse. It is the task of the IT staff to accompany this permanent change and manage it in the best possible way.

There are plenty of different job types in IT. This chapter presents the most important ones.

Something you do all the time becomes somehow self-evident. Every time however, when an IT expert talks to a normal (!) person, he notices very quickly that the public has no clue about the tasks of an IT department. Nothing seems to be self-evident about it. Even PC-aficionados have only a very vague idea about what happens in an IT department.

The tasks in an IT department are indeed numerous. There is plenty of specialized literature about it, but it is written from an academic standpoint. In my humble opinion, that gives the wrong picture to university IT students about what they can expect when reality hits them. I will explain the subject in simple terms and, wherever possible, will illustrate it with examples.

I have been a CIO since 1987. Sounds like a long day. Looking back, I recognize that there has been an immense advancement in the job. I was pretty young in those days, and IT was simple. Today, becoming CIO at the age of 28 is almost a fantasy.

Change is the only constant in IT. Nothing we work at today will stay for a long time. When you start with a project for a new system, you frequently know already when it will be decommissioned. This might be regrettable and psychologically hard to accept, but mentally, it keeps you young.

The IT expert, the bizarre, unknown, and nocturnal creature? The "nerd"? The cliché from the early computer days doggedly lives on. The ivory tower times are surely gone, but the characteristics of IT experts are still hardly known outside of IT. In my more-than-twenty-years in IT, I have met an awful lot of people from all different cultures with very different experiences. You may have met IT experts who are sometimes a bit cranky, often uncommunicative, mostly uncomplicated, but always aware that they work in a very special and important area, and they always have a sense for their mission and its responsibility. They know about their special role in a company, but usually don't exploit it.

Have you ever heard of IT experts going on strike? (Come to think of it, this would be an excellent idea for a novel! Imagine the state of the world if all IT experts stopped working for just three days.) Instead of anger, though, they are more likely to be very disappointed when they get criticized or if their work is not recognized as they expected. It is very rare for IT experts to seek attention; invitations to company parties and events organized by providers are only reluctantly accepted. Party animals are hard to find here.

IT experts are grey eminences—outside IT, they are hardly known, and nobody can describe what they are doing. But they have a big influence in the company.

The IT world is a man's world, and female IT experts are scarce. Different sources provide different numbers, but it seems that the average is only between ten and twenty percent. The reason for this is not to be found in some hidden discrimination. No, the reality is that there are very few women applying for IT positions. This is a pity, as it seems to me that women have a special gift men don't have. They seem to be able to handle "difficult" business users more easily. In every company, there are most likely business users who get up on the wrong side of the bed every day of their lives, and there are those who try to hide their incompetence with arrogance. If you have a man handling the problem, you can count on the situation escalating. I experienced many times that women succeed in taming these types of characters. Women apparently have a unique gift for working in the Help-Desk.

In general terms, IT staff is very sensitive when they get blamed for a problem they didn't cause. Unfortunately, this happens constantly, and users continually bluster about IT when, again, something has gone wrong. IT experts are paid to fix problems, but they have to bear the wrath of the users directly. If you are a computer user and if, after reading this book, you understand that your IT colleagues aren't to blame for your many, daily computer problems, I guarantee that your collaboration with them will be much more fruitful.

Real programmers never work from 9 to 5.
If any real programmer is around at 9 a.m.,
it's because they were up all night.

(Unknown author)

Computers are more predictable than human beings (even if you will doubt this after reading this book), and many IT experts feel well at home in this very special world. I think the work ethic of IT experts is not unlike that of doctors. I almost never came across someone who wasn't prepared to drop everything in order to fix an urgent problem. One call at three o'clock in the morning, and all necessary staff is there. Repeated weekend work? Never a problem. Sometimes the commitment to IT supersedes family.

Over time, the job market for IT experts has been very volatile, and it could well have changed again by the time you read this book. In my country, Luxembourg, the situation in 2009 is temporarily not very good, due to the global financial crisis and the recession. In the past, there has continually been a striking lack of experts, and this situation will return. This lack of experts is due to the fact that Luxembourg is on its way to getting an IT Competence Centre in Europe (more about that in chapter 10: *Luxembourg*).

Managing senior programmers is like herding cats.

Dave Platt

The staff management of IT experts is not always easy and might be compared to the function of a coach who has good players. It is relatively easy to make mistakes here. I made one some years ago. I was somewhat irritated because one of my guys was exaggeratedly huffy in a meeting about a minor incident, and I informally mentioned it to my boss. Well, he had nothing better to do than to bring this up at the next big team meeting. That sparked off a fire! I wasn't forgiven for this faux pas for many years. But then again, this is proof of my argument.

Occasionally, but much less frequently than twenty years ago, there are some who succeed in factoring out the real world. It can happen that a colleague hasn't noticed that a war has started in Iraq or that there is a discussion about Guantanamo.

In order to describe the various tasks in IT, I will list different categories. If you scan the Internet for one of these tasks, you have excellent chances to find a sentence like: "This task is one of the most important ones in IT," which shows that all described tasks are very important. There is no rhyme or reason to how they are presented; it's arbitrary.

This chapter is very long and probably the most strenuous of the whole book. But if you want to understand what your colleagues in IT are doing all day, you should read it to the end.

External factors

IT operates in a very dynamic environment, influenced by many factors. Some of these accelerate our world (business initiatives and priorities, new technologies, new software systems and much more) and others slow it down (IT security, legal requirements, and budget cuts). This area of conflict needs to be managed.

To keep things simple, let's argue that the CIO usually reports to the CEO. A relationship built on mutual trust is of enormous importance. Many CIOs influence business decisions that are not necessarily in the business' interest just by using excessive IT jargon. On the other hand, it can become very uncomfortable for the CIO if the CEO thinks he has sufficient IT knowledge to make and impose unilateral IT decisions. In such cases, the probability is very high that what I describe at the beginning of the next chapter will happen. The situation may become even more insane when the CIO reports to the CFO (Chief Financial Officer). Of course, costs are important, but they are not the most important thing. If IT is viewed purely as a cost centre, it rapidly becomes impossible to generate value for the business or create a competitive advantage. Success requires a well-organized and well-staffed IT that combines drive for innovation with prudence—this combination enables business development and business processes. At the very least, this should be agreed upon, but there are many places where it is not the case.

In companies (as opposed to administrations), the competition is usually fierce, and the pressure to generate revenues is enormous. This pressure is passed on to IT because automation creates efficiency and thus profits. IT is asked to have an understanding of the current and upcoming business requirements and must propose solutions. Because of this mutual influence, a good relationship between IT and the business is a must. IT must be prepared to adapt to ever-changing priorities. All employees in an IT department must love change and accept it as a constant of their work. This may be frustrating sometimes. It is also necessary to have alternatives on hand, as the business frequently proposes a specific software solution (for example, they have heard that a competitor is using the program with great success, and now they are enthusiastic about it). Research may prove that the implementation of that system (cf. chapter 3) would be highly complex, risky, expensive, or even technically not feasible; however, just saying "No" would not be helpful.

Another big influence comes from the regulatory and legal framework. Laws (or, in my case, EU-directives), data protection, archiving requirements, traceability and auditing, outsourcing regulations, and many more play an ever-increasing role.

A constant disruption in all projects is security (cf. chapter 13: *IT Security*). The threats rise constantly, and the technical countermeasures require more and more means and expertise. Each individual security measure increases the running time of a project.

Constant innovation in the computer industry accelerates the creation of new solutions. Imagine how the world changed for almost all companies with the Internet, push-mail technology, or navigation systems. Today, at least as far as it concerns administrative problems, an IT solution can always be found; that doesn't mean, however, that any of these solutions are simple or cheap. However, as we will see much later, the backdrop of this is that new technology is never stable at its launch, and security doesn't play a role at all. New technology needs to be looked at with great prudence.

Strategy

Strategy is a constant topic in IT, and it involves trying to determine the direction the business should take in the upcoming months and years. Which systems will be used, and what technology should be introduced? What services should be offered? What will be the next hype we should keep hands off, and what is mature enough to go for it? Sometimes you may find the wording "architecture management" or "master plan," which mean roughly the same. In small companies, this is, of course, not a permanent task on which someone would work the whole day. But in large, worldwide operating companies, there are dozens of people who do nothing else than evaluate the pros and cons of various strategies. These people are usually big thinkers but are sometimes, quite unfortunately, a bit too far away from reality. There is a clear tendency to produce gigabytes of PowerPoint presentations which contain things that will never see the light of day. One of my ex-colleagues argued, after he had seen another 100-page PowerPoint for the umpteenth time: "The only platform on which this system will run is the beamer." There's a lot of truth in that. Another *running gag* related to PowerPoint is: "A PowerPoint with more than 24 pages is no longer a presentation, but a movie."

When establishing a strategy, there are several influential factors:

Business strategy

The ever-present question is how the IT strategy can be aligned with the business strategy. Usually, it would make sense to have the business strategy lead to the IT strategy. It may happen—and quite frequently—that the business wants to launch a new product, and you would need some software changes in your application for that. But if your provider has decided to develop the product in another direction or does not have resources available to execute your request, you can come into quite a difficult situation.

Headquarters

While there is a worldwide trend in large corporations to centralize IT services, it is still a fact today that even subsidiaries operate their own IT systems. For them, in this scenario, the room for strategic maneuvering is probably quite limited—it all depends on the company's philosophy. As with fashion: if you are there long enough, you will see all possible tendencies. These days, as I said, the trend goes to a more centralized approach. With the background of exploding costs and complexity, it can make sense to run large infrastructures in common and to use the same streamlined processes. But it is as sure as death and taxes that the day will come when it will become obvious that running large infrastructures creates problems in terms of responsiveness to business requirements, thus loosing flexibility and agility. It is a question that will keep us busy for at least the next ten years.

What I observe more and more these days is a trend towards a healthy mix of both. It makes sense to centralize things which are identical everywhere in the world (like data storage or email systems), and to bundle strategic IT components in a limited number of hubs. While this can't, of course, be a general rule that would be applicable to everyone, it is, nevertheless, a scenario which has a lot of charm: it removes the dogmatism from the topic. So it could make sense to have a hub in each time zone and to size it in a way that the complexity is still manageable, it has enough flexibility, and costs remain moderate. If you work at a place where this question is still looked at in a dogmatic way, it could be an approach to just wait for a change—under the condition to stay patient for several years. A strategy which splits the participants will not succeed, and there is substantial risk that key staff will leave.

I plead for pragmatism, meaning that for each system, application, service, or process, it is decided on a case-by-case basis where and how this should be done. Because of the nature of this question, it is possible to discuss it for days and days without reaching a consensus. When sitting in this kind of meeting, you'll see that some participants start to zone out. These kinds of meetings are also a good way to confuse people. Some years ago, I had a colleague who had the ability to drive people crazy by asking questions like: "Is the submitted proposal the journey or the goal?" These kinds of discussions are often led by very young people—surely clever, but inexperienced, and they get tripped up by old stagers. At the latest, when the emcee from New York asks if Luxembourg is part of Europe, we know that we're in for some trouble.

Provider's strategy

Every provider has his own strategy, which may change at any point in time. If you are lucky and you are one of his key customers, you have the opportunity to influence that strategy. But this is quite rare. IT needs to know the strategy of its most important providers and has to align its strategy with the provider's—sometimes merely impossible. There are also providers who don't have a strategy at all or want to keep it secret.

Investments / Supply management

What budget do you get for your strategy? Proposals must be made and must be defended against the master of the budgets. Of course, if a general budget cut is announced, the strategy needs to be adapted accordingly as well. As hardware and software are very expensive and the total investments increase with the size of the company, purchases are often regrouped in a so-called *Supply Management* which allows the company to save a lot of money.

Outsourcing / Insourcing

IT is becoming a cost of doing business that must be paid by all but provides distinction to none.

Nicholas Carr

This is a hot topic, one which is heavily, controversially, and often even emotionally discussed. It is about jobs that the IT department has traditionally done, but are now going to be done by someone else. The IT department may fear losing jobs and losing control. But whatever way you look at it, it is something which does exist and often makes sense. However, it often does not.

First of all, what is outsourcing? I'll give an example from private life. It is about asking someone else to do things which you could do yourself in order to gain time, to be more efficient, or to save costs. You may mow your grass yourself, or you may ask a gardener to do it for you. If you decide for the gardener, you need to define exactly what he needs to do, how much money you will pay, and so on. Applied to IT, it could cover areas as vast as the installation of PCs, doing data backups, administrating networks, or running accounting systems.

For each and every task an IT department performs, it is necessary to ask the question if this could not be done in a better way by an external company. If IT is especially good in a specific area, it may offer its services to others, which would then be called insourcing.

Outsourcing is very much the hip trend these days. The higher the decision makers are in the organization, the more they favor outsourcing due to their dim view of IT. It is obvious that a Managing Director wants to avoid the reproach of having missed a trend. This situation does create bizarre bloopers. Targets are defined top-down, and not very long ago, my boss (of Indian origin) added to my yearly objectives to make three proposals for outsourcing things we had done internally so far—preferably to companies in India. The target was not about making an analysis with pros and cons—no, it was about making three (three! not two, not four!) concrete suggestions. Weird.

Even though outsourcing has become a modern reality, the question of when and how outsourcing makes sense is still something on which most people disagree. This question is not about "yes" or "no." It is just too complex for such a simple approach. Polls carried out by market research organizations to find out if you are pro- or con-outsourcing are downright annoying. This question is too complex for a yes/no poll. (Interestingly, though, I have observed that the more complex a subject is, the more there is a tendency to carry out a poll. It is the recurring attempt to explain the world with a questionnaire.)

By all accounts, the justification for outsourcing something is sometimes hard to believe; extreme care should be taken in this matter. The major arguments raised for doing an outsourcing project are:

- IT does not manage the subject correctly (missing know-how or use of inappropriate systems), and an external provider can do this much better. This may be right very often, but there is a risk that you will just hand over your own chaos to someone else.

- An external company can do this cheaper. To reduce such a decision to its financial aspect is very dangerous and short-sighted.

The trouble with programmers is that you can never tell what a programmer is doing until it's too late.

Seymoure Cray

What are the problems outsourcing can bring along?
- Especially when the financial aspect was the core of the argument, or if the price has been negotiated down aggressively, there will be a rude awakening when the boomerang returns quickly. With every new minor request (like "Change information *customer category* in the database for all customers having a turnover of more than one million."), the insourcer will show the contract and argue that this was not included. But, for a daily rate of, let's say, 1,500 USD, it would

be possible. Need I mention that the number of days that will be proposed for the change will be an ugly number and hard to swallow?

- It is about giving up independence and control. Especially in areas where there is a lot of change (for example, critical core software applications), it is a question of survival to retain control. It won't be very long before you'll need the first major change. This change request will begin a painstaking and lengthy process. A CEO can "force" his IT department to execute the request quickly in a pragmatic way. With an external partner, this is much more complicated, as the whole process of definition, in-scope/out-of-scope, negotiation, prioritization, change of contracts, and much more needs to be done. Because of this heaviness, end-users do self-help and start tinkering with their own solutions—something we call the phenomena of the "end-user-computing-comeback." And by this self-help, they enlarge the IT biotope in their firm.

- The client is in a very weak position, as there is no possibility to ask for alternative offers, and he basically only manages a dependency. A real-life example: a bank had an outsourcing contract containing a clause that did not allow any interventions on an emergency basis, and all change requests had to go through the standard prioritization process. One day, the CEO worked on a presentation that he wanted to give in the afternoon. Suddenly, PowerPoint asked for an additional function (plug-in), but to do so, administrative rights were necessary. Begging did not help: the insourcer refused (and he was right from a legal point of view), saying that the contract did not include this. Finally, an agreement was found, and the extra service was charged at a horrendous price.

- In early outsourcing projects in previous years, the need to monitor the insourcer and provide a coordinator for all its activities was often overlooked. If your insourcer is in India, for instance, it is an excellent idea to send over some of your own staff to make sure that things are going alright. Today, this aspect of outsourcing is recognized, and it is rare to see this mistake.

- A further issue related to control is about the staff employed by the insourcer. It is already tough enough to make sure that you have the right people and allocate them correctly to the tasks you need to fulfill; but when it comes to the insourcer, you don't know this staff, and you have to rely on what their commercials tell you. You have no clue if they offer a long-term perspective or if they treat their staff well.

- India is the country offering the most outsourced IT services. Of course, the salaries are much lower than in the US or in Europe. The problem there is that there is almost no long-term employer retention. Turnover rates of twenty percent or more per year are a reality—for a few rupees more, every expert is ready to resign and go elsewhere. Not to mention that general salaries increase rapidly for the best experts, so it might happen that you will only get the second best.

- The other major issue with India is the cultural differences. Meetings with Indians have their own very special character, and not being aware about these differences will create insurmountable problems.

- When it comes to software development, it is necessary to define with utmost care what needs to be developed. There is no need to explain to a Western-European programmer what the value-added-tax is. It suffices to write down that the VAT needs to be calculated, and he knows what needs to be done. The Indian colleague has never heard of VAT, and therefore, you need to go back to square one. He is paid for executing what is written down—no more, no less. I know about two major cases where massive problems have been encountered because of this. First, there was the conversion to the European withholding tax (introduced in 2005) that a very well-known software company decided to have developed in India. The subject was not understood there, and, consequently, customers received software of very bad quality. The consequence was that this software company had to write letters to its entire customer base, apologizing for the fact that the solution was delivered too late and was full of errors. Second, there was the development of the German tax regulation in a much-known core banking application. This subject is extreme in terms of complexity even for old stager programmers; sleepless nights need to be taken into account. The idea to have this developed in India led to a disaster and burnt millions of Euros. This software company was so discouraged with the subject of German tax that it decided to withdraw from the German market.

- Loss of know-how. Internal expertise gets lost. In the beginning, this might not be so much of a problem, as you get the expertise now from the outside. But over time, the outsourcing company will no longer be able to take strategic IT decisions by itself. A question like: "Should we upgrade from Windows XP to Windows Vista?" cannot be answered anymore. The insourcer might answer "yes" to that question and propose a new project for which the customer will have to pay. An internal IT department would have answered "no" to that question and by this save a lot of money.

It's quite often only a matter of time until a CFO will notice that the outsourcing costs are out of control and recommend to insource again. The way back, however, is hairy and time-consuming.

When is outsourcing useful?

You may think by now that I am completely opposed to outsourcing. This is not the case, and in the past, I have carried out a number of outsourcing projects. For those of you who may have heard about Nicholas Carr and read one of his books, you could get the opinion that outsourcing is the solution to all problems and that it is only a matter of time until everything will be outsourced. He states that IT departments will disappear in the not-so-distant future because IT is on its way to becoming a commodity and should be provided like electricity, for example. A hundred years ago, every company produced its own electricity in the same way that every company has its own IT today. Well, while this statement may impress most CEOs (I would bet that he wrote his books with these readers, and only these readers, in mind), he does not consider enough the very nature of IT. At first glance, his statements have some charm. But, what he totally neglects is the fact that, for most companies, the most important asset in today's business world is the data it owns and not the computers, network, or software.

Declaring data to be a commodity by comparing it with electricity is adventurous. Companies aren't going to give away their business data on a massive, global scale to another company that they might or might not be able to trust. I don't see this happening in the future either. On the contrary, data leakage is a problem of increasing importance. Companies want to retain control of their data. Even Carr's statement about electricity is wrong: companies of some size do not rely on public infrastructure alone for their power supply, but have their own infrastructure (USP—Uninterrupted Power Supply system) to cover power interruption. Companies with extremely critical processes, like satellite systems operators, would probably use their own power first before switching to the public network. Not even electricity is a full commodity today! The only area where his thinking is right is about infrastructure questions: there is not necessarily a need to operate PCs, Help-Desk, or the network with your own staff—things like that can be (and are already) outsourced. The problem with Mr. Carr's books is that he does not differentiate between infrastructure (quite a commodity today) and data, which is a company's most important asset.

Apart from the infrastructure area, outsourcing can be useful when there is not enough internal know-how or if there is no wish to build it up. The amount of new investments in a new project can also be a good trigger. At the end of the day, outsourcing is not a question of "yes" or "no." It needs to be decided on a case-by-case basis, and enough time should be allocated for analyzing the question. One single reason, (cost reduction, for instance) cannot be the deciding factor alone. Involving the business departments in such decisions is also quite important. The eventual unhappiness about IT services should also not be a reason; if such a reason exists, then the management should look for a different solution.

In this context, top management often asserts that IT is not a "core competence" and it would be better to be totally outsourced. As soon as we speak about companies of a certain size, this should be considered as a massive misjudgment at management level. To contradict Nicholas Carr one more time: a well-organized IT department that is under direct control of the top management is a substantial competitive advantage.

Technology and innovation

Does anyone outside of IT have the slightest idea of how many technological concepts and denominations there are? Most likely not. A visit to http://whatis.techtarget.com lists an unbelievable 9,800 different notations (in 2008). This is roughly 2,000 more than two years before. Not all of them are still relevant, of course, but an estimated 7,000 remain active. And behind every denomination are hidden more unnumbered, specific technical definitions.

Since the very beginning, technology management has been one of the tasks of an IT department. It was even the first one, and today, it still is one of the most important tasks, with the only difference that the complexity has exploded. No IT expert will reasonably state that he knows all of them or has even heard of all of them. A job specialization is mandatory (operating systems, databases, web-technology, firewalls, or networks, for example.)

I have prepared a small test for you. I have selected 50 denominations you might have heard about. You cannot win a prize if you know all of them, but, just for fun, take the test:

Active-X	add-on
Buffer	Blackberry
C++	Cache
DLL	Denial of service
EDGE	Frozen zone
Failover	Fuzzy logic
Gigabit	Garbage collection
https	Honey pot
Identity theft	ITIL
Java	JVM
Kbps	Killer application
Linux	MQ-Series
Multithreading	NetBios
Network encryption	On Demand Computing
Object code	Patch Tuesday
PKI	Query
Queue	RAM
RFID	SAN
Saas	TCP/IP
Token	Uptime
UNIX	VISTA
VoIP	VB.Net
WAN	WiFi
Xterminal	XML
Zombie	Zoo

If you work in Europe, with all its different languages, you have to consider that in many countries, the same things have different denominations. When the French talk about *courriel*, they mean *email*; a *computer* is an *ordinateur*, and with *texto*, they mean *SMS*.

Technical discussions and the development of technical concepts are our daily business. We generate highly complex drawings with lots of boxes and connection arrows. The questions to be answered are: *How can a system be integrated in the biotope? How does it communicate? How will it be monitored? Where will it store its data?* When a server is purchased, the list of necessary technical components can fill several pages—many times the number of components you need when you buy a PC. Due to this, the validation of a configuration becomes a lengthy process.

In technology, there are always several options for how things can be done, and each option has its own pros and cons. Compare it to the choice between a LCD and Plasma TV screen, where you have to analyze a list of technical criteria and multiply these criteria by 10, 100, or 1,000, according to the subject. Even experts aren't often clear what all the terminology and listed features mean and how they interoperate. You need highly-qualified experts for this exercise, but it remains true that because of the ever-increasing complexity and permanent time pressure, it is very easy to overlook an important element these days. This means last-minute changes and, possibly, a request for a budget increase. CFOs usually show little understanding for this kind of situation; that's why it is a good practice to add a lot of reserve in the initial budgetary calculation.

Even in Europe, most IT meetings take place in English, and statements which sound like a secret code (for example, "*We will realize a semi-automatic top-down enforcement and a bottom-up monitoring.*") are heard all the time and are perfectly understood by experts. This is the area with the biggest part of gobbledygook. But even the most experienced expert can have difficulties in understanding when the description for some software says for example: "*...offers a vertical tool that binds Web services security to XML financial schema.*"

Something that keeps us busy all the time is the question of how technology will evolve and what innovations will impose themselves. For what do we need to prepare ourselves? At what point is technology out-of-date and does it need to be replaced? What technology can bring business value? More concretely: should the company give up its own email infrastructure and use Google as an email service provider in order to save costs? And if we intend to do so, do we think that the service is mature enough? Is it secure enough, or do we have to fear that Google reads and forwards each of our emails?

Spreading new technology can sometimes be painful. Maybe you have heard about Java programming language, which is based on so-called *object-oriented* technology? For a programmer who has worked many years with other languages like COBOL or PL/1, this requires a radical change in thinking. I started as a programmer, and I am still very much interested in this, so I decided to learn Java in my spare time. Frustration overcame me many times—the textbook flew through the room more than once. It requires several weeks before the concept can be understood.

It is very difficult to foresee the possible problems that can come up when a new technology is introduced. You can bet there will be problems. To stay with the Java example, it is such that Java likes to take some small breaks to allow its internal mechanics to do some clean-up. During the development of a program, this does not play any role, but as soon as it goes into production, this can be really annoying. But you need to look positively at this: it allows the user to make a coffee break.

The introduction of new technology is always a real challenge. The staff doesn't have the necessary experience in the beginning and is often quite helpless when a problem arises. But the production environment doesn't wait until the staff has sufficient expertise. Even if a successful *proof-of-concept* has been done, meaning the validation in a model, the introduction of new technology remains very risky, as problems will only show once they are in production. Here's another example I experienced. Today, there is the technical possibility to replace PCs in a company by simple devices that don't have their own software or a harddisk. They simply display the screen contents, and all programs are executed on a remote central computer. These devices are called *thin clients.* They are "stupid," but the user does not see the difference to a normal PC. The concept behind this is rather exciting, as you can reduce hardware and PC administration costs significantly. It is extremely useful if you want to offer PC functionality to a small and remote office with no local IT staff. Even though this technology cannot be called extremely young, it remains immature. Once production starts, you will find out rather quickly that there are interdependencies you didn't come across before. Simple things, like the mouse pointer remaining as an hourglass, despite the fact that the window has been released for further input, are one of the minor annoyances. But if the situation worsens to the point that the server in the background freezes, then the fun part is over. And being the person responsible for technology, you get defensive very quickly and it is very hard to find the exit. To think that the provider of this technology would help you quickly and pragmatically is a myth that is only believed outside of IT. A decision to introduce new technology should be very well thought out—it is wise to wait until there is evidence that a sufficient maturity level has been reached. The real art in our job is to find the right moment for the introduction of new technology.

Every IT staff member is constantly asked to educate himself further, and he is requested to assimilate new things quickly.

Establishing a technology plan is a further task. This plan documents which technology is already allowed to be used and which is not. For example, it must be decided which PC supplier will be chosen or if DVD-readers will be allowed at the desktop.

Infrastructure

The infrastructure operates in the background, and it is the foundation upon which IT services are built. It can be compared to power supply lines or water pipes in a house, albeit much more extensive and expensive. Generally, the existence of the infrastructure and the people running it are not very visible to the other employees, except in cases when the network is unavailable and they cannot work anymore. For this area, people with very detailed technical skills are needed, business know-how is normally not demanded, and there is very little contact with the business users. In the '80s, those guys were wearing white overalls and operating with soldering irons; today they may wear suits and ties. They are asked frequently to work weekends and at night, because maintenance work in the infrastructure can only be carried out when no business users are working. I know some colleagues who have substantial difficulties and constantly need to fight with their CEOs to get overtime paid by the company. It would be great if everyone understood that this kind of work can only be done outside of office hours.

In the last years, infrastructure has made a quantum leap. The technical possibilities have literally exploded. Because of this (really positive) evolution, it must be said that the complexity has also increased, and more and more people are needed to run the infrastructure. As said earlier, this is an area where outsourcing can make much sense, because the types of questions that need to be answered are of a more general nature and not directly linked to the business.

Every time a user starts his PC, there are complex technical processes running in the background. At its installation, IT has instructed the PC that it is part of a network and must try to take contact with the network when it is started. To do so, multiple technical components are needed (switches, routers, patch panels, servers, and protocols). When the PC detects the network, the user is asked to identify himself. This can be rather complex, especially in networks with a high security level (for example, when access to classified data must be granted) where strong authentication is required (meaning a password that changes every time, usage of *tokens*, a small device that displays a different number after a certain interval, smartcards, or other processes.) Mechanisms must be installed to control whether the connecting PC is at all allowed to do so; this will avoid that an intruder, like the night cleaning lady, will illegally connect to the network with a laptop.

The installation of PCs, printers, screens, and scanners is also managed in this area, and I need to say a few words about that. Rolling out new PCs is surely not a highly sophisticated task, but a labor intensive one. Before moving the PC physically to the user's desk, some manual intervention needs to be carried out. It might be necessary to open every PC in order to install a special graphical card or more memory. As this effort can be nicely defined, it is very easy to charge an external company with this, but of course, it generates costs. When it comes to laptops, the required effort for maintaining them is incredibly high. While a PC can be patched (latest Windows update, anti-virus update, or any other software having a new version) automatically in the firm's network, this is not the case for laptops. You cannot really automate this because, if the user connects remotely in a hotel room, you cannot expect that he will wait the necessary (and unpredictable) time until the patching procedure is completed. Laptops need to be brought into the company, and dedicated staff needs to take care of them manually. Laptops are nice for the users, but maintaining them requires very intensive labor.

Network components can crash. This is the reason why the connection between the PC and the servers are made redundant. This is expensive and requires additional maintenance efforts.

Capacity management is another important task. This concerns all possible components. When a component starts to reach its capacity limit (for storage, the limit is around 60%), this should be detected at an early stage. This requires daily monitoring. A sudden need for a capacity extension is sometimes hard to explain to a CFO, especially when it has not already been foreseen in the yearly budget.

We are in the middle of a data explosion, and some people start asking anxiously if we will not run into a generalized capacity shortage. IDC, the market research institute, is of the opinion that already today there is more generation of digital content than there is storage capacity— something that EMC, provider of storage solutions, contradicts. IDC estimates that in 2011, a total of 1800 billions of gigabyte of data will be generated. Interestingly enough, business isn't mainly responsible for this explosion. Two-thirds of all data is generated by private persons in the form of mp3-players or videos on harddisks. In the professional sector, there are technologies to manage the data explosion, and they develop really fast and are highly complex. A special sector in the IT industry has developed around this topic.

It is indeed the case that companies of a certain size need to develop storage strategies in order to manage the flood. Data graveyards of gigantic dimensions arise. To illustrate, sent emails are stored by the sender and by every recipient—you never know what you will need in the future, even if it is insignificant today. There is a legal requirement in some countries that emails must be archived centrally and never be deleted. In a project, it is usual to send copies of the current status report to many people, and everyone will store every copy of every status report. Computer systems generate log files and audit trails to allow future traceability. Backups and data archiving must be done. Business continuity requirements (cf. chapter 11) ask for a replication of all data in a second disaster recovery centre. Only very little of all this data is really alive or will be needed again in the future. Should anyone have foreseen this evolution twenty years ago, he would have been well advised to buy shares of those companies offering storage capacity.

Infrastructure staff also takes care of the security infrastructure (cf. chapter 13: *IT Security*). This means they supervise if there is no hacker trying to intrude or if the antivirus software is at the latest update level or if the firewall is operating correctly.

The firewall has the task to block undesired content, such as videos. Being a firewall administrator is certainly the most exciting job in IT. He has access to all blocked content and needs to investigate this on a regular basis in order to find potential weaknesses in the firewall setup.

While he is working, he often sees things he didn't even know existed. Once, when I left a job, my firewall administrator burnt a *Best of Firewall* CD for me. Most of it would have been X-rated.

Further tasks are the provision of Intranet, telecoms (connection to customers and suppliers), email, and Internet connection. For Internet, it must be made sure that no inappropriate content is passing through (racism, porn, etc.) and any other specific company-defined content. Emails must be filtered for spam, viruses, and worms. For all this, specific specialized software is needed; it is a fast moving domain. Laymen cannot have a clue about the complex technical processes in the background or the financial means needed to operate all these aspects of the job.

Another task consists in the monitoring of the IT biotope. It can be compared with video surveillance in public places. As soon as something unforeseen happens, an alarm is raised and action needs to be taken. Concrete examples would be:

- Are all servers up and running?

- Has there been an error message or an incident that must be taken care of?

- Are there processes that have not been started (for example: every day at 10 a.m., a certain file needs to be sent to a specific customer)?

- Is the company's webpage online?

- Is there a hacker attack that needs to be blocked?

- Has a PC attracted a virus?

- Has some staff member tried to illegally access confidential data?

- Have all backups been completed successfully?

- Are all external telecom lines active?

- Is the network too slow?

For all these tasks, there is specialized software available, and (surprise, surprise) this software is highly complex and expensive. The large scope and increasing complexity of infrastructure questions is a reason for the large number of staff members in an IT department.

Computer Center

Planning the computer center, also called the data processing center, is a subject in its own right. That's usually an underground high security area. It is not rare to see movie scenes that are filmed in computer centers. The security requirements for computer centers have multiplied over the last years. Because of the complexity of this question (and its related costs), it is today more frequent that companies building a new office no longer plan their own computer centre, but prefer to rent space with a professional provider. Just to name the most important aspects: planning of floor loading capacity, fire load, air conditioning, redundant power supply capacity, uninterrupted power supply system, fire and water alarm systems, modern access control (more and more on biometric basis), telecommunication capacities, and staff security in emergency cases. There are now possibilities to build computer centers as Faraday cages: a terrorist attack with the aim to erase all magnetic data storage would not succeed. On top of that, there are a large number of smaller sophistries as, for example, the fact that a supervision camera can never directly look at a keyboard. If that were the case, the person who monitors the camera would be able to find out the administration passwords!

Day-to-day business

A large part of the employees in an IT department are busy with day-to-day tasks in the production. The word "production" might be confusing because it is used even when there are no items physically produced. It just means the daily operating of the live systems, as opposed to test systems. These staff members are usually not very much in the focus, like those from the Help-Desk who have to deal with business users all the time. This is a bit unfair because the correct execution of their tasks is important for the company. The job specification for these persons is therefore quite different. Very often, they have to do shift work or come in during weekends. It is rare that there is project-related work here. The tasks that must be fulfilled are the following:

Scheduler

This represents the gearing of the execution order of the programs in a system. For example, the backups need to be done first, then the accounting of the daily transactions, then the printout of statement of accounts, and much more. This may sound simple, but it is also a complex task. A computer executes several programs in parallel, and situations arise where it needs to know that it has to wait for the successful completion of another program before it should continue.

When an error is encountered, the computer needs to decide whether the system should be stopped or not. To manage this, there is specialized software (schedulers) for which a dedicated know-how is required. The slightest error in the process can have disastrous consequences and can generate a crisis situation. Let's suppose that all programs have run successfully, but in the wrong order: it may be that statements of customer accounts are mailed, but half of the account transactions are missing.

Modern systems tend, however, to be less dependent on schedulers. They are able to operate on a 24-hour basis and don't need additional software for the execution of backups and similar. The focus of schedulers is now stronger on monitoring and alerting.

Supervision

Either by staff on shift work or by an automatic supervision program, the execution of the programs in the production environment needs to be supervised. When an error is encountered, someone needs to be called on his pager, or he should get a SMS. A problem during the night which is not fixed immediately can have an impact on the availability of the system the next business day. That's why an "on-call"-service is introduced—a predetermined IT staff member is alerted and must fix the problem. He can do this from home by remote access or come to his office, depending on the nature of the problem. Interestingly enough, there are differences in Europe whether staff should be paid extra for such service.

But the fundamental question is: "Why don't systems succeed in passing the night without trouble?" Well, there are plenty of reasons, and chapter 7 gives plenty of explanations, but there is one that I would like to mention here: a database can become *corrupt* (no joke, that's how we call this!) when its internal "mechanics" get disturbed. This can happen when somebody had his fingers in the database and incorrectly updated data elements—a bit like open heart surgery. While this can be understood by everybody, it is also unbelievably possible that a database corrupts itself, loses control, and shouts for help. It may just "decide" to replace some information for a customer (like his account number) with hieroglyphs, and the crash is there. Or the database assiduously counts how many loans there are in the loans file and, at a later time, executes a control if the number counted is still correct. Can you believe the database gets aghast when it notices that the number is not accurate? The guy on-call has to intervene then and repair the internal mechanics.

Data backups

Backups must be done every day; for very critical systems several backups will be executed each day. It should be made sure that backups are still usable for a potential data restore even if many years have passed—something which can be considered being a real challenge considering the speed of technologic innovation.

Backups in a company are totally different than those you do at home on your PC. Dedicated software is used which has been configured to backup certain data from a certain system at a certain time. This backup software must run without failure, and when it encounters the slightest problem, it must raise an alarm. Data loss is critical for every company. The media used for backups are not CDs, DVDs, or USB memory sticks like you have at home. In most cases, cartridges are used. Alternatively, a secondary storage device can be the choice. Cartridges are small boxes that can contain large volumes of data. In large biotopes, robots are used to manage all these cartridges. These robots contain large cupboards—comparable to a big jukebox—where the software guides the robot's arm to the needed cartridge, checks if it is the correct one, writes on it, and puts it back. The robot needs to be fed regularly with the relevant cartridges.

Usually two backups are carried out. It is simply too risky to rely on the hope that a single cartridge will be readable after an emergency. Often, one copy is kept in-house, and the second one is stored far away in a different building. Doing backups is a task that requires an important sense of responsibility.

Not all staff in an organization is aware of the importance of backups. A colleague told me about a person who was in charge of storing the tapes (predecessors of cartridges) in a safe in the computer center. After some time, this guy noticed that the tapes were always written, but never used for reading. He concluded that this doesn't make any sense and decided to skip the backups. By doing this, he could go home half an hour earlier every evening. Then one day, a restore needed to be done. After that, he was allowed to stay at home full-time.

Processing control

System audit trails and protocols should be controlled every day—there's also specialized software for this. This is done to detect any anomalies which are not (yet) critical. There might be error messages which did not halt the process during the night, but which should be analyzed. Let's suppose that there is a program which usually runs for an hour, but one day it finishes in five seconds. This is a strong hint that something is wrong. Software has no intelligence of its own and has no clue for what purpose it is serving. It just executes, does not ask itself any questions, and never thinks it is in trouble. The question whether software does have some self-repair features included doesn't really need to be asked, as you may be able to answer this by yourself.

Software development

A recurring subject among experts is whether a company should buy software or develop its own. There are good arguments for both "make" and "buy," and both have many fans. The fact that "make" still is a valid option may surprise some, because the software market is so extraordinarily vast, and you'd think there should be software around for everything that is needed. When you buy, you get a product that contains the sum of all requirements of all other customers, therefore you get more for your money. But you also pay for things you never needed and will never need. Buying sometimes means that you have outsourced the validation of the results you want to achieve. For example, if you have bought software for tax calculation—a subject of massive business complexity—you must trust, to a very large degree, that what the software calculates is correct. You cannot know every factor in detail. The volumes of data you treat will not allow for having full control of the results. Only samples can be controlled. And there are clever sales people who like to argue that software is a *commodity*, something like electricity. Would someone try to produce his own electricity (after reading about this a few lines above, you might think: "yes!") or build a car instead of buying one? Surely not, but for software, this is the case.

Without wanting to anticipate chapter 7, it needs to be said that in 2009, software on the market continues to be too expensive, too unstable, too inflexible, not standardized enough, and inadequate in required functionality. The integration of a new software system with other systems continues to be bricolage. Not to mention that the decision for a provider and his system means a (very) long-term decision—a possible separation is very painful. At the end, every company needs to decide for itself in its very special own context. Even if the decision is "buy," a minimum need for internally-developed software remains because, as we have seen, it is very rare that interfaces can be purchased and therefore they need to be developed individually.

For the development of software, other dedicated software is needed (SDK–Software Development Kit) with functions that include an editor or a debugger for finding errors. It is mandatory to have version control management in a SDK to trace changes made in the software. It allows only one programmer to work on a program at one time. It documents who changed what for what reason, and it moves the finished program into the production biotope.

Sometimes, however, there is no choice, and a situation arises where there is no product on the market for a specific need. We are still quite far away from products covering all possible needs. In these times, companies show a behavior of addiction to receiving new functionality, and the pressure put upon software development companies is somehow like the pressure a junkie feels for the next high. But software development takes time, and as we don't leave the time to the providers, we, the customers, are part of the problem of bad software quality.

Or it may happen that some software is not sold in every country (and therefore not supported) or that it is above the budget set. The advantage of internally-developed software is, no doubt, the freedom and flexibility. On the other hand, programmers need to be hired, and you can get dependent on them quite quickly, as the know-how of a developed system is possibly only in one head.

I don't understand why cheerleaders won't talk to me.
Maybe I don't throw five touchdowns against Newport High,
but let's see one of those football morons program in assembly language!

Chris Lipe

The profile of a programmer is quite different to that of other IT staff members because he needs to be prepared to work in a concentrated way on one subject for quite a long period of time. A programmer has relatively few contacts outside of his team, and he comes closest to the public image of a "nerd." I generally observe that programmers take the most pride in their jobs. At the end of the day, they are the only ones who have done something visible: a new input screen, a new printout, or some source code. It is also the IT job with the most positive user feedback, because everything a programmer is doing means a solution for some business user's problems.

It is surprising, but the effort required to write a program has not been significantly reduced in the last twenty years. Technological progress has been balanced by an increase in the features a system or program must deliver and new requirements from IT security and traceability. The requirements related to user access rights management have a heavy impact on every development project. You'll find more about the subject of software development in chapter 7. More and more software is developed in India these days. How this evolves will be interesting to observe.

Projects

We often use the terminology "construction site" in relation to projects, as not all activities get the organizational structure of a project. Project management is a key task of an IT department. It is the central place where everything related to a project is assembled. Of course, there is specialized software on the market to manage this area. Every company that takes itself seriously uses recognized methods for project management. Project analyses and preliminary studies are carried out and find answers to questions like: Who decides about a new project? Who will be the sponsor, and who will be in the steering committee? What budget is needed? What are the reporting and escalation lines? What are the risks? What milestones should the project have? Who does what? and many others.

Project managers need to have a high IT understanding and a profound knowledge about the business processes. To manage several dozen construction sites at the same time is tough enough. The largest number I ever saw was an incredible 10,000 projects running in parallel; this was in a very large and worldwide operating bank. When the complexity is really high, then a so-called program management is introduced, whose task is mainly to supervise the inter-dependencies of all these construction sites. To illustrate, it would not make sense to add functionality to a software if another project has decided to replace that software! The "traffic light" mentioned in chapter 3 has a decisive role to play in program management. In order to get global oversight about a large number of running projects, a *dashboard* can be organized on which all red and yellow projects are listed—with special attention to those whose color has worsened.

Program managers in organizations with many subsidiaries fly around the world frequently. As they don't have time for everything, one of them suggested one day putting a red, green, or yellow flag on the roof of the building. Next time he flew over the country, he would look outside the plane's window to see if everything was running fine. A true story.

Project management in IT differentiates substantially from project management in other areas (more details have been described in chapter 3: *One million or one year*). The degree of difficulty in projects can vary a lot. In their very large majority (even though that this is declining), software systems are small dictators: they dictate how the processes in the company have to adapt to the software, not the other way round. This is one element which makes a precise project plan a "mission impossible." Before a system is introduced, it is impossible to know all its aspects. Because of the complexity, the number of tasks, and the high likelihood of upcoming problems, there is permanent time pressure in this sector of IT activity. As a general rule, the given termination deadline for a project is almost never respected.

System administration

A system admin's life is a sorry one. The only advantage he has over Emergency Room doctors is that malpractice suits are rare. On the other hand, ER doctors never have to deal with patients installing new versions of their own innards!

Michael O'Brien

We have reached the heart of IT! System administrators are the IT Gods and Masters of the IT Universe, and they are aware of their power. If they were doctors, they would be heart surgeons. System administrators have full control over the various systems and applications (accounting systems, company's webpage, Office products (Word/Excel), PCs, servers, databases, etc.) For every system and application, one or more administrators must be appointed.

They play an important role in establishing integration concepts and executing implementation projects. They are almighty: they grant access rights and revoke them, install new program versions (for error correction, for example), activate new functionality, define installation parameters, do copies for testing purposes, decide when and how backups are carried out, manage interfaces, analyze future needs, modify the database by bypassing the internal control mechanisms of software, and much more.

A positive recent development, which restricts their powers to some extent, consists in the fact that admin rights can be attributed much more selectively. Until recently, administrators could do everything. Now their power starts to evaporate somehow, at least when it comes to recently-developed applications. Today, many systems have differentiating admin profiles: one can attribute access rights, another can define the installation parameters, and a third can change the contents of the database.

Everything done by admins should be automatically recorded to allow a later investigation if things went wrong. But admins don't like this at all, and frequently, they don't like to document in written form what they did. And not all systems have this technical recording possibility, but if an auditor requires it, someone is facing a nice challenge.

System administrators must be experts with long-standing experience. They need to understand the internal mechanics of a system pretty well: how do the data elements act jointly, which program exercises which function, and what are the dependencies to other applications?

It is an area with a big potential for stress. They must react well to stress in crisis situations. The failure of an application is, in almost all cases, the trigger for a crisis situation. When this happens, they must design and execute unconventional solutions under big time pressure, always considering the risks.

Sometimes, supposed problems aren't problems at all. An administrator can get really frustrated if he has been trying to find a solution to a reported problem, and then it shows that there is no problem. For instance, data which is uploaded from an external source every day at the same time doesn't arrive one day, and an automatic alarm is raised. Several hours of investigation are easily spent on such a problem, and at some point, the administrator gives up. After cross-checking with the business, the feedback is received that they have agreed with the external data supplier that the data is no longer needed and, well, sorry, nobody saw that there would be an IT impact related to that.

A further task consists in accompanying the users in their day-to-day use of the system. They know about their difficulties and can show users how to overcome them. They are the first contact persons when users have questions, and they can evaluate the impact of user change requests.

The more competent a system admin is, the more he facilitates the tasks of an IT department. At the same time, the dependency on these people grows.

Between Christmas and New Year, when everybody tends towards contemplativeness, the most critical time for a system admin begins. In an accounting system, the year-end closing is the most important and critical moment, and having a big party on New Year's Eve is not a good idea. The need to supervise all systems at this moment is even more urgent than on normal days, and only if the last working day in the year is not Dec. 31, he can party as well.

Over the year, there are many program changes in a system, and this means that the year-end programs will run in a constellation that can be significantly different than the previous year. This represents a substantial risk. Therefore, the system admin declares a *frozen zone*, a time period before the year-end when the system is frozen, meaning that no important changes can be implemented anymore. This time period can be up to two or three weeks or longer, according to the system complexity and its importance. This time period is used to test the year-end closing and correct any identified errors. Outside of the question of year-end closing, more *frozen zones* can possibly be declared during the year to make sure that there are only limited time windows when changes can be implemented.

Here is an easy-to-understand example that illustrates the admin's job—taken from the area of PC administration. Dozens of programs usually run on a PC. It is clear that there would be no time to go personally to every single PC and install all programs with a DVD in the way you do this at home on your private PC. Every to-be-installed program (sometimes with different versions and installation parameters) must be installed centrally on a server. Then, a table defines which user (or user group) can have which programs installed. Once this is done, all programs are automatically downloaded to all PCs at the push of a button. This task is often done after business hours or on weekends in order not to disturb the users.

You might think installing programs on a PC should not create any problems once you pushed the button I just mentioned. Far from it! Even in this rather simple example, an IT department is in the clutches of the computer industry. It is very wise to have all PCs in the biotope come from the same manufacturer. They should be of the same type and even be from the same production line. A new PC from the same manufacturer, even of the same type, but from a different production line will (with a high probability) not accept the installation of the same program that works perfectly on the other PCs. At every new delivery of a PC, there are minimal differences in the lowest technical layers, and this makes everything incompatible! This then requires a reconfiguration and a new test of the installation procedure. As this is known, it can be managed, and there can be spare PCs from the same production line on hand. But the day will come when there are no spare PCs left, or you may have an unexpected row of PCs that break down and need to be replaced. Or new hires are communicated too late by the HR department—sometimes only the day before—and panic bursts out. So, if you work in a company and you urgently need a new PC and your IT tells you that this cannot be done quickly, the reason could be that there is an incompatibility problem that needs to be fixed first. Specifically for this example, but also on a general note, the computer industry is not able to make the administrator's life easy.

An example to show the almightiness of system admins: A PC admin can start a user's PC from his desk, even if the PC is shut down. He can take control of this PC and observe everything that is happening. Because of data privacy laws, he is not allowed to do this without your agreement. But when he does not respect this rule, you will not be able to notice it. As administrators have all rights, there must be trust paired with control.

Another area where administrators play an important role: when you send an email, you should know that every admin at every ISP (Internet Service Provider: gateway to the Internet) where your email transits can read what you have written. An email is not better protected against unauthorized reading than a postcard. Companies with a high need of confidentiality either don't use email for confidential data, or they encrypt it. Authorities benefit from this security weakness to prevent many crimes and catch criminals. You should know that your email is stored on a server "somewhere" in the world—maybe in Silicon Valley, if you have chosen an American email service provider. When you send an email, the Internet is searching for the fastest (not the shortest) way to deliver it. This way could lead from San Francisco via New York, Tokyo, and Sydney to Berlin.

Having touched on the subject of emails, read *Who moved my Blackberry?* by Martin Lukes. You will see how you can entangle yourself with emails—a delicious book.

Quality assurance

An area that has gained enormously in importance is quality assurance. With all the deficiencies of today's computer industry when it comes to quality, it has become extremely important to strengthen a company's internal quality assurance.

Along with the word *problem*, the most frequently-used word in IT is, without a doubt, *test*. Because of the expected errors in every software delivery (cf. chapter 7: *Unexpected error encountered*) and the complex implementation (cf. chapter 3: *One million or one year*), everything needs to be tested thoroughly. No other activity swallows so much time in IT and the business departments than testing. Testing is not at all popular because of its frustrating nature. Per definition, a test is only successful once you do it for the last time. There can be unlimited unsuccessful tests before.

The more conscientiously the tests are done, the better the stability in the production biotope, the reputation of the IT department, and the used software. However, tests can never be fully complete, as the number of situations and combinations in a biotope can be enormously high. IT departments need to accept the fact that the quality of their work is, to a large extent, judged upon the quality of the software delivered by an external provider, and they have limited influence on what this external company does. Testing is a boring, albeit important, task. Outsourcing this activity would be ideal. The issue is that the test cases are different for each company, and the IT biotope is unique as well. Therefore, this activity is rarely outsourced.

A further center of activity in QA is the final control before the move into production. It is validated at this point if the user's business requirements are correctly translated into the software that is going to go live. The focus here is not so much the stability of the software, but the question whether the functionality that is implemented is the one that has been asked for. It is self-explanatory that this task is extremely important.

Help-Desk / Support

For many staff members in a company, the colleagues from Help-Desk are the only ones in IT that they ever have contact with. When a problem occurs, they are the first persons of contact. Help-Desk staff is often exposed to the *"kill the messenger"* phenomena. When a user has a problem, he may unload his frustration on the Help-Desk team member, despite the fact that he is not responsible for the problem. If everyone understood that systems can crash because of faulty software, the working conditions of Help-Desk staff would improve. On top of that, every user expects an immediate solution to his problem. But in most cases, this is not possible, and the problem needs to be handed over to an internal expert (2nd-level support) or must even be reported to the external provider (3rd-level support). In this case, the waiting time for a solution can be very long.

Also, questions on how to use a specific system on a daily basis can be addressed to Help-Desk staff. If necessary, they forward these questions to an internal IT expert. Help-Desk is the business card of an IT department: the better and quicker they do their job, the higher the global acceptance of IT.

The job profile is, in many points, different to the one of other IT staff. These people need to be quiet and cool-headed, even in cases when a user has some obvious weaknesses with his IT understanding, or if he has difficulties describing the problem accurately. They need a broad general knowledge about all used technologies and systems. Expert know-how helps but is not a requirement. There's a need to judge about the relative importance of a problem without letting themselves be influenced by the pressure that the user exerts—that's easier said than done! This means they have to fix the most urgent problem, not the one of the person who shouts the loudest. They must be able to treat more than one problem at the same time and keep patient at all times. It is a stressful job, which I personally wouldn't like to do. Help-Desk staff tends to be burnt out after some years, and they must be given a new perspective.

The range of possible error causes is large. It can be anything from a malfunctioning printer to data loss. It is not only a *running gag*: sometimes a reported "broken screen" has had its power cord unintentionally removed by the cleaning lady. But there are also (very few) "stupid" users, and they are a source of continued amusement. Here's one funny story: Help-Desk tells a user to close all windows, and the person gets up and tours the office to see if there are any open. Help-Desk problems (we call them "tickets") get recorded in a dedicated system, so a found solution can so be used again. Care is to be taken not to make this system available to business users, as you may find statements like: "The reason for the problem was sitting 20 cm in front of the screen." There are nice books containing Help-Desk anecdotes.

Providers

Every IT department depends on a large number of providers for hard- and software and on consultants and external experts of all kinds. The management of these providers is a task in its own right.

There is an unbelievably high number of external companies offering IT services, and the number increases constantly. If one would make an appointment with each company that called, there wouldn't be any time left for doing anything else. Quite interestingly, every company pretends to be a market leader in something. Most of the time, this isn't even an exaggeration, as there is a huge number of possible areas. If you search long enough, you will find a point where any company is better than all its competitors.

We have the strongest growth in the last six months may mean the company has grown from two staff members to four.
Our product runs faster than those of our competitors may mean the functionality is low, and therefore it runs faster.
We have the largest number of references could mean the company has a lot of customers, but only very small ones.
With our product, we can reduce your costs by 20% means little, considering another company couldn't know your costs.
We have the best experts might be true, but it can't be proven
And so on and so on.

When a presentation or workshop is agreed with an external company, you are then overpowered with PowerPoint (software that shows presentations on a large screen or wall). By the way, I read in the German magazine SPIEGEL that there are 30,000,000 PowerPoint presentations shown every day. This figure is from 2006—it must have increased significantly since then. Most likely, PowerPoint is the most used software worldwide. If it should stop working all of a sudden, legions of IT sales people would become jobless and helpless. Flights would have to be cancelled. Maybe the world economy would crash.

Originally, the idea behind PowerPoint was to make a simple presentation of complex things—power and point. In the course of time, this starting point has become completely obscured. Today, complex things continue to be reduced to simple bullet points, but the simplest things get converted to highly complex drawings. If I had one wish, I would say: "People! Stop this and keep it simple—there is already enough complexity in our job."

PowerPoint is so popular that there is an automatic reflex for people to use it all the time. It is probably the only application they know. Even in internal IT communication, I have seen this. Rather than phoning someone to discuss an idea, I have been asked many times to prepare a PowerPoint to use as a common basis of discussion. Sad to say this, but PowerPoint has replaced the culture of discussion.

Sometimes, cooperation with a supplier is agreed in order to be the first one to introduce a new product or a new functionality in a product. The terminology we use here is *alpha-site, beta-site, or pilot-site*. Apart from the purely commercial aspect of such a cooperation (a lower price), the customer gets the advantage of having a solution delivered quicker than the competitor. Companies are addicted to new functionality and accept this without complaints. Every provider needs a first customer for his product and is prepared to offer specials conditions. Of course, the risks (for instance, security aspects have extremely good chances to have been neglected) and the testing effort are much higher, and such cooperation must be well thought out. It never takes long until the next supplier asks again for such cooperation. But it also happens quite frequently that a customer is the first customer of a functionality without knowing it. Such a situation is difficult to manage. It requires fighting with the provider, and this happens more often than you would think. Users are constantly abused as beta-testers. This saves the provider money, and, as every provider has this policy, it is not a competitive disadvantage. This quite strange practice has found its way into the Internet. More often than not, you see new software with a "beta" tag behind it. Most users don't realize what this is about. Well, now they should. But Internet users are addicted to new functionality just like business users are.

Choosing a provider for a new system is important and should be well thought out. If the customer is a large company, a provider with a certain minimum size should be chosen. If not, the provider will not be in a position to deploy enough force to react to the company's problems and new requirements. On the other hand, if the customer is rather small, it is dangerous to choose a renowned partner who is significantly larger and stronger. In this case, if you have critical problems, you will not be top on his priority list because you are not strategic enough for him.

A further problem consists in the fact that the provider's staff quality can vary. When you have signed a contract, you have negotiated with management or a salesperson. And those guys tend to overvalue their own staff—always. In the banking world, we experience that external consultancy companies have difficulty retaining their staff because the salary level is higher in banks. Great care must be taken if critical missions are given to an external company.

But I don't want to be unfair. There are providers who deliver excellent quality, and I'm not writing about them here. However, these rare pearls are definitely a minority. And even with those, it is important to insist on having their best staff for the mission (and to conclude this in writing in the contract). These sought-after top people can get a burnout quickly—quite a known and serious problem. I will write more about this in chapter 6.

Providers can become a victim of their success. When they have a good product that everyone wants to have, it is a known problem that the implementation quality decreases because there are just too many customers to be served at the same time. In such a situation, the provider often hires everyone who can count until three or starts to work with subcontractors—and does not consider that the mastering of a new system is an exercise that takes several months, sometimes even years, for the most experienced expert.

Once you have decided on a provider, you can compare it to a marriage. Once operational, it is very hard to get away from the chosen solution with an acceptable level of effort. The more central ("core") a system is in its significance for the firm, the more dependent the firm is on the provider. Of course, all providers know this, and some of them exploit it. Some do it in a very subtle way by slowly but surely increasing the prices for all new requests—others do it in a plump, aggressive, and arrogant way. I know about one case where the provider would refuse any software maintenance work if the customer selected a competitor for another software of lesser importance. Compare it to a situation where you drive a Mercedes and you want to buy a BMW for your wife. The Mercedes dealer hears about it and threatens to stop carrying out any inspection work for your Mercedes in the future. It must be concluded that, when a software system is of central importance, the customer is in the weaker position. Provider management is about dependency management. This is true for all companies in all areas.

Administration and controlling

In the past few years, the necessary administrative effort to be done has grown rapidly. Some tasks in this area are rather clear, like the controlling and payment of invoices. But again, there are some IT specificities in this area:

Change management

Without ever getting interrupted, new change requests crackle into IT—a PC for a new staff member, a new enquiry program, an additional field in an input mask, a new control report, access to a blocked webpage, granting access rights in an application, and thousands more things. For audit reasons, it is not allowed to execute a change in the live environment without a documented request, and the correct execution of the request must be acknowledged by the user. The whole documentation chain, starting at the user's request until the final move of a program into the live environment, must be exhaustive and have no interruption. The volume of generated work here needs to be managed. There is specialized software available to help in this.

Control of access rights

At least once a year, a control of the accuracy of granted access rights should be carried out: Who may put in transactions? Who may authorize them? Who may maintain the customer's address? What external connections does the firewall allow? Who are our system administrators and do they have the correct access rights assigned? Did employees leave the company but still have access to the systems? Or did one employee change his function but keep the old access rights?

Life cycle

Every software and every hardware has its very own life cycle. Every software has different versions (for example, Windows 2000, XP and Vista), which have a life cycle of their own. They are born, grow up, get old, and at the end, they need to be replaced. This cycle needs to be supervised by IT for all components. Every software has requirements for its compatibility with other software components, by which their own life cycle gets influenced. So, a specific program would only run under Windows Vista, but Windows XP is still running fine and does not need to be replaced.

The life cycles get shorter and shorter. For Windows, it takes roughly two or three years until a new version comes to the market. When it comes to functional software (for example, an accounting system in a bank), the time gap between two versions is even shorter: At least one or two versions are released per year. And every time, the full testing effort needs to be repeated.

But when software of central importance, like an accounting system, comes to its end of life, the situation gets extremely critical. Normally, such a situation announces itself a long time in advance, but sometimes it does not. It can arise when a few important customers of that software decide (almost at the same time) to replace that system and, by this, accelerate the decline process. For the remaining customers now, the situation gets dangerous. To replace a highly complex software is an extremely expensive project (several millions of dollars) and takes a lot of time (several thousands of person days). As it gets clear now that the maintenance will be stopped rapidly by the provider, massive pressure builds up. If the source code (more about source code in chapter 7) is not available, it is not possible to maintain the system with its own means. But even if access to the source code is given, it is nevertheless necessary to invest massive amounts of time in order to understand the internal mechanics of the software. At the same time, a migration to a new system needs to be planned rapidly. The firm should make sure that its key people are retained in order to avoid the additional risk of staff resigning. Highly interesting times with a gigantic stress potential.

As there are hundreds of individually-used components in every biotope, a large number of employees are busy monitoring life cycles and carrying out upgrades. With the introduction of a new version, new risks are created, and nobody can say whether the new version will work well with all the other components. It is even rather rare that this is the case. We will see later that this is one of the unsolved problems of the software industry.

Sarbanes-Oxley (SOX)

The biggest nonsense of modern times is the introduction of SOX-controls. After the crash of *Worldcom* and *Enron* in the US, it was decided to implement control mechanisms in order to avoid this kind of faking of balance sheet figures in the future. The idea behind this was that controls do exists, but these controls are not controlled. One reader of the first edition of this book stated: *"SOX is the best invention the Americans ever did in order to increase their competitiveness versus the Europeans—the latter follow the SOX-rules painstakingly (and spend a lot of money for it) and the Americans do it so-so."* I am inclined to agree with this opinion.

Now, we must ask: Where was SOX to avoid the sub-prime crisis and the subsequent global economic crisis? and why do we have excessive controls for the faking of balance sheets and none at all for Investment Banking?

As IT is everywhere, it became necessary to extend these SOX-rules from the accounting departments to IT. I still haven't fully understood why this was decided. A mass of new "control controls" were introduced. Two examples of this amongst many: the CIO must assure that the audit trails from the overnight data processing have been controlled, or when a PC is decommissioned, he must control that the erasure of data on the harddisk has been carried out correctly and has been controlled by someone. The absence of such "control controls" is, no doubt, a question of quality assurance. But where is the link to financial fraud? I found no one able to tell me, and I am still wondering why this had been decided. Even the consultants that I had to work with for the implementation of SOX had no answer to that question. The initial target to prevent financial fraud has completely gotten out of sight on its way.

On a worldwide basis, thousands of people were employed to carry out these "control controls," and audit companies like *kpmg* and *Price Waterhouse* made a lot of money. The SOX-paradox is: if these audit firms had done their jobs correctly in the first place, we would never have seen SOX, and those audit firms would not have been able to increase their profits in that way. These SOX-controls coming from the US are just as useful as the question from *Dell* that you had to answer when you ordered a PC on their Internet site, namely if you would use this PC for the production of mass destruction weapons.

Continuously introducing new controls for fixing problems will probably never change, and it is still too early to know exactly what will be introduced once the financial crisis is behind us. But I bet it will be similar to SOX: we will see some control and reporting mechanisms which will make life much more complicated for everyone. The idea that new controls are needed can't, of course, be doubted. A limited number of clear and commonly-agreed rules, thoroughly supervised, would have avoided the financial crisis in the first place. But with my European background, I have to say that our US colleagues sometimes make us desperate, as they like to fall from one extreme to the other. From total deregulation (financial markets) to strangling controls (SOX), there is no healthy middle ground.

Licenses supervision

There are several price models that can be applied when a software is licensed (purchased): number of concurrent users, number of defined users (the most commonly used model), processor power (a model mainly used for Internet applications where the number of users is unknown), and others. Usually, IT decides the model to choose and is required to supervise the application of this model over time. Should 100 licenses have been bought, it might be that only 90 are effectively used, and the remaining ones are a reserve for future growth. As soon as the number of users passes 100, additional licenses need to be purchased. If this would not happen, the company could be prosecuted.

Software companies sometimes sell blocks of licenses (containing a minimum number of users) as a kind of package. In our case here, it might be that it would not be possible to buy only one additional license, but possibly a package of ten. On the other hand, when the number of users decreases, it is never possible to get the money back. Only if a recurring fee is paid for maintenance services, it can be possible to cancel some licenses. But again, some companies are cleverer than others. One provider of software for the supplying of financial data for Treasury Departments (whose name I don't want to mention), designs its user licenses contracts with a repeating period of two years and no possibility to cancel before maturity. You can only do something like that when you have a sales monopoly.

There is further evidence for the non-maturity of the software industry: it is illegal to sell software (that you have purchased) to a third party when you don't need it anymore. You can't even give it away. Are there other industries with such antiquated regulations?

Inventory

The total value of all hardware assets is usually very high. Several million dollars are reached very quickly. It is obvious that an assets inventory must be maintained and this inventory must be controlled from time to time. Insurance coverage contracts must be established, and it must be controlled once a year if the assurance amounts are still accurate.

Procedures / Processes

The introduction of a new system or new functionality always has an impact on the processes in a firm. Modern software brings along workflow management functionality, giving a bundle of possibilities in the area of process management. Responsibilities and controls change. This needs to be organized and documented. Technical documentation and user guides need to be written or updated.

Reporting

From year to year, the pressure increases to produce all kinds of reports to the whole world. Regulators (more in Europe than in the US) and control instances in headquarters need a view on budgets, projects, statistics on the availability of systems, and . . . you name it.

Customer satisfaction

As every IT expert will agree, there's always some complaining about IT and computer systems. But in order to really understand where the problems lie, it is necessary to do a *Customer Satisfaction Survey*. This should be repeated regularly every 12 or 24 months. The typical questions asked are:

- "Do you agree with the statement 'IT treats me as a customer'?"

- "In what area are your expectations met the most and the least?" where typically this could be about: information flow, applications, Help-Desk, cooperation, project management, training, quality of realization of requests, and IT security.

- "Would you rate the qualitative evolution of IT services since the last survey as better, unchanged, or worse?"

- "How far would you agree with the statement 'I always receive enough information from IT' and 'the information received is always clear and understandable'?"

- "In general, how satisfied are you with the applications you use?"

- "For the most important applications used, please indicate your general level of satisfaction, its user-friendliness, response times, IT support, and stability."

- "How good is the feedback received after having done a new request? And how do you rate rapidity and quality of realization?"

- "How do you rate the Service-Desk for availability, friendliness, competence, rapidity, and feedback?"

- "What can IT do to make your work easier?"

- "Where do you see the strengths and weaknesses of IT?"

- "Do you understand IT's possibilities and limitations?"

While the survey must, of course, be anonymous and should leave room for comments, it should also foresee a possibility for leaving the name at the end of the survey for an eventual feedback discussion.

But, how satisfied are users globally with IT? There are studies available on a global level, and I picked two. *Gartner* found that about one-third of IT users think their IT department is too slow. The *IT Excellence Benchmark 2008* tells us the average satisfaction index is 2.58 (on a scale from 1 [totally satisfied] to 5 [dissatisfied]). So our users seem to be moderately positive about IT in general. My explanation would be that they experience better service with office computer problems compared to the problems they have at home with their private PCs. That would prove that IT departments are generally doing a very good job, considering all the aspects you will understand when you reach the last page of this book.

Budgets

Staying within the given IT budget limits must, of course, be assured—unfortunately. Exceeding the budget generates an immediate reaction from the CFO, followed by unpleasant discussions. It is never a good idea to be too precise in the budget planning: every company has recurring initiatives to reduce costs, and having some room for maneuver in that case is an excellent idea.

IT budgets are divided between investments (*change*) and running costs (*run*).

Contracts

When do the contracts with the providers expire, and when is the time to start new negotiations? Are all contracts still correct after the latest changes in the biotope? Are valid maintenance contracts in place for all used systems?

Escrow

The survival of a company depends on the availability of its IT systems in an ever-increasing way. Depending on the area of business, a few days without a critical system can lead to bankruptcy. The availability of systems depends again on the ability of the providers to maintain and further develop the software. We manage dependency here. As providers can go bankrupt, it is highly important to conclude so-called *escrow* agreements. With these, the provider is obliged to deposit the latest version of the source code (the readable form of the program) with a notary or any other specialized company in that matter. In case of bankruptcy, IT would get access to the source code and would be able to maintain the system itself. While this sounds nice and easy, in reality, it is not so easy to understand a foreign source code, even if it is well-documented and commented. The time needed by a skilled programmer to find his way through unknown software source code is very long. It is obvious that escrow agreements need to be monitored, namely to see if the deposited source code is the one used for the current version.

Error reconciliation

Errors reported by users are usually recorded in a dedicated system (or in an Excel sheet for less important systems). These errors must be reported to the provider, actions need to be defined, and the global list of errors needs to be reconciled regularly between the parties. Priorities need to be defined and, if the response is not fast enough, escalations need to be done at management level.

Service Level Agreements (SLA)

When a new system is introduced, or when insourcing/outsourcing projects are carried out, it is necessary to agree on so-called *SLA*s. This may happen between IT and a business department or with external service providers. SLAs define the service level, as you would expect: what is the maximum allowed response time when the user does an input? May the availability go below 99.9%, and when it happens, what penalties need to be paid? When is maintenance work carried out? What are the business days and hours when the system must be available? What are the communication channels? What is the price of the service? A contract which describes the daily operation mode between partners needs to be monitored. Of course, there is software around to help with this. The number of SLAs in an IT Department can be considerable.

Security

The subject of IT security has such decisive importance that it gets a chapter of its own, and I will not write about it here.

Internal management

The usual management tasks you can find in other business areas are not mentioned here. You will not find anything about topics like management by objectives, team-building, town hall meetings, and so on. I will only describe the singularities of IT.

Communicating with business departments is a subject of utmost importance, albeit an eternal work-in-progress. It helps a lot when the *IT framework*, meaning the specificities of IT (as described in this book), is known by laymen. More than that, it should be made sure that information related to running projects, including their difficulties and possibly also their reasons for failing, is communicated openly. An *IT newsletter* is published in many firms, and it's nice if they are written with a functional focus rather than a technical one. As far as the users will read it!

A regular exchange of ideas with the business departments allows an early inclusion in their reflections about future projects and activities and avoids being put in front of a fait accompli. Hiding in an ivory tower or throwing around gobbledygook was a common practice in the early IT days and is rightfully passé today.

A subject where the CIO community can have quite diverging opinions is which (if at all) services should be charged to the business departments. Everyone tends to decide according to his own experience and principles, and this may lead to global judgments and behavior. On one hand, there are those who reject this idea because of the administrative overhead this creates, including the increase of costs. On the other hand, there are CIOs who charge every single minute to the business. I think neither of these options is valid in all cases. The decision for doing so depends, for one thing, on the size of the firm (in very large firms, this is not really a question anymore, and some kind of charging instrument must be created) and the CIO's preference and experience.

I am uncertain about this question myself. Sometimes I think it's the right thing to do, as it gives the possibility to significantly limit the number of senseless requests, and it avoids the danger that IT is seen as a self-service buffet by the users. Sometimes I think it's wrong, because it generates costs, working time is lost, and it generates stupid discussions with the users. ("What? It took you one hour to replace this lousy printer?") In one very specific case, however, I strongly believe that a service charge is damaging, namely at the Help-Desk. If every problem reported by a user, including its correction, is charged, then it is only a small step until the superior will decide to save costs and will give instructions to limit the number of problems reported. This happens quickly when there are cases where the Help-Desk could not (or only insufficiently) help. Have you every contacted a call center when you, let's say, had a problem with your mobile phone, your Internet connection, or a flight reservation? Quite substantially different when compared to the US, where "800"-numbers are used, we often see in Europe that the user pays high fees when he calls; and in order to increase the fees further, they keep you waiting in the loop for many minutes.

As we know by reading this book, many problems cannot be fixed immediately, and some can't be fixed at all. If a user prefers to live with a problem rather than have it fixed, the firm has a problem, and damage is generated.

The IT world is a jungle, as mentioned earlier. How to manage this jungle and structure all these processes in an optimal way is still being studied. There are tons of articles in the specialized press. The final answer is still being searched for. There are some major methods around, like ITIL (Information Technology Infrastructure Library), which comes originally from the UK and was introduced by Mrs. Thatcher. She was apparently exasperated by the IT jungle and its costs, and she asked for some structure in this mess. ITIL has serious success, but if it is considered to be able to solve all problems, the danger is that new problems are generated. ITIL focuses very much on the internal processes and tends to neglect elements like customer satisfaction, availability of systems, and the responsiveness of IT staff to upcoming user problems. Without a doubt, ITIL brings an increase in quality in many cases in the internal processes, but I know of examples where ITIL was implemented in a dogmatic way and, therefore, created user frustration. It is often forgotten that ITIL requires massive internal resources. If ITIL is introduced and the number of staff remains unchanged, the increased quality in the processes can be offset by reduced customer satisfaction. If a pragmatic approach is chosen, and if ITIL is tailored to the specific internal situation, it is a good thing, and its introduction can be a success for all.

Comparing oneself to others is always useful. To do this, recourse can be taken towards a series of indicators (KPI–Key Performance Indicators) which are valid in the relevant sector of activity. For example, in an ideal world, the ratio between investments and running IT costs should be around 40 to 60, another one being that in average every IT staff member should follow training courses for a defined number of days (8), and much more. KPIs are always worth considering; however, they should be handled with care, as they can never be fully applied to a specific situation. They can also lead to surprising conclusions: not long ago, I experienced that the results of the customer satisfaction survey were significantly above its KPI. Instead of getting applause, I had an external consultancy company telling me that I should consider lowering the level of service (which would lead to lower costs) and the users would continue to be happy!

I know of no other area where the Head of Department has no real chance to know and understand everything his staff is busy with. Several hundreds of projects cannot be memorized by anybody. An outstanding relationship of mutual trust between the CIO and his experts is absolutely mandatory. Otherwise, it will not work. If an expert tells his boss that a technical problem can only be solved in a specific way or that there is no solution at all, the chief has no real chance to prove the contrary, at least not with an acceptable level of effort. This can be compared with a situation where a doctor has his own freedom of decision making. The hospital director needs to trust his doctor and should not doubt him. The problem with this kind of situation is, however, that very few managers seriously live this and believe in it, let alone implement something like personnel development. A mutual relationship of trust towards the staff (and vice versa) does not exist automatically, but must be built up. And it does not sustain itself. It is a continuous process. And if this process is kept alive, the manager doesn't need to know in a detailed way what the staff is doing. It will run by itself. From this starting point, IT experts develop their immense sense of responsibility.

The most various types of staff profiles are required, and all staff members are experts in their domain. The management of experts is quite a delicate task, especially in times when the job market is in favor of the employees. There was such a time until the end of the '90s. It was good to know at all times when everyone's partner's birthday was, and if the dog at home had influenza, it was recommended to check after three days if the dog was better. Otherwise, there would have been a risk that the employee would leave because of discontent. These extreme times are over, luckily, but they might return one day.

And one more peculiarity must be considered. IT experts are closer to their jobs than to their employer. This can be very well observed in situations when services are outsourced and the existing staff should get new tasks. As a general rule, this doesn't work, except if the employee wanted anyhow to do something different. In the same way, as an ophthalmologist does not become a surgeon, a programmer does not become a network administrator. When system A is replaced by system B, there is a real risk that the firm's IT experts will resign and go to another firm that still uses system A. This is a risk that can be managed, but there must be awareness for it. Money can do it (while this is not the only possible remedy), but I experienced a situation where this was not accepted by Senior Management, and the key staff left.

As we have seen, there must be administrators appointed for every system. By principle, there should only be one administrator per system, but as there are holidays, a deputy must be appointed as well. The implementation of this deputy rule is not trivial, as responsibility, if at all, is tough to share.

A strict separation of access rights in a system must be guaranteed between the different staff in IT. For instance, a programmer shouldn't have access to the production environments. While this makes sense in theory, it is, nevertheless, not realistic: when a problem arises in a program in production, who would be in a better position to fix it than the programmer who wrote the program? When we talk about very large IT departments, this is feasible. But, the smaller the IT is, the less realistic this requirement is. This point is very popular with auditors, and is a source of many difficulties with them.

In the production environment, there are regular emergency situations that require a very fast reaction and which make it necessary to bypass the usual cycle of decision making, risk analysis, and controls. If a system is down at three o'clock in the morning, and the solution requires an update in the database, then it is not possible to wait for a form with three signatures. It just needs to be done. Such situations require long-lasting experience from the concerned employee. To manage this, emergency procedures are created to avoid the possibility that an employee gets into a situation where he *must* make a mistake and later be exposed to disciplinary measures. He gets the necessary room for maneuver and is asked to document his work a posteriori.

Reading, writing, sitting

A CIO has a lot of freedom to design solutions, but more often, he is in a defensive position. I think that a CIO's success can be measured to a large extent on how strongly he puts himself into that defensive position and how he maneuvers out of it.

Why does someone become a CIO? Could it be that he gets there because he is the better programmer, administrator, or project manager? Nonsense. The decisive difference between the CIO and any other IT expert is the fact that the CIO has a higher tolerance for pain.

All in all, every day, a CIO reads as much as a small book and writes as much as a small brochure: status reports, project definitions, project plans, requests, business requirements and specifications, security concepts, risk assessments, complaints, customer presentations, software demos, technical memos, professional journals, meeting minutes, agendas, guidelines, problem descriptions, and solution proposals. And when he is not currently reading or writing, he is sitting in a plane, jour fix, briefing, debriefing, project committee, steering committee, management committee, workshop, brainstorming, video conference, telephone conference, strategy conference, security conference, crisis meeting, seminar, training, problem discussion meeting, follow-up, wrap-up, job interview, or negotiation. Often enough, some of these meetings have only one concrete result: the date of the next meeting!

Conclusion

When all listed tasks from this chapter are taken into consideration, it is no surprise that IT services are expensive. No wonder we see frequent press stories where Senior Management is quoted saying: "Our IT is too expensive. We need to reduce staff." Every time I hear something like that, I wonder who missed the point. As a general rule, every time a computer system is implemented, it was because a business department needed a solution to a problem. It might be that, at the time of the implementation, only the purchase costs were considered, possibly also the external maintenance costs, but not the others documented in this chapter. It might well be that this book has not been read or that IT did not communicate enough that a computer system means a life-long need for the maintenance of interfaces, version upgrades, functional enhancements, error management, security, disaster recovery, or the replacement of the system at the end of its life cycle. Usually, a system has been purchased, but there was no clear view on the total costs to be expected over the whole life cycle. Every manager in a company should know that the total costs of a system have to be calculated by multiplying the initial purchase price (according to the size and complexity) by 2, 5, or 10. If this was clear from the start, the decision for a new system would not be made, or a smaller-sized system would be chosen. It shouldn't, therefore, be a kind of reflex to hit on IT when the costs are considered too high, but it should be analyzed why this situation arose. It is very rare that IT costs are too high because IT has continuously purchased the newest technical toys without involvement of the business. If this happens, the wrong people are in IT, and the CEO should have interfered a long time ago.

The Monday morning game

A CIO's job is a stressful one and has always been stressful. "There is stress at almost every job," you might counter. Sure. But during my research for this book, I came across an interesting study from *Gartner Research* which states that 2.6 years is the average length of stay of a CIO in an US company; in Germany, it is 3.5 years. It's hard to believe this figure; it does not correspond to my personal observations. I would have guessed that it would be around 5 years or so.

Being CIO is like sitting in an ejection seat, and the job rotation rate is similar to those of football trainers. This is not because one wants to progress in his career or make more money. Nor is it because the CIO is trying to hide incompetence by running away. No, the reason is that there is a Grand-Canyon-sized abyss between what IT can deliver and what users and management expect. When these expectations are not met (cf. football trainer), management will try again with a new face with the strong belief that the new guy will fix all the problems.

What's worse, consultancy firms make ridiculous claims in their glossy brochures and advertisements that "64 servers can be figured in 15 minutes," "the IT costs will be reduced massively," "with system *xyz* the efficiency will be increased explosively," and (my personal favorite) "with us disappears the complexity in your IT." If the CIO fails to explain to management that the truth does not correspond to these fairy tales, the going will get tough for the CIO.

Although working in IT is fun and can be the most exciting office job in the world, it can–quite literally–drive a person insane. A study from the German Institute *RISP* revealed that IT experts suffer from psychosomatic illness four times more often than the average population, and they consume 91% more of psychotropic drugs. The consumption of antidepressants is 60% higher in IT experts than in the rest of the population. This is common industry knowledge: in October 2008, the largest producer of microprocessors in the world launched its "New antidepressant for IT managers" marketing campaign, introducing a new processor which would give to the IT manager less stress and more control. This isn't funny.

If, by the time you reach the end of this book, you understand that the IT world these days is anything but easy to master, then I could say: "Mission accomplished." On one hand, every IT department is fully responsible for everything related to IT systems within the business and needs to constantly explain instability, lack of project control, and rising costs. On the other hand, IT isn't able to fully control such things, because it strongly depends on external providers, who are far away from becoming adult. This unsolvable conflict produces frustration both for the IT department and the users. The gap that I mentioned is a minefield that claims many victims.

As a CIO, there are always moments when massive technical problems come up and one wants to throw it all out the window and have a serious chat with Bill Gates (or any of his consorts) about the mess he created–preferably alone in a dark forest. These are the moments when it is good to remember that IT jobs are the most diversified and interesting jobs in the world.

The CIO magazine published an annual list of CIOs who earn the "Elephant" award (*elephant*, because the most discerning characteristics of this pachyderm are required to be successful in this job). There are a number of criteria in order to qualify to receive an "elephant," and two of them are especially revealing:

- To be employed more than 10 years as CIO at different companies (!)
- To be at least for five years in the same position (!!)

I know many colleagues who are depleted after years in this position and give up. Others, who want to avoid the psychotropic drugs, react to the stress by venting their anger in an uncontrolled manner. My very first boss opted for the latter. It went like this: during all those years, every Monday morning, every member of his department participated involuntarily in the same game. They all tried to avoid being the first one to encounter the Head of Department. During the weekend, it seemed, an enormous anger had built up which waited to be unloaded, and he took advantage of the very first occasion for an immediate explosion. It was sane to be far away at that moment.

Everyone had a tactic of his own to be out of the way. Some arrived very early and hoped to be in the office before the boss, determined not to leave their desks even when a strong nature call urged them to do so. As soon as the roar could be heard in the corridor, it was enough to wait a few minutes until the storm had calmed down. This tactics often worked, but not always.

Then, there were those who intentionally came later in the hope that the thunder had gone by already. But the boss had adapted to this tactic, and sometimes he also came in a bit later in order to give everyone the opportunity to enjoy his outburst. There was a side effect for him as there was a larger audience then.

One time, about six months after I was hired, I was the victim.

"Mister Roeltgen," he shouted in the corridor with maximum strength in his voice. He was not very tall, but robust and had a frightening glare.

"This is an enormous mess. Your Atlas project is a disaster–such as I have never seen in my whole career. You will have to account for it. You are a goner in this department, and I will personally take care that you will be downgraded as night-watchman. In my whole life, I have never ever seen a project being managed so badly."

A careful attempt to open my mouth failed miserably, and he interrupted me and shouted even louder: "What the hell! Do you dare contradict me? No word anymore!" He slammed his office door and disappeared.

I received pitiful, but self-content glances from everyone in our office. I started thinking it would be a good idea to take off every Monday morning in the future.

Never before had I ever heard one single word about the Atlas project.

The computer community lives to the ground rule
that the presence is a program error,
which will be corrected in the next release.

Clifford Stoll

Unexpected error encountered

Why do computers crash?

The fact that badly-developed software could be a profitable business was already known by Elliot Carver in the James Bond-movie *Tomorrow Never Dies*:

Elliot Carver: "Are we ready to launch our new software?"

Mr. Jones: "Yes, sir. As you requested, it's full of bugs, meaning that people will have to upgrade for years."
Elliot Carver: "Outstanding."

I wouldn't go as far as to insinuate that the software industry builds errors into their products deliberately just to be able to sell new updates in the future. However, the computer industry is fully aware about the fact that it produces error-prone products. The only surprising thing about this is the fact that there is no public outcry. Software users are used to crashing programs.

Every time I open my laptop, the first word that appears on the screen is: *Problembehebung* (German for problem correction.) So, it is possible to work on problems before having made the first click. Very impressive indeed.

The computer industry is still in its storm-and-stress phase; it tries out many new things and rejects them quickly. To cite Mr. Resch again in his interview in the magazine *Computerwoche*, he goes even further than I do and considers the maturity level of the software industry as "infantile."

The market permanently asks for new software, and most software companies need to produce positive quarterly reports. This mix is the ground on which bad quality grows.

Rebooting is a wonder drug—it fixes almost everything.

Garrett Hazel

This chapter is about why systems crash and produce errors. Nothing that happens in a system is based on random factors. For every crash, it is possible to trace the precise cause. However, the effort needed to find out the cause bears, in many cases, no relation to what needs to be done to correct it. It is a fact that most errors only happen once and cannot be reproduced. In about ninety percent of all cases, it is enough to restart the program or reboot the PC and try again; the error usually won't happen again. For the other ten percent, investigative work needs to be done, and you will read more about it in this chapter.

One observation I've made over the last twenty years is quite interesting: in those old times, hardware was the main cause of problems. Computers failed often, and we used terms like MTBF (mean-time-between-failure, meaning the average time between two system crashes) and MTTR (mean-time-to-repair, meaning the average time needed to repair the problem.) Today, it is possible to obtain an almost one hundred percent availability of the hardware if you invest enough money. When hardware crashes, it is almost always because of the software that controls it.

If builders built buildings the way programmers wrote programs,
then the first woodpecker that came along would destroy civilization.

Weinberg's Law

Software, on the contrary, has developed in the opposite direction. Twenty years ago, it was not necessary to have a lot of thoughts about its stability. Today, however, hundreds of thousands of people worldwide are busy with keeping software running and working on fixing the problems and their consequences. The problems started when PCs got popular and subsequently when client/server technology was introduced. Developing software became democratic and it is undoubtedly right to say that all the wonderful software programs we have today would not exist without this happening. But the downside is that from that moment on nobody cared about how all these software pieces should fit together. Every software developing company focuses solely on its product but gives only insufficient thoughts about how it can be integrated with all other existing products. This task is left as far as possible to IT departments.

Publishing MTBF and MTTR values for software would be a fantastic breakthrough, but I cannot imagine that the software industry would be prepared to publish such figures because, without a doubt, they would be extremely bad. This situation is really worrying, and, according to a study done by *Corporate Quality*, the total damage in companies due to faulty software is as high as 100 billion Euros—for Germany alone! Another 20 billion Euros need to be added as loss of profits due to inefficient software—again for Germany. Imagine the total amount on a worldwide basis! Knowing that there is no obligation for a company to officially report any loss due to software problems, it could well be that this is only the tip of the iceberg. Indeed, unbelievable amounts. Elliott Carver would be pleased.

To illustrate what kind of damage failing software can do in a professional environment, take the following example I came across recently. Banking software used to print customer account statements behaved strangely on the first working day of the new year. It was configured to reset the sequential number of the account statements to 0, so the first account statement produced in the new year would start with 1. Nothing very complicated, you might say. Well, this software was *thinking* that, if the statement number is 0, it *must* be a new customer, and the starting balance must therefore be 0, so there is no need to fetch the starting balance from the database. Quite logically then, the printing of the starting balance on all statements was 0 for all customers. Fortunately, someone noticed the problem during the mailing process, and nothing was sent to the customers that day. If not, the bank would have had to install a crisis team to manage the furious phone calls from customers. To correct such a problem, it is not enough to change the program accordingly so it will run correctly the next time. No, it is necessary to roll back everything that has been done so far (like the already-carried-out archiving of the account statements into the archiving system), build up a second correction database (to rerun the whole process of account statement production), and move the updated second database to the live database. Some people spend a number of days on such a correction scenario. Just as an aside: in an outsourcing scenario, such a problem correction is extremely hard to manage and would take much more time. Being too far away from the customer's business, the insourcer would possibly not have noticed the problem at all and would, therefore, not care. Running an improvised process, added to the need of updating the database manually, cannot be clearly specified in an outsourcing contract. End of story. The example illustrates how a small program mistake can lead to a huge necessary correction. Needless to say, the software provider cannot be made liable for the damage caused.

The reasons for the problems created by software and how these can be handled are quite different depending on whether they happen at home or in a firm. That's why this chapter is split in two parts.

At home

Even we, the IT experts, who deal every day with new software, are repeatedly fascinated and amazed about what newly-released software can achieve. Even if this book is mainly about what is going wrong behind the scenes, the enthusiasm about new functionality remains intact. Every time I open a computer magazine, I detect something totally new. In the same way as laymen, we are amazed about things like *Google Earth*, navigation systems, the software in Apple's *iphone,* or computers that constantly improve the quality of weather forecasts. This ongoing astonishment over decades is one of the excitements of IT jobs. It is fascinating that computers can compose music and that these songs make it to the charts; however, there is still a lack of creativity in this which you can clearly hear. But never mind.

But precisely because there is constant innovation and new products get released relentlessly, instability is created.

Your PC at home is quite a simple biotope—compared to the biotope in a company—but it still generates enough problems to have you regularly on the edge of despair. In the following paragraphs, I list some of my favorites—you may have your own.

> *The message "bad command or file name" is about as informative as "If you don't know why I'm mad at you, I'm certainly not going to tell you"!*

(Unknown author)

Who hasn't received messages like: "Unexpected error encountered?" Well, if the computer doesn't know, how should a normal user know? Microsoft's idea to manage this problem under Windows XP was too simplistic: after every crash, the user was asked if the PC should send an error report to Microsoft. Users have answered "yes" to this question hundreds of millions of times, and obviously, due to the sheer mass of reports, it was impossible to work on them. If Microsoft had done so, it would have created a massive amount of new jobs.

Optimistic messages, such as "Software successfully installed," are nice to see, followed by "Program cannot be started" at the first startup attempt. Or "Program *abc* doesn't reply." What the hell is program *abc* at all, and why doesn't it want to answer? And did I ask program *abc* a question in the first place?

Or: "File *xy* cannot be opened because it is in usage by another user." It would be nice if the system would tell me who this other user is, especially if I am the only one working on it.

Imagine if, every Thursday, your shoes exploded if you tied them the usual way. This happens to us all the time with computers, and nobody thinks of complaining.

Jef Raskin

Messages like "Remaining time: 30 seconds" are not really acceptable, when you then notice that the time decreases first, then increases again, and it can't decide how long the current process will run. I understand that the calculation of the estimated remaining time can be difficult, but it should then be omitted or a clear indication should be given. The user's trust in technology is not strengthened in these situations.

On my mobile phone, I can see the number of unread messages in my mailbox. However, when I decide to open these messages, I get a totally different number. After a while, you get used to these small deficiencies.

While surfing the Internet, everyone has encountered a notice in the lower left corner of the screen that says *Done*, but the page is empty. Or *Error on page* without any further explanations.

Or you click on a program on your desktop and nothing happens.

What really gets on my nerves is the habit of software to jostle itself by hook or crook into the foreground. Users get permanently ejected from the window they are currently working in because any other program running in the background needs help urgently and requires full attention. It's like a cat addicted to caresses. If you are looking at your keyboard, you might not notice this. Then, when you look at the screen the next time, you see that some of what you have typed in is lost. I wish a small message would open without taking away the focus from what you're doing, in the way Apple already does.

You can get really angry when you encounter data loss because some company has abandoned a product. You have created files with some specific software, and after an upgrade to the next Windows version, these files become unusable. This happens because the program that always managed these files is not compatible with the new Windows version, and there is no available compatible version supplied by the software company anymore. A request for support from this company is answered with arrogance: "*CPO-files can unfortunately not be opened with the current C…-program. The last program, with which this was possible, was (…). Kind regards.*" It is, perhaps, better for those people that they are far away from you when you read this.

Software can put you on very thin ice: "Your registry is damaged," followed by: "Use Regedit." God beware; don't do this under any circumstances if you are a layman.

Or totally confusing messages displayed in a window: "SERVIC ~ 1.EXE ~ Application Error," followed by "Error in application: The instruction at '0x645030a8' referenced memory at '0x02f51f4e'. The memory could not be read." Phew!

Let's stop here. The list of similar errors and problems is endless.

The computer industry has a poor reputation with the public and IT experts as well. For many people, PCs come straight from hell— machines that do a lot, but are downright stubborn und capricious. Today's PCs are too complicated and unstable, and it will be this way for a long time. The industry is still in a state where it can produce marketing slogans without being immediately punished, like: "No one guarantees you more reliability" or "Solutions that work." Well then. At Christmas, I got a greeting card from IBM labeled "All I want for Christmas," where I could tick the boxes "solutions that work," "ease of use," "scalable IT," "rock-solid security," "lower IT-cost," and "stress free IT." The only problem is that I don't believe in Santa Claus anymore.

The computer industry is quite a young industry. Computers for private usage have only existed for about twenty-five years. It all started with devices that addressed younger people's drive for bricolage. After some time, useful programs were developed for daily usage. How this has evolved can be observed in computer magazines. In the beginning, they were full of programs that you could type into your computer yourself. Today, they contain DVDs with programs ready to use. This shows, to a large extent, that the public has matured. The industry, however, seems to have the view that its main customer profile is still the *nerd*, someone who is more technology-interested than solution-driven. But the ignored fact is that the overwhelming majority of people want to use the computer without worrying too much about the underlying technology and the problems it creates.

Over time, PCs increased their performance and took on new tasks. Since the demand for functionality that needs to be developed has been enormously high (and still is), the focus has always been on the development of this functionality, not so much on the ease-of-use or stability. An IT department takes care of this situation and helps the users in their problems, but at home, you are on your own.

The decisive reason for system crashes is errors in the software. To simplify, it can be said that software is not much more than a text in a technical language; programmers write this text. You may compare it with a large book. To get an example of what a program looks like, you'll see below a small extract from a game written in the *Java* programming language. It is part of a program that contains several thousands of lines, and this small part is executed by the computer when you click with the mouse on a field called *startnewgame*:

```
public void mousePressed(MouseEvent e)
{if (e.getSource()==startnewgame)
        {
                new_game=false;
                if (!user_plays) return;
                if (lstcoi!=0 && lstcoj!=0)
                {
                        if (!nd)
                        {
                                cbox(10*lsti+lstj);
                                rf.repaint();
```

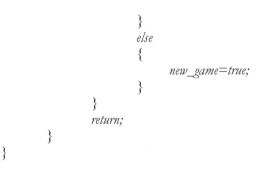

```
            }
        else
        {
                new_game=true;
            }
    }
        return;
        }
}
```

Every reader can understand the text in a book. A programmer understands the above technical text (the terminology used is *source code*). When you see a typo in a book, this distorts the meaning only in very exceptional cases, and the reader will understand the author's intention without problem. With software, this is unfortunately very different. Software shouldn't contain a single error, however large the program may be. Compare it to sending an email. If you want to send it to John Smith at his yahoo account and you type *johnsmit@yahoo.com* instead of *johnsmith@yahoo.com*, the email will not reach its destination, and what you intended to do is totally missed. If the account *johnsmit* doesn't exist, the email will bounce back, and you can correct the address immediately. If, however, there is such an account, your email will have reached the wrong person, and you won't know it. With software, it is quite similar: an error can be noticed immediately by the programmer if the syntax is wrong. But if the syntax is correct, the error might only become a problem once the software is being used. One single wrong line can make the program crash or produce unexpected results and unexpected errors. When you write a book, you usually have an editor who corrects your mistakes. A programmer's source code is, by principle, never checked by someone else—only the result of what the program does is checked. Since every software must be able to handle an enormous number of situations (of which many never went through a testing process), it is impossible to have error-free software.

> *Real programmers don't comment code.*
> *If it was hard to write, it should be hard to understand.*

> (Unknown author)

It must be said like this: there is no such thing as error-free software. The number of errors is counted on the basis of 1,000 lines of code (*error density*). Thirty years ago, the error density was around 20 (meaning, on average, every 50th line of code was wrong) and has decreased since then. Today, studies come to diverse results (it is not possible to measure the number of errors in a program as they only show up when the program is used in all kinds of biotopes), but a density of 0.5 could be a benchmark. On the other hand, software has exploded in its size and functionality and has more interactivity with other software than in the past. The latest evolutions, being SOA and Web 2.0, have added another dimension of complexity to software development.

Windows XP has about 40,000,000 lines of code. If we apply an error density of 0.2 (which would be an excellent value), we come to a total of 8,000 errors. You understand now why software needs to be updated permanently and why there are constant reports about security holes.

Large programs are not written by a single programmer, but different teams develop different parts in different places in the world. Often, these teams ignore each other, have different skills, and make decisions for their programs that need to be communicated to the others. The different elements of that puzzle are then assembled, and often the puzzle comes out loose, or it contains errors that will only show up when the customer uses it.

When Microsoft was working on Windows Vista for replacing XP, it had to announce at some point that the already-far-advanced development was stopped and needed to be restarted with a new concept. The reason given was that the integration of the different software components was too complex, and it would generate too many errors. Vista has been launched meanwhile, and the press reported extensively about the many problems it had; finally, the market did not accept this new version.

Many products available on the market are many years old and have been continuously extended with new functionality. By this, the software has become a patchwork of program instructions, and this is a jungle in itself that is very hard to manage by the software provider. In these cases the source code is called *spaghetti-code*.

When you buy software, you buy a faulty product. Always. The larger the software, the more errors it contains. One possible conclusion from this is: if software doesn't work, don't blame yourself right off the bat. It is always a good idea to give it a second try, maybe after having rebooted the PC. Most errors simply disappear because something in the biotope is a little bit different compared to the previous try.

It is interesting to take note that there is very little money being invested in the development of new programming languages. It would be very hard to earn any money with that. Also, there is very little effort in the development of methods to improve the quality level of developed software. Of course, every software producer does some kind of quality control, but there are just too many situations that can happen in a real-life usage situation. It is not like in the automobile industry, where hundreds of thousands of test miles are driven on all different kinds of surfaces, in all weather conditions, and where all encountered problems are corrected before the car is presented to the public. Over time, every software gets more stable as errors are reported by the customers, but avoiding any problems from the start is not possible with today's methods and possibilities.

Would it be possible to imagine that you bought a car and, today, the direction indicator doesn't work and, tomorrow, you lose a wheel? Surely not. When it comes to software, this seems to be accepted by everybody.

Software has uncounted features and installation parameters (take a look at Microsoft's Excel) which, when combined, create a massive number of possibilities. The fact that a user can put in the most stupid commands has to be managed by the software as well.

It will be an awfully long time until we will see the stability we have in the automobile industry. It is interesting to note that the automobile industry reports that the highest number of problems reported by customers comes from the area of electronics. Every time you take your car for an inspection, you can be sure that the car's software is brought up to the latest release. While writing these lines, I had an *ipod*-adapter built into my car, but this thing has a life of its own—it jumps from song to song, stops playing in the middle of a song, freezes and requires a reboot, and shows that song *a* is playing while I am listening to song *b*. Clearly a software problem that will be fixed at the next inspection. Only a question of patience.

It is not only the fact that software contains errors; it is also how software functions that leads to problems.

In Europe, we are especially confronted with language clutter. If you have configured Windows for the German language, and you buy software that is only in English, you will be confronted with quite a mess in all the messages and menus. But language considerations can be more than just a mess. Last time I was in Florida, I rented a car with navigation system. I configured it to give me instructions in German, but apparently nobody had tested this. Every now and then, the software instructed me verbally to turn right, but the display showed a left turn. From time to time it gave instructions that were totally unknowable: "Rechts retten," when translated into English giving something like "Save to the right". Well.

Much more than the fact that the software industry delivers faulty products, my biggest reproach to the industry is the missing error management in their products. When they know that every software has errors, necessary steps should be taken to address all possible errors. A crashing program is the most critical point for a user and should be managed. I have never come across software that handled unexpected errors and gave relevant information to the user about what happened, what needs to be done, or proposed concrete alternatives on how to proceed. What you usually see is a window with the message: "Unexpected error encountered. Do you want to proceed?" possibly with the options "Yes" and "Cancel." Not to mention an eventual attempt by the software to repair the problem itself. It needs to be stated clearly: professional error management does not exist in software. The software producers prefer to have the program crash and leave the problem to the user or the IT department.

I was a programmer, and I know that there is potential for a very large number of problems in the usage of a program and that it takes a lot of time and money to handle it. But this does not change the fact that the situation is not acceptable. Software should be able to manage exceptions. How does a software provider imagine what happens when "Unexpected error encountered" is displayed on the screen? Basically, such a message is a software provider's declaration of bankruptcy, and the message behind it is: "I don't know what I should do. Please, user, fix the problem for me." The way the software industry manages this problem is just not good enough. Either the problem is avoided with a better development quality and more tests, or the software's reaction must be managed correctly. Storm-and-stress or really infantile?

Would it help to use the *Help* function? No. This function consists only of static text that does not adapt to the current context. (Of course, there might be exceptions, probably as many as there are solar eclipses.) The text in the *Help* function is most often only a repetition of the obvious, and its usefulness is limited to explaining how the software should be used under normal circumstances.

You don't have to complete any studies to develop software. The tools needed for doing it can be obtained very easily, and you can start programming right away. The resulting product does not have to go through any quality control processes, and it can be put on the market for sale just like that.

When you drive a car, you don't need to know how the motor works, but whoever buys a PC and software has no other choice than to make the necessary effort to understand the technology. The alternative is to have someone around to help you.

Here's another problem you might experience: your computer gets slower and slower from month to month. Nobody would accept a performance loss with his car, but with a computer, it is a generally-accepted software problem and complaints are not formulated. If you want to fix the problem, there is no other choice than to buy a book or a magazine that deals with this problem and dive deep into technology.

Strange incompatibilities can be a problem in software. Printing one document on two different printers can produce different results—even going as far as one printout missing some parts without having produced any error message.

Maybe you have experienced that your PC freezes for some time (a few seconds up to a few minutes), and if you are lucky it comes back. If not, you have to hold the power button down for a few seconds to shut it down abruptly.

As I said, books could be filled with examples of problems generated by software. The reasons for these problems are the general bad quality of software. But can you do anything about it?

The answer is: "Yes, you can. You may ask fellow sufferers for help!" The Internet is ideal for such situations because you can easily find people from all continents with similar interests and problems. There is no software for which you can't find a user forum. (But note that this is only true for software publicly used. For functional software, as it is used in companies, this does not apply, and a different approach needs to be taken, as I will describe later in this chapter.) Ask your question in a forum and you will see that there is hardly a situation that hasn't been experienced before, and someone in the world will be more than happy to help you. How can you find the right forum for your problem? This is quite straightforward. Type in the error message you received into your search engine, and you might get a direct link to the solution of that problem. If that doesn't work, just type in the *name of your system* and "*forum.*" Usually, you will get a list of available forums in different languages. Register in that forum, follow the rules, and you are a member of a worldwide community. As a general rule, you will get a meaningful answer. In rare cases where there is no immediate answer to your question, some people in the world will take pride in finding a solution for you. The software-producing companies are very happy with the existence of these forums, as they can save money because it allows them to build up a support infrastructure of lesser size. The other side effect for them is that there is lower pressure from customers to develop high quality products.

In the company

Most likely, you are also confronted with the described problems in your job, but there, you will just call your Help-Desk and your problem gets fixed. Often, you will get the recommendation to reboot your PC. This is not a sign that your IT department doesn't know what to do. No, it is true that rebooting fixes the problem in probably 90% of all cases. This can be explained by the fact that your software has "lost" or "changed" some important control information, like knowing if a printer is connected or not. When restarting, the software is re-loaded, the needed information about your printer is recollected, and your problem disappears.

It is not without some irony that the world's largest producer of PC-software (guess who that would be?) announced some time ago and with some pride that, alone in Germany, 76,000 jobs were created at their customers and partner firms in order to install and maintain their software products. What was not announced was that their customers would save a lot of money if their products were simpler and more stable. To be fair towards this software provider, it needs to be said that this applies to a lesser extent to all other software products as well. People from my generation, who haven't earned their money with computers, or elder people who have grown up in an atmosphere of unconditional acceptance of authorities have enormous difficulty believing that such world-famous products can have so many errors in them, and that this is totally clear to the producer. "It can't be that M… is doing this!" I hear then. Well, it can!

The relation between small errors and huge effects is unchanged since the existence of software. As big software packages contain millions of instructions, it is not possible with today's methods to check for total correctness before the software is shipped. It can be said without any doubt that the total effort made by software companies for the testing of software stability has not grown in the same way as the effort for the development of functionality. Twenty years ago, software was dramatically more stable than today.

Computers are obstinate about precision.
Miss a period here or a semicolon there,
and you'll get pistachios instead of caviar every time.

Bill Weinman

In a company, you will find additional problems that you will not find at home.

We must mention the non-compatibility of the different components in the biotope (cf. chapter 3: *One million or one year.*) IT biotopes are as unstable as the weather: when a bicycle tumbles down in China, there will be a storm in the US weeks later. Sometimes a wrongly-placed comma is sufficient to cause a program crash. Faulty behavior of components in the biotope is a problem that is almost impossible to manage. I'll give one example. We installed software that had been designed as if it would be the only software product in the world. When you started it, it grabbed all the memory it could obtain in the PC. If you tried to start a second program, there wasn't any memory left. Upgrading memory did not help, as we reached the end of the possibilities quickly, but the software continued to grab. In a professional environment, the number of programs running simultaneously by a user is usually quite high. Well, Windows manages such situations and tries to keep all programs running for the price of decreasing response times. But in this case, it didn't help, as the application immediately grabbed all the memory it could get hold of and refused to release any. There is never an immediate solution to such a problem. You need to argue with the provider and persuade him to redesign his product, which of course, he doesn't accept easily. Even if he does, the time needed for changing the application is very long. The most likely answer from your provider is that he wants you to participate in the costs of redesigning the application. Something which may lead you quickly into a situation for which you need legal assistance.

As I mentioned already: when you are a customer of a software provider, you are always in the weaker position, because throwing that provider out and replacing its system with another is always a complex decision, and there's no guarantee the new product will be better. Managing the dependency to providers is tough and is often the cause of a degrading reputation of the entire IT department.

Is this a rare example? No, in any decently large IT department, you come across similar problems on a daily basis. IT departments are in charge of trying to manage the dependencies between components, but this task can never be fully executed to total satisfaction as not all relevant information is available. We usually get the information of compliance with other components, but hardly ever do we receive non-compliance information. A producer of database software might say that his version X requires at least Windows XP SP3 (Service Pack 3), but it hasn't been tested with Windows Vista yet. Therefore, it would be a good idea to stay with SP3. Another provider, however, states that his product requires Windows Vista as a minimum. Decide now what you will do! Such analyses can be tedious and expensive; at the end, there is a residual risk that needs to be taken. You might be obliged to go for a specific version of the software even if it is not recommended by the provider to do so.

As there are thousands of software products around and no two identical biotopes, there is always a situation where software runs in a specific environment for the very first time. To find out if a product will be compatible with the existing biotope is a task every IT department needs to do. This question is like the relation between medicine and the patient. Every new medicine has side effects. These need to be known before it is put on the market. Because of this, it takes many years to be approved by the authorities. The software industry should, in fact, make the same effort, but this is not possible as there is no official authority that would validate software before it is released. Of course, this comparison lacks something. The human body does not change the way an IT biotope changes in a firm. And, needless to say, software in most cases is not a question of life or death.

The situation degrades in cases where functional software (like a stock management or accounting system) is used and only installed a limited number of times. In these cases, there is always some functionality in such software which is running only for one specific customer. It is then the case that this functionality is so specific that no other customers are interested in it. Every reasonably large company has such a situation. These scenarios are a pest: they generate many errors and frustrate a lot of people.

To remain fair, I must say that functional software needs to be adapted constantly to changing requirements, be it because of legal requirements or because of needs from the business departments. Especially in Germany, it is true that their worldwide leading tax complexity, combined with a frenetic political will to make major changes in tax questions every year, creates massive pressure for software providers. As I wrote already, we, the customers, are addicted to new functionality. Business constantly creates new ideas and wants to have the necessary software changes almost immediately. We never leave the software providers enough time to develop high quality programs. Our requests are formulated as follows: "We want to offer this product to our customers within the next three months. Your software will be able to do this, right?" We are part of the problem, and as long as there is still a big demand for new functionality in software, there is no chance that things will get better.

Software gets very faulty when it is developed as a specific request for just one customer. In this case, you get exactly what you want (which presumes you are able to define it precisely!), but you also get a very high error density because no other customer has tested the result or reported errors.

This book is written from the perspective of an IT department, and the software providers cannot defend themselves here and now. Maybe in short there will be a book from the other side with complaints about the customers?

What makes life even more difficult for software companies is the fact that those who understand the business best are sitting at the customers', not the software providers', side. Some of them hire experts from the business to buy-in the necessary know-how, but this is more an exception than a rule. When it comes to the definition of new business requirements that should be translated into software, there is a necessity for a know-how transfer from the business to the software companies. But we, the customers, are not necessarily good in doing this know-how transfer, and this leads also to problems in the final software—a small omission can lead to a big problem. This situation is a major risk for software companies developing functional software.

Software debacles are part of the business, and when talking to colleagues, it is possible to hear of new examples all the time. When there are substantial debacles, they sometimes find their way into the media:

- In April 2008, a software failure paralyzed baggage handling at Heathrow airport for several days.

- The problems with the construction of the new Airbus A380 are very well remembered. The rollout of the new planes was delayed for several years because there was a problem with the cables being a few centimeters too short. It was shown that a software problem caused that. The engineers in Germany and France were using the same software, but different versions of it. Everything seemed to work fine, but when documents were exchanged, some comments added in the one version were not transmitted to the other version. That's why the engineers made mistakes—they didn't have all necessary information. The damage caused by this quite minor software error was 4.8 billion Euros. (Source: *Basex*).

- The US-based company *Shane* explained its request for protection under Chapter 11 by the fact that the introduction of a Point-of-Sale solution took too long, was four times as expensive as planned, and didn't work correctly for a number of years.

- The 2008 US Presidential elections produced a number of cases where the election terminals crashed and voters had to be sent away.

> *If a program is useless, it must be documented.*
> *If a program runs right, it must be obsolete.*

> (Unknown author)

In IT, we explain the instability of new software away by saying it's new: "It has only been on the market for two years; it cannot be stable yet." Then, after only five to seven years, it has reached the end of its life cycle and needs to be replaced by a new version or product.

Very dangerous, however very popular and sometimes absolutely necessary, are requests from business departments to the software providers to make a *quick-and-dirty* program change "only for us." The provider is asked to include commands in his programs like: "*If customer=x, then do a else do b.*" There are legitimate cases for such requests—namely when the software is not able to handle the specific situation of the customer and it needs to be adapted "locally", as we call it. If you are using software in a subsidiary, it could be that your headquarters require special codes which are needed for a balance sheet consolidation. Or the software that is being implemented does not run in your country at another customer yet, and you need to fulfill local legal requirements. There are techniques available to manage such requests which avoid changing the software source code, but such an ideal situation is more an exception than a rule. Normally, software providers handle specific customer requests by changing the programs individually, and changes like the one above are added into the programs. Changing the source code specifically for just one customer should be avoided by all means. It is easy to understand that this change requires never-ending maintenance work from the provider (in new releases of the software) and has an increased need for testing. It adds instability to the biotope. Providers react quite differently to these kinds of requests: some refuse them, but others accept them easily. While it is a source for short-term revenue, it creates long-term problems.

And then there are so-called *design errors*. During the analysis phase for the creation of a new functionality, it has been rightly decided to do things in a very specific way, and the translation into a program has been done correctly. But it is possible that the decision was wrong from the start and nobody knew it. This kind of error is only detected much later, once this functionality is used in a production environment. A rather simple example to illustrate: "If the balance on the account is zero, then do not calculate interest." This seems to be correct at first glance, but when you take a closer look, it should be like this: "If the balance on the account is zero *since the last calculation of interests*, then do not calculate interest." It could well be that the customer had some movements on his account in the meantime and interest should be calculated; the fact that the current balance is zero doesn't mean a lot if taken as the only criteria.

Another example how a horrible software error can contribute generating the mentioned 100 billion Euros of damage: software in charge of moving money transfers from one system to another was configured to collect all events for ten minutes or, alternatively, start the transfer if the quantity of 5,000 transfers had been reached. Due to a banal (and easily correctible) program error, every ten minutes, the program transferred a maximum of 5,000 transfers. Transfers above the 5,000 limit were simply ignored and never transferred. Five thousand transfers within ten minutes is really a lot, and this situation does not happen often and apparently has never been the case at any of the software's customers. Similar situations happen all the time and can get dramatic very quickly. And again, the Help-Desk or the system administrators must play their role as firefighters. Possibly the business users must do overtime and write letters of apology to their customers.

It can happen that the translation from solution-design to the actual program is wrong due to a small lapse, which is caused by the fact that the programmer didn't understand what he was supposed to do. An example (perhaps too simplistic) is: "If the sun is shining, then do not take an umbrella" gets translated into "If the sun is shining, then take an umbrella." Scenarios like these are frequent and can only be detected if enough tests are carried out. Today, there are no mechanisms to detect errors like these automatically. And as software providers outsource the lion's share of the testing work to their customers, we have massive quality problems in software delivery.

As seen in a previous chapter, customers pay every year around 20% of the purchase price of the software for maintenance fees. When we consider that the license price of a software is the result of a negotiation rather than a list price (software, once developed, can be sold for any price, as selling an additional license doesn't create additional costs for the software producer), it becomes immediately clear that the maintenance price is also arbitrary and does not reflect the coverage of the real maintenance costs, but is a source of revenue—a business model. Indeed, the customer pays for the correction of errors for which he is not responsible, for the adaptation to technological evolution, and for the generation of profits.

Let's have a look at how the relationship between a customer and a software provider works.

> *If McDonalds were run like a software company,*
> *one out of every hundred Big Macs would give you food poisoning-*
> *and the response would be "We're sorry, here's a coupon for two more".*

Mark Minasi

It is highly astonishing how often the customer gets the following answer: "You are the first to report this error." Thank you, very nice, but this doesn't really help. It's rather the opposite, because the provider needs more time to fix the problem than if another customer had reported it earlier. The provider needs to find a time slot to investigate the problem and subsequently fix it. During that time, the business departments wait, and the IT department builds a workaround.

Responses like this one from providers are especially frustrating: "We were not able to reproduce the error." This happens permanently. This doesn't mean the provider doesn't recognize that there is a problem (which does happen as well and usually triggers the start of a nice discussion), it only means that his biotope is in at least one significant point configured fundamentally different than the customer's. Saying so is rather a nice statement. In reality, the situation is such that the software companies usually have a tiny little testing environment, likely with static data (meaning there is very little data fed into it), that has probably not been modified for years. Its setup doesn't even come close to the customer's complexity. It is not interfaced to any other system that the customer has, and, therefore, the error can't show up there. This is one of the reasons why new software is almost always delivered in poor quality. It's like trying to repair a broken car with just a screwdriver and then giving it back to the customer. In all my professional life, I have never come across a software company that applied high standards when it came to the question of quality assurance in its software correction processes.

Another typical discussion: "The error is not on our side. Totally excluded. We believe that it happens because there is a problem in the database software. Please check the database provider for support." We do this, even if we don't believe the database is to blame. And the database provider answers: "Sorry, it can be totally excluded that the database answers incorrectly in this constellation. We suspect a problem in your operating system. Did you load a new patch recently?" We contact the Help-Desk of the operating system provider, who answers: "How can someone have the idea that the operating system can be the source of your problem? This is clearly a problem with your application. We're closing your error ticket." As there are plenty of individual components in the biotope, this chain can be extended almost endlessly. This is a situation where you have plenty of valid maintenance contracts for which you have paid a lot of money, and every provider blames someone else and, at the end, you can hold no one responsible. A horde of choirboys. Is this situation exaggerated? Not at all. This game is very popular, and every provider only covers his little part in the biotope and ignores all the rest. What can be done about this? IT invests time, tries to find the real cause of the problem, and then leads the one responsible company to the core of the problem.

We have cases where the cause of an error can be identified easily but the correction is tough to implement. These are cases where the correction ("fix") needs the addition of a field in the database. A database is entangled with so many other components that it is very dangerous to do such a thing quickly. Other programs reading that table (in a database, a file is called a "table") need to be checked or possibly modified for that purpose. It can become necessary to make a full test or, if urgent, to develop a workaround for the solution of the problem.

Sometimes we receive the answer: "Yes, we are aware of this error. We will send you a correction immediately." The business user is happy because he receives an error correction quickly, but IT is rightly frustrated because it is, again, a situation where the stable door is locked after the horse has bolted. Preventative maintenance is every system administrator's dream, but it doesn't exist for functional software. In fact, it only exists for those software systems which are highly standardized, such as operating systems (Windows, Unix, etc.). Changes in functional software are much more complex and can have much more negative effects if they go wrong; therefore, they require huge testing efforts before being put into production.

It should be general knowledge that an IT department does not possess the source code of purchased software. Therefore, IT is limited to analyzing what goes wrong, but not why it goes wrong, and cannot fix the problem itself. The role of the IT department is, therefore, limited to reporting the error to the software provider and is dependent on their reaction time. But, since this is not general knowledge, an IT department's reputation can suffer if the correction time takes too long.

Some errors have more than one cause. Please remember this when your IT department tells you that the problem is fixed, but you still receive the error. It is human nature to think that the first reason for a problem is the only one.

And now it gets interesting. A relatively new player on the market for banking software has decided to give the source code to their customers and allow them to perform (under some restrictions) modifications to it. The provider guarantees that future versions of the software will be compatible with all changes that the customer has done in his source code. Indeed a highly interesting experiment, worth observing in the future. How this can be achieved without having the maintenance fees reaching astronomical levels and without running into chaos is not clear to me. The only thing that seems obvious is that this company has to hire a lot of new staff if it continues to grow its customer base.

Software is created individually every time and is, therefore, not an industrial mass product. Programs are written by a person (programmer) and, to some extent, the wheel is reinvented with every new program. Developing software is still handicrafts. Computers are not able to write software. From time to time, some news pops up about attempts to create software factories. As far as I can see, the theoretical basis for doing so exists, but nobody is prepared to invest the necessary millions to do so. It seems to me that the pain threshold has not been reached yet: as long as the customers pay outrageous maintenance fees and are prepared to accept bad software quality like an act of God, not a lot will change. But since the beginning of 2009, there is hope, at least when it comes to the question of ever-increasing maintenance fees. The German company SAP announced an increase of their maintenance fees to reach the level of 22%. It was the first time in IT history that the customer base united and started a rebellion against this increase. And the rebellion was successful: SAP had to withdraw this increase! I sincerely hope others will follow this example.

Software does not break. It is wrong from the first moment on. Therefore, errors cannot be fixed by exchanging it with a new piece. Errors must be investigated and corrections must be found each time.

We have already seen the necessity for regression tests in a previous chapter. If you work in a company and if you are using functional software, you have most likely come across the situation that an error that has been previously fixed has shown up again after a new release has been installed. It is possible that a programmer has corrected an error but has not reported his correction to his (ever existing?) Quality Assurance department, and the erroneous program remains the official one. Or, the software-developing company has been working on a new version of its product and has been correcting errors in the old one at the same time. If the changes in the new version are very substantial, it could have been very difficult to integrate these error corrections into it. This problem of errors coming up again after they had been fixed already is, indeed, a totally unacceptable situation, but it is very common. Until proof of the contrary, I do not believe any provider of functional software has this situation under control. It seems to me that the programmers working on error corrections have no connection whatsoever to the programmers working on new functionality or new versions. It is daily business in each IT department to explain to the business users why this is the case. I do not want to repeat everything I wrote in the chapter 3, but this situation is, indeed, a scandal. For me, more than anything else written in these pages, the fact that we have old errors coming back in new versions documents the unbelievable immaturity of the software industry.

A further reason for problems resides in non-documented functions. By this, I mean a behavior of the software that is not documented in the user handbooks or has not been explained in the *Release Notes*. In every line of code, the software makes some kind of decision, and this cannot be viewed from the outside. Non-documented functions are also to be seen in the light of a general poor level of quality assurance. A customer has basically no means to protect himself against such situations. Each and every possible business scenario should be exhaustively tested in order to detect any potential problem. For obvious reasons of time and money, this cannot be done. Especially when minor changes are delivered, it is very often decided to take the risk and trust the *Release Notes*. Too often, however, this is not a good idea.

When there has been damage due to a software problem, it is important to know that this does not give the customer the possibility to claim damages. Software producers know their products are faulty and always refuse to sign contracts which would oblige them to be liable for the financial losses caused to their customers. You can find clauses like this in contracts: "It is known to the customer that the licensed software, as it is the case for all software products, can contain errors, which have not been detected in controls and quality assurance." It can be considered as true that every company of a certain size suffers damage due to software mistakes, be it of financial nature or of reputation.

A permanent source of agitation is the interfaces (cf. chapter 3: *One million or one year*). As systems communicate between each other, the crash of one system directly creates problems for the subsequent systems. A chain reaction can result. If a system crashes during the day, it is possible that the last backup must be restored and that the day's activities need to be redone. Extremely popular in business departments! But when data from that system has already been subsequently transferred to a second system, these two systems are no longer in sync after the restore, and it is very risky to continue normal processing. Experts need to take control of such a crisis situation.

This program posts news to billions of machines throughout the galaxy.
Your message will cost the net enough to bankrupt your entire planet.
As a result your species will be sold into slavery.
Be sure you know what you are doing.
Are you absolutely sure you want to do this?

(Unknown author)

Besides what I have mentioned so far, there is a further reason for computer crashes: human error. You might shrug your shoulders and ask, "So what?" But the problem goes deeper than you would think. Obviously, the administration of computer systems is complex, and it presents a lot of risks. I guess you have understood this already. Making a bad choice because of lack of understanding of interdependencies, or just because the guy worked 16 hours in a row and is terribly tired, is to be expected. To be able to avoid this possibility of bad choices, the administration of computer systems should have a four-eyes principle. But such a principle doesn't exist. We see this as a standard in functional software, where a user is allowed to input a transaction, but cannot authorize it, and vice-versa. In the area of responsibility of computer systems administrators, we search for it in vain. (Ok, there are extremely rare exceptions, but it is not risky to state that 99.9% of all administration parameters are "free.") The best we see are confirmation messages, such as *Are you sure?*, with the options *Yes* or *Cancel*. But this is totally insufficient. Administrators can potentially destroy for good any computer system without needing a second person to authorize the move. As we speak, we have retraceability only. This allows us to determine *afterwards* who did what. The absence of a generalized four-eyes principle is just another proof of the immaturity of this industry. You would think that such a principle would require additional staff in IT departments, but I don't agree. The consequences of bad choices would be almost eradicated, and we can, therefore, expect a decrease in total IT costs. But, in any case, the choice to use or not to use a four-eyes principle should be left to the IT department. Today, such a choice doesn't exist.

While I have written a lot about problems due to bad software quality and their reasons, there are two further homemade causes for problems. Many input masks in programs have fields which are not used because they are not relevant for the business needs. I could take the example of a field like *mailing instructions* in an accounting program, which is not needed because mailing to customers is handled in a different system. A user could now develop the wonderful idea to use that field for whatever special purpose he decides. As there is no processing linked to the contents of that field, everything goes fine—until the day it is decided to use that field for its original purpose. There is not a lot of fantasy required to imagine the chaos this will create.

Somehow similar is the difficulty that will pop up if data was supposed to be maintained in a system for potential future use. As there is no immediate processing behind this data, it is obvious that the quality of the data put in will be horrible. Before the new processing can be activated, it is absolutely crucial to carry out a control of the contents (*health check*); however, such a control is often impossible to carry out.

Dating a girl is just like writing software.
Everythings going to be just fine in the testing lab (dating),
but as soon as you have contract with a customer (marriage),
then your program (life) is going to be facing new situations you never expected.
You'll be forced to patch the code (admit you're wrong)
and then the code (wife) will just end up all bloated and unmaintainable in the end.

(Unknown author)

After all that has been documented thus far, it should be more or less clear with what challenges system administrators and Help-Desk staff are fighting. All this contributes to the growth of IT departments.

But it is unacceptable that hundreds of thousands of IT experts worldwide are busy analyzing and correcting errors, while the source of the problems, namely the bad software quality delivered by software companies, remains untouched. On top of that, it is, indeed, a scandal that every company pays 20% (or more) of the purchase price as maintenance fees to get errors corrected that others have committed.

To put it into one statement: "Software providers have, to the largest possible extent, outsourced Quality Assurance to their customers." While everyone discusses outsourcing IT services to service providers, nobody discusses the biggest outsourcing business case in the world—a business that is offered free-of-charge by the service providers (the customers) to the service takers (software providers). The customers pay a license to receive the errors. They pay salaries to their employees to find the errors. They pay 20% of maintenance to have the errors corrected. They pay salaries again to have the corrections tested. And they pay for the damage caused by all errors that they haven't detected.

The problems related here refer to buying software (cf. chapter 5 about the advantages and disadvantages of "make" and "buy"), but is the picture better when software is made, meaning developed internally? No, not really. This kind of software contains errors as well, and it is necessary to have enough programmers to fix these problems. A study from IDC calculated that newly-developed software contains around ten critical errors in its first year after release, and that the correction of one problem can keep a programmer busy for up to ten days.

This chapter contains a lot about problems, but so far, not very much about solutions. Therefore, here's a list of some proposals on how the situation can be improved. They may sound straightforward to non-experts and should be standard, but they are, in fact, quite revolutionary, even provocative:

- Software should control itself. It should have an understanding of what it needs to achieve and should monitor itself. It should know if a calculated result is realistic and if it is likely to be to the user's expectations. In the same way that software knows what data is acceptable in an input field, it should know what result is acceptable as output and take action if it is not the case.

- We need to define the standards of how software is developed. There are a lot of discussions around this subject, like SOA (Service Oriented Architecture), but I think this is not going far enough, as it applies only to developments done within a single organization.

- We need standards on how software is tested by providers before it is released to customers. This is a potentially huge market for new products. However, there is little activity around this subject.

- We need standards on how software communicates and how it integrates in unknown biotopes. SOA is supposed to do this, but when you take a closer look at it, it is like trying to fly to the moon with a bicycle. As long as we don't have a way to buy a piece of software from company A and another one from company B and combine them without huge efforts, it will not be sufficient. As long as IT departments in companies need to take care of things like interfaces, security, integration, implementation, migration, and everything else described in chapter 3, we need to state that the industry is not mature.

- Software must be robust enough to handle unforeseen events without crashing or saying *"Unexpected error encountered."* Professional error management must be included in all critical software. It must either be able to get out of difficulties by itself, or it must give enough information at hand to the users to be able to find out what went wrong.

- We need methods to check the quality of software and an institute which attributes (and removes) a quality label. Quality labels can be found almost everywhere, but in one of the most important areas of the modern world, it is totally missing.

- The software industry must assume responsibility for its products, just like other industries do. Warranties must be mandatory, and contracts must be designed differently. While this might be unacceptable for software companies today, it would create opportunities for those very few who focus on quality. One of my colleagues said: "This will re-launch the old discussion: *It's not a bug, it's a feature*," and judges will have difficulty making the right decisions. Maybe, but this is not a reason to abandon this requirement.

- Companies should no longer expect to pay 20% maintenance fees every year for the correction of errors created by others. I am happy that a first rebellion has been made, and that it was successful to boot! I know no other business area with similar practices. We should limit our payments to the development of new functionality and the adaptation to new technology. By this, we would get back to the 10% maintenance fees we had twenty years ago.

Please don't tell me now that all these requirements will make software more expensive. It needs to be said that the software industry is extremely profitable. Of course, many small companies are at subsistence level. I speak about the big players. The margins in the software industry can reach 70%! What other (legal) business areas have similar margins? The money to come of age would definitely be there. But if we accept the current situation, these money printing machines will run and run.

We see the woodpecker in our companies every day, and fortunately, it hasn't destroyed the entire civilization yet! The situation does not improve; it gets even worse from year to year. It is necessary to say that we have a software crisis in terms of quality. Software is launched on the market too quickly, and it is not tested enough. In fact, testing is outsourced to customers to the largest possible extent, and to make things totally unbelievable, it is the customers who pay the full price with their internal testing efforts and maintenance fees. While everyone will agree that software is extremely important and extensive, it must nevertheless be said that in this industry, the atmosphere is more like in a gold rush than being characterized by professionalism. The way things are done today is just not good enough.

The punchcard sorter

First of all, a hint for all the super-stressed people in these modern times: this chapter may be skipped. I guarantee that I won't be upset. Although its content is interesting.

640K ought to be enough for anybody

Bill Gates, 1981

Let's do a short excursion together into the medieval times of IT. Until the beginning of the '80s, these famous punchcards existed. They had been introduced roughly ninety years before (in 1890) by Hermann Hollerith for the population census in the United States. Strangely enough, they were still partially used in the US at the beginning of the twenty-first century and—who could forget?—caused massive problems in the 2000 presidential election in Florida. In the '80s, then, when computers were already able to calculate—albeit much slower than today—but had huge difficulties in storing data, storage capacity was rare and almost more valuable than gold. Hard to believe nowadays! The predominant storage was the punchcard.

There were eighty columns on one punchcard, and every column represented a number or letter. By the punching of holes in every column, a different value was created. Such a card could hold eighty so-called bytes (letters or numbers).

To illustrate how computer technology has evolved, references are usually made to processor speed. Such a comparison does not give much information to a layman, because what does it concretely mean if a computer can compute a few million instructions per second more than the previous generation? More illustrative is a comparison of storage capacity. A comparison between a punchcard and Apple's *iPod* would work nicely. In its maximal configuration, it can hold 120 gigabytes—which corresponds to up to 30,000 songs, or roughly 2,500 CDs. To store this information on punchcards (which, technically, would have been impossible) would have required nearly two billions of these cards! A further comparison can be drawn between the internal memory of a simple PC (1 gigabyte) and the first professionally-used computers (16 Kb) more than thirty years ago. In a modern PC, related to the internal memory, you could hold more than 60,000 mainframes the size of a living room.

You must imagine that, with every program execution, computers had to read a huge number of cards, and a new pile of cards was punched as output. It was very easy to remove a card manually from this pile— either intentionally or by mistake. That's how, in a very simple way, it was possible to delete customer data. Or to exchange a card and, thereby, the customer's holdings on his bank account! When you think of today's requirements for guaranteeing traceability of changes in a database, then it must be said that we have come a very long way. But this doesn't mean that this kind of manipulation wouldn't be possible in modern systems. I have experienced a loan accounting program that crashed during the night after it couldn't find the loan's customer reference in the customer file. In a perfect world, such an error would never happen, but you already know that we are not operating in a perfect world. The guy at the provider's Help-Desk proposed to change the customer reference information in the loan so the program would be able to continue processing. With a few clicks, an innocent customer would have suddenly had a new loan in his books. Administrators have the technical power to do things like that.

But not only did the computers punch. In every company were employees who did nothing else all day but punch cards—a job description that has, of course, totally disappeared. There were many of these punching machines in one room, and the noise was horrific.

A pile of punchcards could hold customer information, such as account numbers and account balances. The sorting order might have been the customer number. If you needed a printout of all customers with all holdings—sorted by balance and not name—you had to sort the pile into a different order. In those days, computers were not able to read a big bulk of data, sort it internally, and continue the processing—no, it was necessary to somehow find a way to sort the pile before the computer could work on it. Of course, this could not be done manually. For this, we had a punchcard sorter. This was a grand device, roughly the size of a wardrobe and made a lot of noise. The principle was simple: the whole pile was put into the machine and—by reading the columns that were used for sorting, combined with an ingenious physical process—the sorted pile came out at the end.

Sometimes, the whole pile fell on the floor and needed to be put in the right order again. This was an exhausting thing to do, and such a machine was, therefore, very useful.

When the punchcard sorter was launched, it was a sensation and produced a small anecdote which was reiterated many times.

IBM, producer of this machine, had invited the CIOs of their most important customers for a presentation. To make the presentation more understandable, they had prepared the pile in the expected order. Then, they marked different blocks at the back of the pile in different colors so, at the end, blue would follow red, which followed green, and so on. After that, they had thrown the whole pile on a big table and mixed it thoroughly.

The now-unsorted pile was put in the punchcard sorter, a few buttons were pushed, and after some time and noise, the correctly-sorted pile came out. As foreseen, there were blocks of blue, red, and green. The CIOs were enthusiastic, and IBM was happy.

The next day, the CIO of another company called my boss and told him that, unfortunately, he had to cancel his attendance at the presentation at the last minute, but he had heard that it was a big success.

"But there's one thing I don't understand," he added. "I have talked already to another participant of the presentation, and he told me this machine would be able to sort colors. I was thinking about it the whole day, but I have no clue how this bloody thing can possibly recognize colors on a punchcard!"

"Is it true that working with computers drives you stupid?"
"You don't need to be afraid. Computers can drive you
crazy, but not stupid."

Egmont Kakarot-Handtke

Training

A wise approach for using software and choosing a computer.

Software usability

Much more perfidious than error messages or an unexpected behavior in a system are "normal" behaviors where it's not clear if the program really does what the user intended. Software is limited to executing what its programmers told it to do, and it has no idea what a user expects. To illustrate what I mean, let's take opening an Excel attachment in an email as an example. You start working on it, and you do a save at the end. Later, when you try to find your Excel document again, you will search in vain, because the system has saved it in the email contents, not your documents folder. To avoid such a problem, you must first be aware of it, but the software will never warn you. Another example could be the synchronizing of your Outlook calendar with your mobile phone. The program may tell you: "Synchronization completed successfully," but after a few days, you may realize that you missed a meeting because your mobile phone never received a calendar entry. The software just didn't do what you wanted it to do. It is especially tough to manage these kinds of problems, as there are no error messages generated. In order to work correctly, a second (and independent) program would have to control whether all calendar entries are identical in both systems. Should that not be the case, an alarm would need to be raised. In a professional environment, an IT department would have typically developed such reconciliation functionality; with purchased software, you will search for such features in vain.

> *A computer program will always do what*
> *you tell it to do, but rarely what you want to do.*

(Murphy's Laws of Computing)

Software does not learn. It will ask you the same questions again and again (where a human being would have understood very quickly what your intention is), and it will continuously repeat the same thing all the time.

Missing such ability is comparable to a car without a navigation system. If you get on the wrong road, the car doesn't know and can't inform you. Software with that kind of navigation functionality would be an enormous step in the right direction. It would then have a premonition of what the user intends to do and could discern a pattern. This is by no means a revolutionary idea; in 1995, Bill Gates was already proposing in his book "*The Road Ahead*" that software should have an assistant functionality. This assistant would recognize what is of importance to the user and would do part of his work. Well, Mr. Gates is surely a visionary, and he is at the source of this question, but he hasn't done very much about this subject in the last fifteen years. Let's hope we will have something by 2015.

Another idea is to develop software that orients itself to the expertise level of the user, as with games. According to the level (beginner, advanced, confirmed), the user guidance could be different. Some programs offer wizards, which guide you step-by-step in the process. This is quite helpful for beginners, but is seen much too rarely.

With the proposals above, I don't think software would become much more expensive.

Every software has its peculiarities that only experienced users know how to manage. To get around this cliff, you have two possibilities:

either wait until the industry gets mature or invest time to find out at what you need to be attentive. You can take some training courses, if possible, or read books and magazines of the kind: *tips and tricks.*

Every day, you see small and funny situations linked to software deficiency—things that won't make the world fall apart, but bother the user. One example: the software in some of Microsoft's mp3 players refused to work on Dec. 31, 2008, because the software didn't know that 2008 was a leap year! Microsoft recommended waiting until Jan. 1, and the problem would disappear automatically. An excellent recommendation, unless you had invited friends for a New Year's Eve party and you needed your mp3 player for the dance music.

You can find minor, but still annoying, software problems everywhere. The HDD (harddisk recorder) I use sometimes likes to tell me: "Timer recording started, but not finished successfully." Why? What should I do about it? Will it happen again? Where do I get help with this problem?

Enough so far for software behavior, where a lot of progress still needs to be made.

In the area of user-friendliness, the situation has much improved. We have come a long way from the early days of a black screen with 24 lines at 80 characters each. Then there were the times when we had function keys that we had to know by heart (F2=Save, F3=Exit, F5=Calculate). Later, we got the mouse with all the functions arranged at the top of the screen with pull-down menus. Menu structures in all popular software now tend to be built up in more or less the same way. Today, devices like Apple's *iPhone* show the way by introducing icons which are largely self-explanatory. Adding to that the possibility of touch-screens, and the comfort starts to get pretty good. In a short while, I think user-friendliness in software will no longer be a problem.

In general however, the picture is far from perfect. Something is going wrong with computers all the time, and user frustration is a global phenomena. It's ideal if you have someone around to help you; otherwise, you can get really lost. Maybe it's an idea to marry an IT expert? There were times when it was good to have a doctor in your family. Later, it was preferable to have a doctor and a lawyer. Nowadays, it is ideal to have a doctor, a lawyer, and an IT expert in your circle of friends or in the family. But there is a restriction about that which I need to mention. Younger people don't have too much difficulty finding their way through the function jungle in a software system—it is usually the elder generation (who didn't grow up with computers) who have these kinds of difficulties.

There's an old story about the person who wished his computer were as easy to use as his telephone. That wish has come true, since I no longer know how to use my telephone.

Bjarne Stroustrup

The days when computer users abandoned new technology because of its complexity, seem to be fading away—software usability for the public market improves constantly. Not more than two or three years ago, digital cameras were good examples of how it should *not* be done. Loading pictures on a PC was just too cumbersome. But now things are good enough and the navigation is quite intuitive so that even laymen can find their way out of the jungle. Exchanging documents between programs is no longer a problem; just copy/paste or drag/drop an object from one place to the other. The future looks good, but we aren't there yet: 61% (out of 4000) mobile phone users in the US and UK think configuring a mobile phone is as frustrating as changing a bank account, and 19 out of 20 users stated they would use mobile services more intensively if the setup was easier. (Source: *Mformation*)

Microsoft also seems to have learned in this area. When the development of the new Office 2007 suite was started, it was decided that the user interface should be designed in a way that he would only see functions that make sense in the specific context. An excellent idea. However, the implementation of that idea into the final software product was not done so well. Finding a specific functionality is now even more cumbersome than before, and user complaints for the new Office are numerous. But, don't despair; things are nevertheless moving in the right direction.

But, to make this totally clear, this applies to publicly-used software for the mass market. In the area of functional software, we are still in the dark ages. Copying data from one application to the next requires the development of an interface by IT. I have a dream: an IT world where a stock exchange order in system A is dragged and dropped by the user into system B for accounting without IT having to develop anything. I will long have retired by the time this sees the light of day. Functional software providers don't like opening their systems to the outside world—we have jealously-protected environments here, and nothing at all is standardized. Even the normal usage of functional software is ages behind what we see for mass market software.

While I said before that the usability of software for the public market has vastly improved, there are still many areas where this is not true. Have you ever watched what happens when a passenger wants to self-check-in at an airport? Have you seen the despair in his eyes when he is given unclear instructions and the whole process is cancelled at the very last step without explanation? Maybe you have experienced this yourself? And then you don't know if the check-in is done or not! From a software point of view, such a process is not really difficult, but is very good at producing anger. Frustration generated by software happens millions of times every day worldwide. Personally, I have to travel to Munich frequently, and I am now used to buying a ticket at the suburban train. But I continue to be amazed when I see a tourist trying to understand which one of the dozens of buttons he needs to click just to get to the city center.

How to find the right software?

The software jungle is enormously big and grows every day. To make the right choice here is not trivial. If you take a look at the provider's website to understand what a specific product really does, you have very often started a digital adventure. The impression I get is that providers think visitors to their website already know about the product and, therefore, only display some cryptic descriptions. It is quite a good idea to ask someone else about his experience, be it personally or by browsing through the various forums you can find on the Internet. It is not hard to get an overview of how satisfied the community is with a specific product and what functionality it covers, and, more important, does *not* cover. IT departments are not the right place to ask, as the software you use privately is only in rare cases used in a company.

Choosing a PC?

586: The average IQ needed to understand a PC.

(Unknown author)

The list of features for a normal PC is breathtaking and not easily understood by laymen. The following description was taken from an ad in a newspaper:

Intel® Pentium® D 820 DC Process. 2x 2.8GHz
800 MHz system bus
2 x 1024 MB L2 Cache
1 GB PC-3200 400MHz DDR2 RAM
250GB Hard Drive SATA 7200 RPM
160GB Personal Media Drive
16X DVD-ROM drive
DVD HP ±R/±RW 16x/2.4x drive
ATI RADEON X600 graphics card with 256 MB DDR Video Memory
10/100 network card
Wireless LAN 802.11 a/b/g
56K ITU V.92 modem
Digital Media Reader (9 in 1)
1 PCI-Express 16x slot
3 PCI slots
6 USB 2.0 ports (2 on the front)
2 Firewire IEEE 1394 ports

It would be possible to make this better, no doubt about that, but I believe this isn't wanted.

Roughly speaking, there are two categories of customers. Firstly, there are PC freaks who have no difficulty understanding this gibberish and expect it to be that way. The second category is average software users. This second category can easily be bamboozled and led to a purchase with slogans such as "Powerful processor." In cases like these, it is intentionally not mentioned that this slogan was correct one year ago, but is no longer true today.

As we are still in a storm-and-stress phase, it is unfortunate, but true, to say that the computer industry doesn't look too much (if at all) at customer satisfaction. I experience this again and again. I had a problem with my laptop some time ago: the DVD reader didn't open any more, and this was after only a few weeks of moderate usage. When I sent the laptop in for repair, I was told the repair would take up to four weeks. In the end, it took six weeks for something that didn't probably take more than one hour of work. To think that a letter of complaint would receive a response is quite naïve. Make sure you have at least two PCs at your disposal and that you have backed up your data accurately.

In opposition to professional business hardware, PCs break very often. It is also true that after two or three years, they get outdated and should be exchanged. Why produce for a long lifespan? Few people know that PC producers have very low margins and that there is, therefore, only little room for higher quality.

When you buy a car, you know that the more expensive it is, the more power and comfort you get. The options are mostly self-explanatory (and if not, the reseller will happily give you all necessary explanations). If you buy a PC, things are different. There is little chance that a salesperson will have the necessary patience to explain everything you need to know. Also, for resellers, it must be noted that the margins are very small and do not allow for hiring highly-qualified staff.

The best way forward is still to ask a friend or relative who can guide you in your choice. Maybe your company's IT department offers this kind of service and can get you the same discounts. Another good idea is to order your PC online. Some vendors offer the possibility to configure your PC individually according to your needs and explain the different options; you can then make your choice accordingly. Even if you don't end up placing the order, you nevertheless get a very good idea about current market standards.

You are, however, left totally alone later if you want to make a configuration change on your computer. Installing a second internal harddisk or an integrated blu-ray writer is a real challenge. It is better to connect them via USB—this is more or less worry-free.

When it comes to network connections, things get really bad. This is an area where I see no progress at all. The reasons for such connection problems are numerous, but the error messages are always the same—something such as "Connection could not be established." "Contact your network administrator" is the best possible help your computer will give you before it gives up. And, unfortunately, you are the "network administrator." Tremendous effort needs to be undertaken here. Configuring a router, a WLAN-DSL, or anything like that is not possible without assistance or without deep-diving into technology. Answering the question of which technology to choose, whether you have to put new cables in your home, or whether the WLAN signal will be strong enough is impossible without help. Let alone the question of whether this is safe or not. And even if you are successful in making it run, it is sure as amen in the church that, pretty soon, you will have the error message that no connection could be established.

Why do I have to dig into the question of whether my PC can read DVD+R or DVD-R when I find out that a movie from a friend doesn't play on my system? Why can't the industry leave me alone with this rubbish?

For laymen, PCs are an endless bundle of insurmountable hurdles, machines straight from hell. If you are one of these deplorable creatures, you may ask a *PC-doctor* where you live or, as I said, a friend or relative. For this kind of problem, your IT department will usually not be able to assist you, except if you have a friend in the IT department who can help you privately.

> *Imagine a school with children that can read or write,*
> *but with teachers who cannot,*
> *and you have a metaphor of the Information Age in which we live.*

> Peter Cochrane

PCs are, without a doubt, enormously powerful, but they are too complicated, too technology-focused, and not reliable enough. The problem might get fixed somehow by itself, as the younger generation has less difficulty in finding its way throughout the jungle. This might also be the reason why the industry is not making all the effort it could. Someone once said the elderly amongst us are immigrants in the digital country, whereas the younger ones are natives.

Professional training

Leaving the world of public software and entering the business world again, we find ourselves back in dark ages. The more complex functional software is, the more cumbersome it is to use. There are just not enough efforts being undertaken to make it easily usable. The focus is almost entirely on continuously adding new functionality. Of course, there are pull-down menus and a mouse and icons, but in the cases I have seen and heard of, this is rudimentary. Starting to use and administrate such software without an in-depth training is just not possible.

For training (future) IT experts, there is an ocean full of available training programs. This training is very expensive and needs to be budgeted for. The training fees depend on the complexity of the subject. Spending several thousand dollars for a one-week course is quite normal. To become an expert in one area (like UNIX or Windows 2007), one week is not enough, and several weeks (however, not in a row) need to be planned. To send a staff member on training for a whole week has a direct impact on the department's internal organization; it is never easy to find a five-day window of time. Some clever people calculated the necessary number of training days that need to be organized in order to keep IT staff up-to-date with new technological evolutions. This KPI (key performance indicator) seems to be at the number eight. Well. The probability for training success is increased by the employee's personal interest in the subject.

As I said, it is not conceivable to introduce a system without organizing sufficient user training. The consequence would be chaos and non-acceptance by the users. Also, the changes from one version of a system to the next can be substantial (like from one version of Microsoft Office to the next) and require training. In large companies, you will find special training centers; smaller firms would rather charge external companies or work together with professional training centers.

Who offers training for functional software? You may see software-development companies with extensive training measures on offer, and you may have the possibility to tailor these training measures to your specific needs. But there are just too many providers of functional software who focus solely on the development of their software and leave the training aspects totally out of sight. When the decision for a system is made in a company, it is usually such that the quality of the training program does not play a role; this is understandable, but not good.

Training in a firm is an ongoing process. It is not enough to organize some training at the introduction of a system and hope that this will be enough. All software systems change constantly, and therefore, training needs to be a continuous effort as well. On top of that, users tend to forget about available functions they don't use regularly. Every IT department is regularly faced with requests from the business asking for new functionality when that functionality is already available. The users might not have been informed about it, or they have forgotten it since the last training. To illustrate what I mean: in Excel, a user normally only uses about ten percent of the available functionality and ignores the rest. Repeated training, therefore, has the positive side effect that existing solutions are used more efficiently and new software development can sometimes be avoided.

It is a good practice to monitor which system functions are really used and which ones are not. When it is noticed that some specifically-developed software is not used, it is possible to take appropriate measures.

Requests to the Help-Desk can be analyzed to find out which area has the biggest need for additional training. Users generally don't volunteer for additional training themselves. They suffer and rant. One more reason for a constant dialogue with the users.

There are several different ways to organize training. It can be done interactively in seminars or workshops, or it can be by listening to a presenter. Interactive online training courses *(webcasts)*, in which experienced presenters explain the usage and functionality of a software system and give useful tips and tricks, are becoming more and more popular. Very often, these webcasts are free of charge and don't require the installation of software. The participants in the webcast simply connect via Internet and follow the presentation. When there are questions, it is possible to send them directly to the presenter, or they can comment and rate the presentation.

After each training, feedback must be given by each participant. Was the training too long or too short? Was the level appropriate? Was the speed too quick or too slow? How competent was the trainer? This feedback makes it possible to improve the training program.

Foolproof systems don't take into account the ingenuity of fools.

Gene Brown

Another thing which is often forgotten is the fact that it is necessary to train new hires. Otherwise, existing staff try to explain "on-the-job" how to use the systems. Such a situation produced the following story:

About twenty years ago, we were regularly confronted by total system crashes. The main computer powered down all by itself, and we had to restart it many times a week. In spite of intense research, we didn't find the cause of the problem quickly; you may imagine the rising anger in the business departments. It was pure coincidence that we finally found the reason for it.

A new employee had been hired in the Payments department who, unfortunately, had no knowledge about banking. She was in charge of putting payment tickets into the system. She was shown very briefly what she should do, and then she was left alone with her mission. As there was a move in that department, she was asked to sit in IT for a few days until the move was completed. The very first day she was sitting next to us, the computer crashed again. And one of my guys observed that—just before that crash—she had switched her screen (PCs didn't exist yet) off. We realized the source of the problem! At that time, computers had enormous difficulty managing the loss of a connection to a screen and could react very badly. Today, this is no longer a problem since modern systems can handle such situations.

But why did she do that? We asked her, and she showed us the last ticket she had put in. In the *currency* field, the value was DEN in handwritten form. This was, of course, a mistake, as it should have been DEM for Deutsche Mark. Quite logically, the system didn't want to accept DEN. She hadn't understood the meaning of what she was supposed to put in, and she didn't dare ask. The input mask was blocked, and the only way out was to switch off the screen and hand over the ticket to another colleague. After we explained to her how to handle this in the future, we didn't have any more crashes. A few days later, however, the Head of Department called me and accused us of advising this lady to put DEM into the *currency* field every time she couldn't decipher its contents. And now there was a myriad of customer complaints! Needless to say, this lady didn't reach the end of her probation time.

Another example to illustrate the difficulties users can have with computer usage happened with a colleague who was a Head of Department. He was asked to move to a new office—much nicer by the way—which included a brand-new PC. But, without giving an explanation, he refused to move. Finally, he agreed to move under the condition that he could keep his old PC. To make a long story short, it finally came out that he opposed the move because he didn't want to have to recreate all the documents he had on his old PC. Is this too farfetched? Not at all—the number of users who think their data is on their PC and not somewhere on a server continues to be high, even in these modern times.

Luxembourg

Working like the Germans—living like the French.

There has been a lot of evolution in Luxembourg over the past several years. This country didn't have the reputation of being an international center for IT services. This has changed significantly. It is still true that software isn't developed for the world here, but I bet this will change in the future. The government has been very active and successful in persuading internationally-renowned e-commerce companies to bundle their service offerings in Luxembourg. The most important examples are:

- Amazon

- eBay

- Skype (now belonging to eBay) has been a Luxembourg based company from its start

- Paypal

- Apple's iTunes

- Japanese company Rakuten for their e-commerce platform

The complete list of these "Success Stories," as well as additional information, can be found on http://www.luxembourgforict.lu

In preparation for new projects of this kind, there are currently substantial efforts underway to build new computer centers in the country. There is a real boom in this area right now. Additionally, telecommunication capacities are continuously being enlarged.

Many banks have decided in recent times to bundle their IT services in *hubs* in Luxembourg. As IT gets more complex and companies can no longer afford to have individual subsidiary IT departments, the bundling of IT services in *hubs* is the big trend, and Luxembourg is perfectly positioned for this. One German bank even went as far as to transfer its headquarters to Luxembourg. There are very good reasons for this because of the right and necessary technical and legal measures that have been taken. To illustrate this, here is an excerpt from the speech *Declaration of the Government's Political Priorities* by our Prime Minister, Mr. Jean-Claude Juncker, on Oct. 12, 2005:

"We intend to make Luxembourg the main address for e-technology in the world and in Europe. Well-known brands like AOL and AMAZON are already today the flagships of this politics...The headquarters of SKYPE, the world's largest international Internet-telephony-provider...is here, and they will stay here. There are highly promising contacts with other international players. This future-oriented activity is based, however not exclusively, on a positive taxation framework that has been created here in Luxembourg. This framework is what we want to keep, and therefore, we are opposed to the EU-Directive that intends to change the indirect taxation rules. But this is not enough: in the next months, we will change our data protection laws, we will fix the deficiencies in the area of telecommunication infrastructure, and we will improve the pricing structure. We want to profile ourselves intensively and aggressively as a Center of Excellence for Information and Telecommunication technologies worldwide."

To be added to this declaration is that Luxembourg has quite a unique regulation for banks concerning in- and outsourcing.

These political decisions are accompanied by efforts in the area of research. The University of Luxembourg has created an interdisciplinary center called "Center for Security, Reliability, and Trust." As computer systems and networks continue to have a growing importance for society, it is very important to make sure that the necessary levels of security, reliability, and trust are achieved. In five to ten years, it is expected that Luxembourg will be strongly perceived in Europe as being able to answer these questions.

Since the beginning of 2008, the new "Intellectual Property" law is in application. This law grants a tax exemption of 80% on income generated from copyright protected material like software, trademarks, domain names, patents, designs and models. The aim of this initiative is to promote the development of intellectual property and new technologies in Luxembourg. The hopes are high: should this law have the expected success, we will see major software developing companies settle down in the country. Silicon Valley will be history!

All these laws and initiatives have led to a rush of IT experts into the country, and it was expected that this rush would continue for quite a while—until the worldwide financial crisis arrived. At the beginning of 2009, it is uncertain if, when, and under what conditions the need for IT experts will pick up again, but there is reasonable hope that things will return to normal soon. If you are an IT expert, you might come to the point one day when you will consider moving to Luxembourg, and then you will find the following lines quite interesting. If your focus as a reader is purely to learn about IT, you may very well skip to the next chapter without missing anything.

It is hardly known, but Luxembourg is a very pretty country, which has experienced an extraordinary, positive change in the last few decades. My grandparent's generation was mostly small farmers who, according to today's criteria, could be considered as poor. The next generation made a much better living because of the booming steel industry. In the '80s, the steel industry was replaced by the financial sector for the generation of wealth. As a next step, should the financial sector decline in its relative importance, we are confident to see the IT sector take over and make Luxembourg a Centre of Excellence.

The level of prosperity in the country is quite hard to increase, even though the times are also getting harder here due to the consequences of the worldwide crisis. The rise of the financial sector has brought along a fundamental change in the population structure. Around forty percent of the population is foreigners, but the integration does not create major problems. Just the opposite: the majority of the locals believe that foreigners enrich the culture of the country. Of course, it helps to consider that these foreigners contribute to rise the level of general wealth.

The typical local mentality is quiet and observant, but after a certain time, the relation becomes uncomplicated and hearty.

If you take a ride through the countryside, take time to visit the villages away from the main roads and take a look at the newly-built houses. Nowhere is there such a diversity of construction styles in such narrow space. You may find a Scandinavian-style house close to one that looks like a medieval fortress. Communities only define some basic rules, such as the distance to keep from neighbors, the maximum height, and so on. Apart from that, you are free to build whatever you want. It is worthwhile doing some housing tourism.

Luxembourg is in the geographical heart of Europe and has been (and still is) heavily influenced by the neighboring cultures of France, Germany, and Belgium. Over time, it has been proven that it is a good strategy to pick out the best pieces from the other cultures. This is one reason why Luxembourg is not hackling breathlessly after each and every new trend, the way you see in New York or other big metropolises. We love to "wait and see." A *bon-mot* says that we work like the Germans, but live like the French. In numerous excellent restaurants here you can observe this: French cuisine with German portions.

There is another "soft factor," which, with the exception of Switzerland, exists nowhere else: the multilingualism is deeply anchored in the daily life of the people here. The locals usually speak four languages: Luxembourgish, German, French, and English. Luxembourgish is a language of its own right with a lot of elements coming from other languages. Some don't want to hear it, but it is closest to German. When we are confronted with this, we like to answer that Luxembourgish is not a German dialect, but German is a Luxembourgish dialect. Whatever it is, we are proud about it and do all possible efforts to maintain it for the next generations.

Luxembourgers are probably the only ones who understand the specificities and cultural finesse of both the Germans and the French. This is not only a major asset in politics, but also in business life. At many occasions, we are preferred contact partners—at international conferences, for instance. Additionally, the competencies acquired by speaking several languages are very useful when it comes to bringing different people around the same table.

The quality of life in this small country is extraordinarily high—independent of the material aspects. The social stability is exemplary. All involved parties dialogue to decide on changes, and no yellow press will kill every new idea with big headlines on the front page. With its 490,000 inhabitants, the country is really small; the capital has only

83,000 people. The country has a lot of green—one-third of the surface is woods alone. Needless to say that the quality of our infrastructure is excellent.

Our administration shows enormous flexibility and adapts legislation quickly when necessary. It is rather straightforward for companies to open new business here and to negotiate details with the government.

When it comes to sports, our possibilities are, of course, limited. We have some professionals in cycling and tennis who play at a top international level; apart from that, our last major international success happened decades ago. We tend to change subjects quickly when foreigners start a discussion with us about local sports.

The City of Luxembourg is an insider tip. Its fortress (which is more than 1,000 years old) was classified in 1994 by the UNESCO as *World Heritage*. This alone is worth the trip. Luxembourg is one of the most beautiful cities in Europe, a fact that is little known. Also, there is plenty to see outside the city: the "Small Switzerland" with its wild and romantic creeks; the northern part with its castles, old mills, unspoiled nature and the small towns like Clervaux and Vianden. Not to forget the picturesque town of Echternach and the region around the Moselle river.

Luxembourg cuisine? Well, even the locals have diverging opinions about it, and it is difficult, but not impossible, to find it in the restaurants. Should you come to Luxembourg, give it a try with: *Gromperekichelcher, Huesenziwi, Kuddelfleck, Rieslingspaschteit, Fierkelsgelli, Feierstengszalot, Kachkeis, Kwetschekraut, Bouneschlupp* or *Judd mat Gaardebounen* and a glass of Moselle wine.

Living in Luxembourg is easy and good. Should you, however, desire nightlife like that of Paris, your time will be a bit more difficult here.

Damage in the millions

About the difficulties of implementing business continuity

In August 2007, the Internet telephony service *Skype* was unavailable for several days. Investigations showed that the reason for the problem was that millions of PC users were automatically updating Windows on their PCs at the same moment and rebooting after the installation was completed. Due to this, an enormous mass of connection requests was sent to *Skype* in a very short time frame, and the server couldn't handle this. It just said "good-bye." It took several days for the problem to be understood and a correction in the server configuration to be made. While the extent of the financial damage wasn't disclosed, it can be surely said that it must have been substantial. The interesting fact about this incident is that *Skype* is known as being a comparatively robust system, but still such a disaster happened. What is frightening about this is that, if we imagine for one moment that the automatic updates users load on their PCs contained a serious problem, the entire computer world could come to a standstill. Such a scenario hasn't happened yet, but it is possible at any time and would surely deliver enough material for a good novel or movie. The described incident shows how computer interactions create dependencies and instability.

Incidents happen all the time, but very few of them make it to the news. There are no reliable figures about how often and for what reasons breakdowns happen, as no firm is publishing such information.

In a previous chapter, I wrote that hardware is very stable these days and does not often fail. Therefore, it might be surprising that there are such things as computer breakdowns at all.

When such an event does go to the media, we hear something like this: "Good evening, ladies and gentlemen. Because of a generalized computer failure, all services at *xyz* were down and unreachable by the public. First estimations report about a possible financial loss in the millions."

Every user has repeatedly experienced, when surfing the Internet, that a specific page is not available. The most likely reason for this is that the server hosting the site is down. And most likely, when you check the next day, it is up and running again. You may also have experienced an Internet application crash during use—an incident that can be very tricky, as you would possibly not know if the flight you were booking was accepted by the system or not.

Over a long period of time, everyone working in a company regularly experiences that one or more systems, if not all applications in the biotope, become unavailable unexpectedly. You must be a lucky devil if this has never happened to you.

Broken-down computer systems are very stressful for system administrators. On one hand, they don't know how much time it will take to repair the breakdown, and on the other hand, they have the users (and, very often, important company managers) urging them to announce the timeframe needed to repair it. How should the users be informed about the status of the problem? Communication via email is ideal, but when email is down, you still have Intranet. If this is impossible, you can send break messages in Windows (there is special software that can send information to a workstation even if the user is not logged in). In an Internet scenario, this doesn't work, and communication is almost impossible. In times of globalized financial crisis, with banks dying like flies in autumn, a non-available bank's webpage can lead to panicking customers.

One of the most feared expressions in modern times is:
"The computer is down."

Norman Augustine

Who among us hasn't heard a friendly voice on the phone, saying, "We apologize, but we had a computer breakdown. Please call later." Or: "We have a problem in our IT, and we currently don't have any information about the status of your order." (The statement "we have an IT problem" is a very popular excuse to get rid of a complaining customer on the phone. Everyone believes this immediately, as we all know that "IT" and "problem" are synonyms.)

An important system which is offline for a day or two can very quickly create damage in the millions of dollars. If a company doesn't know which orders to handle, or if it cannot produce invoices (or pay invoices) in the right time, then it gets into difficulties very quickly. A bank without IT systems for three days in a row would most likely go bankrupt.

Considering that companies of a reasonable size all have backup computer centers, called disaster recovery (DR) centers, it is surprising that such things continue to happen. (By the way: some firms should have DR centers, but they prefer to save the money. It is known that roughly half of all companies do not have a DR center.)

What can be the cause of such breakdowns? Well, the difficulty in this question lies in the fact that there are quite diverse triggers for a failure, and each scenario requires a different protection approach. To illustrate this, I list here the most frequent failure scenarios, sorted by the effort required to manage them correctly.

Software errors

The only way for errors to occur in a program is by being put there by the author.
No other mechanisms are known.
Programs can't acquire bugs by sitting around with other buggy programs.

Harlan Mills

The overwhelming majority of breakdowns in the IT biotopes is due to software problems, and it does not help to switch to a DR center in this case. Because, when a software problem happens, it would also happen at the DR center. If, for instance, your bank credits a payment instead of debiting it, the copy of the software will, of course, do exactly the same. Switching to a DR center would, therefore, be total nonsense.

However, this fact is communicated very rarely or not at all. The reflex of business users to ask for a switch to the DR center when a problem has occurred is frequently observed and hard to get out of people's mind. I had a case where a colleague in a business department didn't want to accept this. He insisted on having a second (but different) software with similar functionality that would be able to pick up in case of problems. Apart from the purely financial aspects, it must be known that each functional system stores its data in the way it wants and also calculates with its own algorithms. None of this is standardized in any way. Because of this, migrating from system A to system B is always quite a task, as we have seen in a previous chapter. When it comes to functional software, we are decades away from any standardization; this is surely true for software used in the banking world.

Every vendor is reinventing the wheel and tries to hide his product from the competitors. In software used by the public, things are getting better rather quickly. In the most popular products, you can copy/paste objects between the applications from different vendors, and you can use two different programs for, let's say, image enhancing. However, as soon as such software uses data stored in databases, it doesn't work anymore, and the situation is comparable to what I wrote above about functional software: imagine you have bought a program to manage your wine cellar on your PC. All of a sudden, it tells you: "DLL incompatible" or some other Chinese-sounding stuff. You buy new software, install it, launch it, and what happens? Correct, nothing! Your new program doesn't know your old data. If you are technically skilled, you may write a migration program. If not, you have to key in all the data again.

Software cannot be protected against failure. In all cases of software failure, the only choice is to wait until the IT has fixed the problem. Business departments need to decide what to do during the waiting time, and according to the nature of the business, the most important tasks could be executed manually.

On a general note, it must be said that software providers only send program corrections when the customer reports an error—even if the problem was already reported by other customers a long time before. Would the industry apply preventative maintenance, a lot of breakdowns would be avoided. But as I mentioned already, this is only the case for technical software (like Windows XP, databases, etc.) and does not exist for functional software. For functional software, it is necessary to plan the implementation of new versions (once or twice per year), and it requires a massive effort on the customer side every time. The installation of program corrections is a tedious and risky task, and therefore, most of the time, it is preferred to lock the stable door only after the horse has bolted.

Hardware crash

Of course, hardware can crash, as every PC user will confirm. But professional hardware is extremely reliable these days, and should it fail, it proves most of the time that it was due to a problem in the software that controlled the hardware—which brings us back to the previous scenario.

To manage a possible hardware crash, it is necessary to have a disaster recovery concept in its simplest form: it is enough to switch over to a second hardware. There are several approaches on how to achieve this, and at the end of the day, it is simply a question of budget in order to have a more-or-less comfortable switch-over. The mistake that can happen here is the decision for a second hardware which is too small— a Piper does not fly as fast as a Boeing. It is possible to build up an infrastructure where the DR hardware picks up the processes "on the fly," meaning the users will not even notice that there has been a breakdown. In this scenario, it does not matter whether the hardware is physically located in the same building or hundreds of miles away.

Disaster in the Computer Centre

Slowly but surely, the scenario gets more dramatic. If the Computer Center (CC) becomes unavailable because of fire, water, or something similar, it does not help to have a backup computer in the same room; a second installation in a different location is mandatory. To know whether such a thing is really required depends very much on the firm's type of business activity. If the CEO is convinced (or lets himself become convinced) that a short period of computer breakdown would be sufficient to endanger the stability of the company, he must put money (a lot of money!) on the table in order to run a second CC.

In order to keep the IT disaster biotope parallel to the IT main biotope, the IT department has a choice of different approaches. According to the type and size of the firm, different decisions may be made:

Data backup and data restore

When the disaster has happened, the last data backup (probably from the previous business day) will be reloaded in the DR center. This scenario is the cheapest, but works only for small firms with simple processes. Very quickly, you come to the conclusion that:

Clustering / Replication

is needed. With this solution, the data is copied fully automatically (and in real-time) between the main CC and the DR center. Such a solution is enormously expensive and technically very demanding.

In order to save money with the installation of the IT disaster biotope, it is often decided to make it smaller. However, this is a big mistake, because, as soon as the business grows, the IT disaster biotope becomes useless. It is then necessary to upgrade this biotope very quickly. Special care should be taken that both biotopes are configured identically as much as possible.

Another money-saving method consists in establishing the second biotope only for a limited number of applications: only those that are declared critical for the firm's survival. But here's the rub: how do you define "critical" when you know that everything is entangled, and who should define this? And who will monitor that this definition remains valid over time? Such a decision is not really recommended in complex environments.

When IT has decided for the above-described concept of data backup and restore, it is confronted with the dilemma of when to align all future changes from the main biotope with the disaster biotope:

- *Before?* In this case, the disaster biotope is ahead of reality, and there is a risk that a short-term change in the plans of the main biotope won't be reflected in the disaster biotope.

- *Afterwards?* As you know at present by the lecture of this book, there are always problems in the main biotope after a major change. The alignment of the disaster biotope will possibly be delayed too much.

- *In parallel?* As changes in the systems are often carried out under major time pressure, it is often the case that there is simply not enough time to do both things at the same time. Nevertheless, this would be the ideal choice.

The scenarios described to this point do not, in principle, affect the user's daily work in the firm. If IT did a good job, business departments might not even notice that a system crash has happened.

The building is destroyed or not available

This scenario is about cases where not only the CC is affected, but the whole building or the grounds on which the building is located is affected. These are cases involving fire, explosion, or blocking of the building due to hostage-taking, strike, or another unpredictable event. There's quite a good chance that these events find their way to the media as they are very rare and spectacular. However, the media will most likely report about the problems with the building, but leave out the resulting IT aspect.

A disaster that got special public attention happened May 5, 1996, at the bank *Crédit Lyonnais* in Paris. A fire destroyed the entire trading floor and its related IT infrastructure. Luckily, it happened on a Sunday, and nobody was harmed. They had a very good business continuity concept which had foreseen that all data was replicated automatically into a DR center; therefore, they were able to get a working emergency service in place by Monday morning. In a bank, the trading floor is of outstanding importance, and if it is unavailable, the losses start to accumulate very rapidly. It is very popular to rail against IT in general and its employees in particular. IT has only a once-in-a-blue-moon chance to become a hero. In this case, however, they were indeed heroes.

This scenario is much more difficult to manage than the previous ones, because the problem is added that for some unpredictable time, there will be no building available. DR concepts define the technical aspects of this question, but there's more that needs to be done: a so-called Business Continuity Concept (BCC) must be developed. Such concepts have to answer questions like:

- A DR center alone is not enough; there is also a need for office space for the employees. So there's a need to find this space, and its size must be decided.

- As disasters don't necessarily happen during the night or on weekends, it must be taken into consideration that some employees got hurt or worse. Whatever it is, measures must be decided to keep the business up and running.

- Who is needed in the crisis team, and how can they be reached during holidays?

- How do the employees get to the DR center? Is it possible to park there? Is there a public transport infrastructure?

- In order to be able to continue to work in an efficient way, it must be made sure that the business processes work in this scenario. This can indeed be harder to achieve than the already-complex computer technology. Folders with important contracts might have gotten lost, and they haven't been scanned into an archiving system. (But even if they are usually scanned, you have to take into consideration the possible delay between the signing of a document and its scanning.) Even in a "perfect" organization—something which doesn't exist—there are undocumented processes that have established themselves over time between the company and its customers/suppliers that can be very important for the survival of the company. The larger the company, the more (documented and non-documented) processes there are.

- In normal business operations, there is an infrastructure for receiving customers/suppliers (reception area, meeting rooms, and storage space) which is not available in a disaster situation. This needs to be taken care of as well.

- Every company these days has electronic data exchange that needs to be rerouted.

- Incoming emails need to be rerouted as well. But, as simple as this point may seem, it presents a difficulty quite of its own: in a real crisis situation, only a subset of all users will work at the DR location. Therefore, emails sent by business partners will not be read. Organizational measures need to be taken to assure that all emails are handled.

- The usual phone numbers don't work anymore, and there must be a way of rerouting phone calls to the new location.

- How should the communication with the press, the public, and the business partners work? Who decides this? How are they kept up-to-date about the measures that are taken?

- How does the company get its brochures, forms, and computer output paper delivered to the DR center? Does it already need to be stored there before a disaster?

- Especially in France, a country which is regularly afflicted with strikes, the question of keeping the location of the DR center secret is of great importance. A strike at both locations could amplify the problem to a level of being unsolvable. The possibility to change the location from time to time (when it has become public to too many people) must be considered in this country as well. Imagine the costs of such a decision.

- The BCC must be kept up-to-date permanently. Therefore, a test should be conducted at least once per year. When these tests are carried out, it is to be expected that deficiencies will be detected. Major things will have changed since the last test, and the concept (and most likely its technical infrastructure) must be adapted. Organizing a test is a project of its own. It needs to be decided to what extent the tests are carried out, and doing this swallows a lot of resources in IT and in the business departments. After having run such a test, the appalling conclusion is, very often, that, should the disaster have really happened, the plan wouldn't have worked properly.

In summation, it can be concluded that having this approach generates a lot of costs and is extraordinarily complex. Additionally, loss-of-use insurances can be done, but these can only cover a short period and are very expensive, too.

Acts of God

But at some point, the limit of what can be done for protection is reached and the best concepts come to their end:

- Power failures over a short time period can be managed. So-called UPS (Uninterrupted Power Supply) systems can handle this by generating their own electricity. But they can only cover a short period of time, and the electricity needs to be supplied by the public network again. Quite frequently in the world, the public power supply fails for too long of a time. On Aug. 14, 2003, the power was unavailable in New York for more than twelve hours. For most companies, this was beyond the acceptable time limit. In summer 2005, there was a power failure at the railway company in Switzerland and no trains could run for many hours. In this case, a BCC can only try to manage the impact on the travelers; a disaster recovery solution on such a large scale with an autarkic power supply is, of course, not possible.

- Terrorist attacks are not acts of God, but present the same aspects. On 9/11, there were cases where companies had their main computer center in one of the towers and the DR center in the other one. The geographical distance between the two centers must be big enough to avoid that a local catastrophe would impact both. But, what is far enough? This is very hard to answer. In tiny Luxembourg, this is also an important question as the border is reached really fast, and the authorities don't easily allow the banks to have their DR center abroad. Also, massive natural disasters show the limit of what is feasible. Hurricane Katrina in New Orleans proved that having the DR center many miles away was not sufficient.

- Should all IT experts and other key people in the business lose their lives, the best concept will not work.

One more question remains that hasn't been asked until now: once the catastrophe has been overcome, how do we get all data from the disaster biotope back to the main biotope? Planning something like that is not really possible, let alone that it would be hard to get budgets allocated for it. All IT experts hope they will never be exposed to such a situation.

Like everything in life, it is possible to exaggerate things. My colleague Mike from our subsidiary in New York was possessed by DR and BCC in a way that he totally lost sight of the target to achieve. All his activities were exclusively turned to business continuity, and he sometimes forgot to take care of his other tasks. At every international IT conference in our group about this subject, he surprised us with a highly-professional presentation he must have spent hours on. We envied him for his talent to get astronomical budgets approved. As far as I can remember, he was allowed to spend more than a million dollars a year for an entity that employed roughly 100 staff members. He had developed an interesting concept, something that I hadn't seen before and never came across again afterwards. He not only demanded that all computer systems be redundant in two locations; no, he also required that each business department have half its staff working in New York City and the other half at the DR location! The impact on daily operations was quite substantial, as you will imagine. His dedication was rewarded. He was elected into the *Contingency Planning and Management Hall of Fame* (yes, there really is something like that!), and he shook hands with Colin Powell.

Once, I succeeded in leading him up the garden path. When he had finished his presentation, I asked him about his recommendation for a case in which his headquarters in Europe would be destroyed. As there was a lot of daily business interaction, this would have consequences for New York. Mike got as pale as clay, and I noticed he hadn't thought of this scenario yet. But his uncertainty didn't last long. He answered, "This is a good point. We must streamline DR and BCC worldwide and include headquarters. I would willingly accept the task." The headquarters representatives kept a straight face, and nobody picked up his proposal.

"My husband has a PC"

IT job interviews

No doubt, this chapter isn't compulsory reading. It is more of interest for younger people who are thinking of starting a career in IT.

Here is an excerpt from a job application I received once:

"Leonardo da Vinci applied for a job at the court of Ludovico Sforza in 1482 by naming thirty-six different skills. Compared to that, I think my main skills are well-grounded experiences and know-how in dealing with the support and implementation of networks as well as user support and user training."

First of all, I am not Ludovico Sforza, and secondly, I don't think a candidate should compare himself with Leonardo da Vinci. Either this guy is a megalomaniac or he applied at the wrong place. Or he got the suggestion from some clever book.

How to apply for a job and know what is expected from the candidate in an interview are things that every person asks himself when he applies for a new job. I checked a few books about this subject, and I must say that I have come to the conclusion that many of these authors have probably only looked at it from a theoretical point of view, but have never led any job interviews. Otherwise, they wouldn't write such nonsense.

As Luxembourg attracts people from all countries, we see some substantial cultural differences in how a job application is written. The Germans like to do it very laboriously by sending in a kind of glossy folder containing all (really all) the school certificates they have ever gotten.

This is just as much overdoing as the French are understating. Their applications are very short (one or two pages) but densely written. Others love to write their cover letters by hand. Reading unknown handwriting is displeasing and should not be done; an IT department does not employ graphologists.

The best way is to write a short cover letter so the reader gets a first impression and then to add a CV with the most important experiences. If you have some extraordinarily positive degree, it can of course be added, but never should all possible certificates be added since birth.

It is not wise to list special abilities if they are not linked in any way to the position that will be filled. In one example, I had a candidate whose biggest professional accomplishment was that he was nominated "captain" of his company's soccer team. In some other application, I read: "I love spicy food—I have a high resistance level to one of the hottest chili peppers in the world!"

Due to the Internet, today you get masses of emails for every open position: a butcher from Argentina or a political sciences student from Sydney. Human Resources departments are pretty busy filtering these kinds of job applications. The Internet can really be a plague.

To everyone who is interested in the computer world, it is a good idea to go into the field of computer science. The media give a lot of confusing messages about the prospect of the IT business: one day, there are too many experts, and the next day, there are not enough. We must recognize that the IT industry is very young and that there is still a long way to go. So, starting studies in this area should provide a bright future, considering the fact that there will always be times where the demand is less.

Strangely, considering that the young generation uses computers and software very naturally, there are not too many youngsters who want to begin IT studies. In the public perception, there's still that picture of the spotty *nerd*, and the industry has not been able to show young ones how interesting a job in IT is and what career opportunities it offers.

Studies in IT have changed a lot over the last thirty years. At that time, I had to explain to everybody what an IT study would be; the focus was on electronics and programming. IT management was unknown at that time. Today, there are so many different IT jobs that every taste can be served.

I guess I must have had around 200 or 300 job interviews in my career, and I can use this experience now to give some hints. Over time, things have changed, but not exclusively for the better. What worries me is that there are more and more job applications in which the candidate lies or massively exaggerates his abilities. Skills about MS-Access, for example, are listed, but the truth is that the candidate only knows what MS-Access is, but has no clue how to develop with it. "Windows XP expert" means that he has installed it on his PC and simply uses it. One question is enough to overthrow the whole construct.

Then it must be noticed that some training programs with an issued certificate are partially useless. There are always candidates who show their MSCE (Microsoft Certified Engineer) certificate but can't answer the simplest questions. I guess (but I cannot prove) that the same questions are always asked in these tests, and you can find the answers beforehand on the Internet. Learning the answers by heart is then enough to pass the test. The problem is, on a job application, you can't distinguish a real MSCE from a faked one.

Then, we experience continuously that the real world of an IT department, with all its specificities as described in this book, is totally unknown by newcomers. The real world is not communicated in schools and universities. Job starters have the strong belief that an IT department somehow resembles a Silicon Valley Research and Development lab. But we're far away from that. As I stated a few pages before, IT is like working in an open pit—new galleries need to be dug while old ones risk collapse.

As the business world is moving very fast (well, in normal times outside of recession periods), what is needed most are people who can adapt to such environments. What special abilities should employees of IT departments have? Here is a (non-exhaustive) list:

- If the job is in a company which doesn't produce technological products (a bank, for example), then the candidate should have a certain level of know-how about the business in this branch and should show interest in extending this know-how. Technology freaks are only needed in limited numbers.

- In one of the previous chapters, I compared the mentality of IT experts with those of doctors. Character traits are very important (of course, not only in IT, but also especially here): respectful treatment of others, open and clear dialogue (especially important for the numerous occasions when project delays occur), keeping promises, and sticking to arrangements made (not always easy, as there are many external factors upon which you have no bearing on and of which the user is not always aware).

- Permanent readiness to learn something new and to question yourself. Because of the short life cycles of systems and technology, it is necessary to change job orientation several times during a career. This is true even if the employer remains the same.

- A mindset which wants to achieve something and commits itself to the objectives of the company. An "it's only a job" mindset doesn't work in IT (just as it wouldn't work for a doctor). An IT job, in whatever position it is, never becomes routine.

- The general perception is that the words "IT" and "problem" are synonymous. But the majority of problems is due to faulty software and is not caused by IT staff. Differentiating between person and problem is absolutely key. The person who is in charge of solving the problem is almost never the one who caused it. Regrettably, only a small percentage of users have read this book and are, therefore, quick to criticize the colleagues in the IT department. IT staff members must be able to ignore this and patiently explain the cause of the problem to the user.

- Ability to analyze a situation very quickly and come up with a pragmatic solution, as unforeseen situations happen every day.

- Unusual situations require unusual solutions. Some of these solutions are obviously not always compliant with official rules and guidelines and may come into conflict with auditors, should they become aware about what is done. A firm instinct for the tightrope walk between improvising and following the rules is extraordinarily important. Studies show that all (!)

system administrators break rules from time to time in order to be able to fulfill their tasks.

- Resistance to stress. Variable working schedules, including late hours and weekend work, are part of the job. The one who doesn't accept this should stay away.

- A platitude, but nevertheless worth mentioning, is that no one knows it all. IT is always teamwork; trust in others is a minimum requirement.

- Maybe less true for the US or UK: multilingualism in an increasingly globalized world is important for success. If working in Europe, speaking your customer's language is a real asset.

Many errors can be made during the interview, but many things can be done right as well. Maybe it's a cultural thing, and what follows could be different in the US and the UK. But as far as Europe is concerned, my best tips and tricks would be the following ones:

- Before the invitation for an interview is sent out, a decisive error can be made—namely if you drop in at the company (or even call) and ask to talk to the Head of Department in order to ask about his impression of your application. To hand your application in personally is not a clever idea either. A Head of Department usually has dozens of things to do at the same time. Thinking that he would have time to see you is quite arrogant and naïve. The one who hires must stay in the driver's seat at all times; don't try to push him to do something that is not agreed on beforehand.

- Starting a new job is a far-reaching decision. It should be well thought out because, if things turn out right, the employer will not be changed so often. It is all right to be a bit nervous at the first interview. Compare it with the first rendezvous where some nervousness is quite okay. A totally "cool" candidate is displeasing and not authentic.

- During the interview, a real interest, even enthusiasm, must be noticeable. The interviewer must detect that this person really wants this job and be convinced that he can handle the task. The candidate must ask questions: he needs to know what the job responsibilities are, who his colleagues are, what special challenges there are, and much more.

- It's a bad idea to ask about salary at the very beginning. This should only happen around the end of the interview and only if the whole atmosphere was positive. Early questions about parking spaces, restaurant vouchers, and similar things are also very unpopular. It only shows that the candidate is more interested in the details of his personal advantages than in his new task.

- As you might get asked about your salary expectations, it is useful if you have informed yourself about what you may reasonably ask for given your experience. The Internet can help you in figuring this out. If you don't want to answer with a precise figure, a statement, such as, "According to the usual market practice," or, "A reasonable increase of my current salary would be very welcome," are quite acceptable answers. If you were significantly underpaid in your previous job, it is possible to mention this and state that you would like to have a higher salary.

- If you apply for a position which is below the level of what you did until now, you should expect some distrust from the interviewer. You should have a good and honest answer to explain why you want to downgrade.

- If you apply for a job where the requirements are above the old level, you must be able to argue credibly why you believe you are up to the higher challenge.

- Avoid talking too much about technical details from your previous job. IT is so multifaceted that there are good chances that the interviewer doesn't know as many details as you do. Explain your work in words that can be understood by an IT expert who doesn't know details about the specific technology (or system) that you used. Should the interviewer have precise technical know-how, and should he insist, then of course you should answer at the same level.

- Something that surprises me again and again is the question of career planning. Our German candidates are especially good at asking this kind of question. I suppose it must be written in these clever books for job applications. Don't do it. Life is so full of possibilities, and we live in a free world. If you are good enough, you can become president of your country or the CEO of any company. Such a question shows that the candidate wants others to do the planning for him or that he wants to know already now with which position and salary he can expect to retire. (Ok, exaggerating a little bit.) A competent employee will always have the opportunity to progress, and if it doesn't happen in the place where he works, he will seek an opportunity at another place. It is not possible to eternally block someone against his will if he really wants it and if he has the skills to do more. You should have at least an idea of where you want to be in three to five years. Should this question be asked, you should have a plausible answer. If you are an expert in a specific field and you want to stay in that field, then it is all right to say so.

- It is of outstanding importance that there is good chemistry between the parties. If this is the case, half of the crop is yielded.

- Just be yourself and don't try to play a role that you can't master. Sooner or later, you will be detected.

- Give some thought to your major strengths and weaknesses. If you are asked about this, it is always very impressive when the candidate can reply to both aspects without hesitating.

- Own up to your weaknesses: nobody is perfect, and it is embarrassing if you turn out to be somebody different after you have been hired compared to your behavior during the interview. If you can't reply to a question, just admit that you have no answer. Avoid improvising—an experienced interviewer notices this immediately.

- You should have a picture of what you expect from your superiors in the day-to-day contacts. It will tell the interviewer how you function. The answer should be honest, and an answer should definitely be given.

- If you are asked about your hobbies, give a short, but informative answer. If the interviewer picks up the subject, as he may have the same hobby, don't let him feel that you have the better golf handicap or that you have caught the bigger fish.

- Include references in the application. If one of your previous bosses was very satisfied with you, you can mention this—under the condition, of course, that you have previously asked his permission. A solid reference is a very good argument.

- Collect information about your potential new employer. Their Internet site will usually give enough information. It is indeed very worrying to have a candidate in the interview who doesn't know what your company is doing.

- Ask if the job you are applying for is a new position, and if so, ask if you may see the job description. If such a thing exists, then consider this a good sign: the company has given serious thought to what you should do. If such a description does not exist, the interviewer should at least have it very clearly in his mind and should tell you details about it.

- If you are supposed to replace someone who has left, it can be risky to ask why this person went away. Tactfulness is necessary at this point. A question, however, about the general working atmosphere in the company and the working mood of your immediate future colleagues is surely appropriate.

- If it is applicable for the offered job, you may (no, you must!) check the maneuvering room for making decisions. Fix it with a concrete example (such as: Who decides what PC-supplier we take? What influence does the IT department have on the decision-making process for new projects or budgets? Who decides when the upgrade to the next Windows version will be done?). If it is a job in a subsidiary, you may also ask about the influence of the headquarters on your job.

- And a last tip: ask what is expected from you. You must know where the real challenges are (be it upcoming projects, current problems with staff, cost cutting exercises, or whatever).

Even if the interview went well, it is still possible to make decisive mistakes. Don't call the next day to thank the other person for the interview. In fact, you only want to know how you were evaluated and what will happen next. As I said, a Head of Department has many other things to do. Consider that he surely wishes to see other candidates as well. Give him time; if you want to avoid negative reactions, don't push. If you're on the black list, pushing won't get you back on the white list.

One day, I had a chat about interviews with a colleague of mine, a CIO in a hospital. And he told me that he has further criteria to consider. With a twinkle in his eyes, he said that he was sure he could never do the job in his Help Desk. To my surprise, he said, "We ask every potential candidate if he can see blood. He must be able to replace a defect screen under high pressure in the operating theater while there is blood everywhere while looking at opened human bodies. Should he faint, the doctors would have two patients to take care of and still have a defective screen." Well, personally, I am surely not adequate for this job.

Interviews are never really a laughing matter. However, there was one such situation when we could only laugh after the lady had gone. We were looking for a part-time job starter for simple tasks on one of our computers. We couldn't ask any expert questions, as she was indeed a job starter. To get an idea about her affinity with IT, we asked her where her interest for this job came from and what she knew about computers.

"My husband has a PC," was her answer.

IT Security

About the risks related to IT and how firms and private people can protect themselves.

The fact that using computers brings risks should be public knowledge by now. The public is continuously informed—though not very systematically—every time a specific security topic gets newsworthy. In summary, the volume of IT-security-related press articles is growing constantly. But I am afraid most people just ignore them in most cases. The aspects related to IT security in a firm, however, never become part of a public discussion, and the information contained in this chapter related to companies will probably be quite new to most readers.

IT security is a wide and complex field. Those who are responsible for it have to find ways of protecting systems against all kinds of risks, like general computer failures, unauthorized data access, or attacks from the external world. It is a subject with a literally exploding level of importance.

Until the mid-'90s, this area was limited in essence to questions of physical security, meaning that the computer center must be inaccessible to unauthorized persons. Apart from that, the biggest danger was that someone would ruin his keyboard by pouring coffee on it. Only with the success of PCs and the Internet, combined with private and commercial usage, were new threats created. Meanwhile, this area is so large and complex that a huge multi-billion-dollar industry has been created around it.

What has remained constant over time is the fact that security measures are always at least one step behind technology. The market requests new functionality in systems and soaks up anything new. Only when there has been enough damage around a new technology do the security aspects come to forefront.

To get introduced to the subject, let's look at a small example:

I don't think there is a need to explain what push-mail is. (Well, if there is, it is a technology that allows having your office emails sent to a mobile device.) It is a very interesting thing, and there's probably nothing more exciting than being on a ski slope and getting a beep from your mobile phone, informing you that a server has crashed at home or a customer has cancelled an important contract.

When the Canadian company RIM introduced the first Blackberry years ago, there was massive hype around it, and every top manager wanted to have one immediately. As we know already, first comes the new technology, and then, much later, come the security concerns. And it was the same with the Blackberry. This technology was a real open door for anyone wishing to gain access to confidential data. This new technology was, at that time, a real nightmare for any IT security officer, as there was no technical solution available to make the device safe. At the same time, it was surely not good for the career and the yearly bonus to say "no" to a top manager—especially when you were faced with the argument that a CEO-colleague at another company had such a new toy.

Simply stealing the Blackberry or listening to the phone communication (by using easy-to-find software) would give access to all the emails that the owner of the Blackberry received. Today, this problem is fixed, and the devices are reasonably safe. But history repeats itself: Apple's *iphone* created now the same hype and every manager wants to have one; but from an IT security point of view it returned us back to the early dark times. Only very slowly do we see that security solutions become available. As a minimum request (among many others), IT administrators should have the possibility to remotely erase all data in the case that the user reports a stolen or lost device. But of course, first we have the incidents, and then countermeasures are developed. It would be ideal to analyze the risks first and then define (and implement) countermeasures. This describes in short the framework in which an IT security officer works: he has to find out how a system or technology can be used without unacceptable risks.

There are two categories of risks, depending on if we talk about security at home or in a company. That's why this chapter is split in two parts.

At home

It's surely not the result of a scientific analysis, but in the area of private PC usage, I haven't met anyone so far (apart from IT experts, of course) who was sufficiently aware of the risks linked to computer usage—let alone knowing how to organize a sufficient level of protection. A private user is left quite alone with this subject—a fact that is really worrying, considering it only takes minutes to get attacked when you connect your PC to the Internet. The media don't really help here either, as some individual risks are talked about from time to time (spam and phishing are the most popular ones), but there is no global picture of the threats and countermeasures to take. Now, a possible approach to that question could be that every PC and every piece of software you buy comes with appropriate security. You might compare it to buying a new car, where the safety belts are already installed. But this is just a dream that will not become reality in a near future.

So, what are the risks?

Internet

Internet, is that thing still around?

Homer Simpson

The Internet is a new surprise every day. Even old stagers like me are continuously amazed about the creativity and inventiveness of what you can find on the Internet. But that's not the subject of this chapter.

The Internet contains very real dangers. Anything forbidden in the real world can also be found in the virtual world. But there are country-specific differences.

Without much difficulty, the Internet allows users access to all kinds of information, including forbidden content. Even if search engines block forbidden elements, there's not a lot of research required to get all the data you want. Studies say that about half the Internet is "bad." Just imagine! In the year 2009, the Internet continues to be an anarchic space where the law can't easily impose itself. There is a legal gap of gigantic dimensions: on the one hand, we have country-specific legislation, and on the other hand, we have the Internet, where country borders play no role. To illustrate this, just consider the effort that a country like China undertakes to block (through a gigantic firewall) all Internet content which is not compatible with their laws. Another example could be the effort undertaken by India to block the Internet telephony from *Skype* and others. The beginning of this chapter is confirmed here again: first there is the technology, and then, at a later stage, come security and legislations. It will take some time (probably a lot of time) until the laws from the real world will have the same effect in the virtual world. To achieve this, international coordination is required between governments, and this is, as we all know, a very painstaking process.

So, whatever you want, all possibilities are at hand. Here is a non-exhaustive list:

- All sexual variations ever detected by humans, including all possible and forbidden perversities can be found really fast, maybe sorted nicely by alphabetic order, and including explicit pictures and videos.

- Pedophiles have easier ways to get into contact with children than in the "old" times. Fortunately, this problem is closely monitored by the authorities, and many persons get arrested. Germany undertakes massive efforts to oblige all Internet access providers to block sites with such material. The "don't climb into the car of a stranger" of our childhood corresponds today to the "don't meet with unknown chat friends."

- Purchase and sale of all kinds of forbidden material is easy to organize.

- Instruction manuals for the construction of bombs are only a few clicks away.

- Extreme agitation documents of all kinds are online.

- *DRM* (Digital Rights Management)
  Now, this is interesting. This is the third edition of this book,

and the part related to DRM has already changed substantially. In the second edition (mid-2008), the question of how to avoid illegal copying of protected material was totally open. Now, in the first quarter of 2009, it looks as if the industry will withdraw all technology enforcing copyright protection. Once you have bought music, you can copy it as many times as you want. Away from the question of music, another aspect is important here: how can it be assured that a document (Word or Excel, for instance) which has been forwarded to another person can't be read by a person who is not explicitly allowed to do so? And how can it be made sure that there is a time limit on reading a document? The industry is still working on this question.

- Protection of minors
  It is no longer a question of whether parents should monitor what their children are doing on the Internet. The question is now how to best achieve this. There is software around today to configure specific firewalls, but the bad news is that they don't work properly or have very big loopholes. I tried it with a very popular one, and it required an enquiring mind to get it working. But even if you succeed, many pertinent pages continue to work. Upon a request sent to the support center, I got the answer that the specific webpage had a problem: *"There is a problem with the structure of the HTML on this site that may cause some clients not to recognize the label,"* whereas the tags in the webpage tell you that you will see *"Naked breasts, naked buttocks, visible genitals, etc."*. If you are not satisfied with this result, you may activate an *add-on* called *Parental Control* that you can download with another popular security product. Even if the result is visibly better, there are still too many pages getting through. Some doubtful webpages try to give themselves a picture of seriousness by adding a message of the following kind at the entry page: *"Protection of minors is important for us. If you are older than 16 years then click OK, otherwise CANCEL."* Aha. Even the webpage for *Hostel*, an extremely sadistic torture movie released for 17-year-olds, can be reached without barriers, even when the category *Violence* is blocked in the *Parental Control* setup. It is really a fiasco: the blocking and filtering of web content is not working properly.

- The problem would be significant enough if it was limited to webpages, but there are many other ways to get access to all kind of data. Everything, really everything, can be downloaded by so-called *Peer-to-Peer*-programs totally hassle-free and, in most cases, even free-of-charge. No control mechanism snatches this. Another way to the PC's harddisk is, of course, email or the USB port. As long as the data loaded from there doesn't contain a virus, everything can get in without control.

There can only be one conclusion: "There is no protection of minors, and there is no solution available that would justify such a label." But is there hope for the future? Will the current young generation, once they have children of their own, accept that their kids will have the same access to everything they had, or will they insist on better technical solutions? Technically speaking, it would not be so difficult to reach that goal. In a professional environment, it is possible to block web content very precisely and to monitor the other open gates to a very large extent. But this software is expensive and not available to the public.

Wireless Lan (WLAN or Wi-Fi)

is a fantastic thing, no doubt about that. As is always the case with new developments, first we see the enthusiasm about the possibilities before we see the risks. When you buy Wlan for yourself at home, you get a device which is configured for a totally unprotected access, which means that everyone near you can use it too. When you live in a house, it is more likely that the signal is too weak for your neighbors to catch it, but if you live in a flat, then, if you use the default setup, your neighbors can browse on your Wlan.

Wlan security is quite a disaster. The major risks that you (or your neighbor) are exposed to are:

- Somebody else listening to your entire data traffic and getting hold of your passwords.

- The data transfer can be manipulated. Thereby, a money transfer could be changed to a different beneficiary, or an important email may be voluntarily deleted.

- Your neighbor surfs with your Internet connection and uses it for illegal purposes. There is a risk that someday the police will ring at your door and ask you to explain why you did certain things. Proving that it wasn't you is not easy. To show that this risk is not purely theoretical, here is an example of how this approach was used for terrorist purposes: *"MUMBAI: City policemen will be soon seen roaming the streets with laptops in their hands in search of unsecured Wi-Fi connections. In an initiative taken by the Mumbai police, in the backdrop of terror mails sent before blasts and terror attacks, policemen will be sent to various locations in the city in search of unsecured Wi-Fi connections. 'If a particular place's Wi-Fi is not password protected or secured, then the policemen at the spot has the authority to issue notice to the owner of the Wi-Fi connection directing him to secure the connection,' DCP Sanjay Mohite said. The notice will be issued by the police under section 149 of the Criminal Procedure Code, which is to prevent the commission of a cognizable offence. The step was taken at a conference today (January 9, 2009) where around 80 police personnel were present to learn about Wi-Fi connections and cyber crime. Terror mails were sent through unsecured Wi-Fi connections prior to the Delhi and Ahmedabad blasts. While the mail sent before the Ahmedabad blasts was traced to the residence of US national Kenneth Heywood in Navi Mumbai, the mail sent prior to the Delhi blast was traced to a residence in suburban Chembur. The Wi-Fi connections in both the cases were unsecured, which was used to send the terror mails."* (Source: The Times of India)

- Inward transfer of viruses, trojan horses, spy programs, or the usage of your PC as a *zombie* (will be explained later).

- Your connection may get massively disturbed, and you may have lower bandwidth or no connection at all.

It is hard to find the ratio of protected versus non-protected Wlan, but my guess would be that the majority is not protected. To avoid all these problems, encryption of the data transfer from and to your PC needs to be activated. Usually, your Wlan should be capable of doing this, but unfortunately, it doesn't come along preconfigured. And how do you achieve this? If you are not an expert, you are confronted with a tangled mass of technical jargon. Not surprising, then, that many people just capitulate. The adapter I used at my home refused persistently to activate encryption, even when I followed the manual's instructions. I complained at the product's user support site, and I received the following instructions:

1. Start by configuring the adapter over the already-existing Ethernet or USB adapter in order to establish the connection between these devices.

2. Make sure that the PC/laptop from which you want to configure is in the same IP range as the wireless adapter. At shipping, this one has the IP 192.168.0.252 and the subnetmask 255.255.255.0 configured.

3. Change the settings of the wireless card on your PC/laptop in the way that the SSID has the value «xxxxxxx» and that the encryption is deactivated.

4. Open a browser in order to connect to the address of the wireless adapter. It is of no importance whether you do this directly over wireless or over a connected Ethernet/USB adapter. It is important, however, that you don't run a wireless and a cable connection simultaneously.

5. Should you use one or more Access Points (AP), you should configure the wireless channel in a way that there is the highest possible distance between the configured channels of all other used AP.

6. Provided that you have changed the IP of the wireless adapter for the value of the existing network, you should now also change the IP of your PC/laptop.

Any questions? A nightmare for everyone who can't explain the difference between "bit" and "byte." To disappoint even more: if you overcome this hurdle, you need to know that the encryption password can be cracked quite easily if you selected the wrong method (WEP). But does anyone tell you this? It is cheaper for the producers to come up with technology that works rather than safe technology. The day will come when all this will be better, but until then, as the customer, you bear the full risk.

Backups

The risk of losing data is very real. PCs can crash, and documents can get lost forever. Or you may have accidentally deleted a document, and it is impossible to recover it. And did you ever want to restore a document with the previous week's contents, as all the changes done are rubbish?

Data must be backed up regularly. This point can't be repeated often enough.

But it seems that the seriousness of this question is ignored by the computer industry. It is indeed totally unacceptable that this basic requirement of any system is not handled in the PC's operating system. Microsoft Vista hasn't fixed this issue, and I don't know yet if Windows 7 will do so. In any case, we have now had computers for private usage for roughly twenty-five years, and no solution has been integrated in all this time. Imagine buying a new car without brakes: it would be the same. It is still the user's responsibility to think about this—to buy a product on the market and to configure it correctly. Surely not a problem for technically-interested people, but undoubtedly an unacceptable situation for normal PC users. Some PC vendors are aware about this and have added backup functionality on their own initiative. Even if some license fees need to be paid to activate it, it should be done.

Execute backups regularly. It is good practice to do it every day or at least every time you have changed something you want to keep. Give some thought to how you want to structure your data on your PC. If you have folders which clearly indicate their contents, then executing backups will be easier. You may compare it to the organization of paper folders. And don't forget that your data can be lost tomorrow—it happens to a lot of people all the time around the world!

Create a cycle of five USB memory sticks (rewritable DVDs work as well, but are prone to scratches that make them unreadable) to hold your backups. Use stick #1 for your first day's backup, stick #2 for the second day, and so forth. The backup on day six will use stick #1 again. If your data is really important, consider repeating every backup on an additional media, as your memory stick may become unreadable or you may lose it. Take this question really seriously.

Something more to consider: when you have bought a new PC, it is not possible to copy programs from the old PC to the new one. There is special software around to handle this, but this costs money. Normally, you have to reinstall all your programs again—a cumbersome task if you don't have the installation programs anymore. Normally, nobody keeps installation programs! And even if you did, they are probably outdated, as you have received error corrections (fixes or patches) or new versions of them in the meantime. Backing up the "Programs" folder is useless as well. PCs have the annoying tendency to give up their lives abruptly, but every program you ever downloaded "thinks" it will stay on that PC until the end of time and that a move to another computer is a fairy tale from a different world.

Virus protection

In God we trust, all others we virus scan

(Unknown author)

Meanwhile, "virus" is a very popular word. But what is a "virus," in fact? The term is irritating because it is a biological term. Computer viruses (including variants like worms and Trojan horses) are, in fact, programs—a piece of software developed by someone with the intention of doing harm to others. This proves that computer programmers are not necessarily better people than others. Viruses are developed on the basic understanding that computers have open doors (faulty software) and that not enough is done by software developers and the PC user to close these doors.

A virus is comparable to a home burglary. If you leave a door or window open, the burglar can get in. The only difference is that a virus can only create material harm, not hurt you physically.

Today, every new PC comes with a virus protection program, but with a limited right of usage (trial period). It is strange that the industry handles this basic problem in this way. A virus protection program should be part of the operating system and fully configured when you buy your PC. Asking for extra money for this is like asking for additional money for safety belts in a new car. Forcing a user to analyze different products and make a final choice without being an expert in that matter is an unbelievable process. This is downright bad.

If you think your data is so extremely valuable that you don't want to take any risk, it could be an idea to have a second anti-virus program from a different vendor installed. In this case, you might also consider implementing encryption. A regular complete check of all your files on your PC is absolutely necessary because some viruses "sleep" and wait for a specific event (like a date) to be activated. Thereby, the virus avoids detection when it is loaded on the PC.

It should be rightfully expected that providers of this kind of security software have an increased sensibility for security questions. However, this is not always the case. I experienced a situation in which the update to a newer version produced an error message, and the solution proposed by the vendor's support was to uninstall the old program fully and then install the new version. Not at all an unusual situation— the only strange thing here was that there was no recommendation to close my Internet connection during the process. Obviously, once you start removing your protection program, you are no longer protected. You might be sensitive enough to think of this problem and close the connection before removing the program. It is, then, quite a surprise when the installation program moans and insists on having an open Internet connection during the installation process! You have to live with a situation where your PC is unprotected for a non-negligible period of time. This is profoundly dangerous and wantonly negligent. I can easily imagine a court would judge in favor of the PC user in the case that such an "upgrade" had caused damage by an intruder who used this window of time for his attack.

It is also important to know that the providers of such security software are always at least one step behind. Their process is to monitor threats that are spreading around and then develop an update when a new security hole arises. It is a defensive strategy. It would be extremely difficult to have a proactive approach in such a situation, and I guess having a defensive strategy is their only choice.

Firewall

What is a firewall? It is a program designed to block intruders, and it can be compared to a physical fire door in a building. In opposition to a virus protection program, where the attack is normally done via email, the firewall is designed to block direct attacks coming over the Internet. To see how many times you are attacked, you may configure your firewall to inform you when an attack is blocked. You will see this is often the case, and the situation is definitely more dangerous than leaving your wallet unattended in a public place.

Cyber crime is the fastest growing "business" in the world. In the first edition of this book in 2006, I wrote that, according to a study published by the *US Organisation Consumer Reports*, there was a total damage of eight billion dollars the two preceding years. Since then, the amount has multiplied many times. The estimates are that every third Internet user has already been a victim of an attack. I cite Eugene Kaspersky, head of an anti-virus software company of the same name: "The problem of Internet and virus risks will not be solved before long." His proof: "The security industry had a turnover of 15 billion dollars in 2007 and, at the same time, there was damage in the infrastructure of 13.3 billion. And this does not include the costs generated by stolen data." Now, at the beginning of 2009, the experts at the *World Economic Forum* in Davos have reported the unbelievable figure of one trillion dollars of damage caused by cyber crime. Cyber crime is definitely starting to seriously threaten the economy.

But the public is not as anxious as it should be and the laws are not sufficient. Furthermore, technology is not mature enough to prevent this.

What should a user do? Well, a firewall is a good start, an absolute, and a non-negotiable "must have." With the success of "flat rates," many users keep their Internet connection open at all times, which also means that potential intruders have endless time for their attacks.

Keep your firewall up-to-date. But even then, there is no 100% guarantee against successful attacks; consider that a firewall (as well as a virus protection program) is only a piece of software and can contain errors.

What makes me lose a bit of hope is the fact that there is no real need anymore to have profound technical know-how in order to hack a computer. You can find software pieces on the Internet and create your own attack scenarios. Cyber crime has become extremely professional.

The problem of Internet security must be of interest to everyone for purely egoistical reasons. It's still a wild world out there, and it looks like if the "bad guys" will continue to outrun the "good guys" for quite a while.

Software updates ("patching")

Using software updates, errors get corrected and security holes in operating systems get closed. For reasons of stability and security, it is enormously important to keep the operating system (Microsoft Windows, Linux, Mac OS X, etc.) on the latest level: your firewall might not work properly if your operating system is not up-to-date. Be prepared for technical jargon when a software update is carried out, and don't be surprised if you read something like: *"The webpage uses ActiveX elements in order to find out which version is installed on your computer. If an ActiveX warning is displayed, make sure that the element is digitally signed by Microsoft before you install it."* Good luck!

Since the beginning of 2007, software updates are also available for mobile phones, and it is not a bad idea to keep yours updated. However, the technical process is still very cumbersome, and we need to see much more progress here.

Browser protection

The most widely-used Internet browser is Microsoft's Internet Explorer. Functions like JavaScript, Java, and ActiveX allow it to execute programs embedded in the webpage on your PC. This is nice, but represents significant risks. Every browser can configure the security level you want. Click on Extras | Internet Options (with Internet-Explorer) and define the security level with which you feel comfortable. Obviously, the higher the better. This book is not about describing all possible configuration elements. Take some time to understand the available options. If necessary, search for related books or ask someone for help.

User accounts

You should protect your PC against access by other people near you. If you can't have one PC per person, you should make sure user accounts are defined for each user. If not, it will be possible for every user to see all data on the PC—something which you might not want. Define your own password-protected user account, avoid using "Administrator," and deactivate "Guest."

Don't leave your PC unattended for your kids, but buy them a computer of their own. Kids like to download all kinds of software and data from all kinds of uncertain sources. The Internet contains tsunamis of malicious programs and webpages; downloading new software without taking great care is not a good idea. Malicious software looks harmless at first glance and is not easy to recognize.

Phishing

Phishing is one of the very few security subjects which receive broad coverage in the media. Therefore, I don't want to go into details here—

only just to explain it: it is an (increasingly successful) attempt by criminals to gain access to extremely sensitive data, such as your passwords of your online banking. Their methods are extremely professional, and their faked webpages look like the real ones. Even emails sent to you look as if they came from a trustworthy source. In spite of media coverage, the dangers linked to phishing don't seem to be taken seriously by everybody. The security recommendations of your bank (or similar) should be followed by all means. What I consider as a very positive trend in recent times is the usage of colors in the browser to indicate whether the webpage you are viewing is safe or not. The advice can only be: if you see red, go away immediately. As a general rule, your sensitive data is never requested by email.

Downloads and games

I wrote already about this question in the paragraph "User Accounts." Great care needs to be taken when downloading software from a webpage. It is, however, not easy to make sure whether a source is trustworthy or not.

Social networks

I rigged my cellular to send a message to my PDA,
which is online with my PC, to get it to activate the voicemail,
which sends the message to the inbox of my email,
which routes it to the PDA, which beams it back to the cellular.
Then I realized my gadgets have a better social life than I do.

Tom Ostad

Social Networks (also called Web 2.0 or online communities) are the next big problem in terms of IT security. Even if I repeat myself: the possibilities offered to communicate with each other are so great and so accepted by millions of people that the security aspects are left aside. It is worrying that people like to tell the most private and intimate things in online communities—things they would never tell anyone face-to-face. There are plenty of studies which prove that social networks are like the "Wild West." The security requirements are in the area of data protection and are roughly the following:

- Personal information must be protected against unauthorized access.

- Personal data (like uploaded pictures) must be invisible to search engines if the user doesn't explicitly allow it.

- The user must be able to change his data (and delete it) and all copies, traces, and search engine entries of that data must be handled in the same way.

The consequences for a participant in such a community can be devastating, and many cases are documented: pictures of a party with drugs or excessive alcohol consumption can lead to a person losing his job if the HR department sees it. A radical political opinion, however changed with growing maturity, will still be visible in some search engine's cache, and it can have consequences for that person. He may never be invited again to an interview for a decent job. Social Networking systems slowly start to grow into the business areas, and *Gartner* considers that by 2010, more than 60% of the Fortune 1000 enterprises will use Social Networks for communication with their customers and providers. This will be very interesting times for criminals.

Mobile phones

Viruses for mobile phones are appearing now as well—not yet at the same severity level as PCs, but nevertheless. The usage of Bluetooth technology makes it easy for hackers to read the data you have stored on your mobile phone (like secret phone numbers, for instance). Make sure you have Bluetooth deactivated by default and check the security settings.

Stop of usage or sale

If you decommission your PC or if you sell it, you will want to make sure the data stored on the PC is not readable by someone else. Most people don't know that the data you have on your disk, USB memory stick, DVD, or mobile phone can still be read after you have erased it. Deleting a file usually only removes an entry in the system's table of contents—the data still remains there. Even after formatting a disk drive, there are specialized companies around that can rebuild the data.

If you have sensitive data, you could consider destroying it physically (hammering the drive or breaking the DVD). Your employer might offer to give your PC to a professional who specializes in disposing of computers correctly. It is frequent to read reports about data that got in the wrong hands due to this. On eBay, you can buy decommissioned harddisks, and it is a piece of cake to try to restore the data that was on it. The latest example I heard of was a harddisk containing credit card numbers, names, and addresses of more than one million bank customers, purchased for 45 Euros. The New York-based forensics agency *Kessler International* studied this question and found that 40% of all harddisks offered for sale on eBay contained readable data, such as financial information, emails, or pictures. There seems to be very little public awareness about the gravity of this problem.

Sometimes there is no need to destroy a computer, because there are enough staff members in an IT department who have IT as both a job and a hobby. Those guys happily take these old boxes home and build them up again in their cellar in order to experiment a bit. Computers need a lot of electricity, and well, it might happen that the power supply in the area where these people live collapses.

Credit cards

It has been said so many times in the media: be careful with your credit card number on the Internet. *Symantec* reported that a stolen credit card number is worth between 25 cents and 25 dollars each in the cyber crime space! Modern security protection software indicates today with a green or red color in the browser if the webpage you are visiting is safe or not.

Theft or repair

PCs need to be repaired sometimes, and laptops get stolen frequently. There is a good chance you will have to hand over your computer to someone else some day. So, you can never be sure who will read your data one day. In this respect, considering encryption software is a valid option.

Spam

The advent of electronic mail has provided people throughout the world
with an expedient and cost-effective means of communication.
Unfortunately, it has also created a whole new territory
for the high-tech version of the door-to-door salesman.

Pete Wilson

You might be surprised that "spam" is mentioned only at the end of this list, as this subject is probably the most popular of all security topics. But spam is, in fact, nothing more than annoying advertising material (if we make abstraction of phishing emails and emails containing viruses), except in incredible volumes. Those spam emails are annoying, but not direct threats.

Spam volumes are growing exorbitantly fast. Back in 2007, the messaging expert *Retarus* had calculated a growth of 165% compared to the previous year. According to the *Panda Security Spam-Report 2008*, 91% of all emails are spam. The only good news is that spam filters get better and better, and the number of spam mails which overcome the filter hurdle does not grow.

A study (*National Technology Readiness Survey, Center for Excellence in Services in Maryland*) found that 14% of users read spam, and 4% buy the advertised products. But as spam filters remove most of those emails, in the end, just one in 12,500,000 spam emails is opened by the recipient (Source: *Computer Scientists from the University of Berkeley*). While this sounds like almost nothing, it still generates millions of dollars in revenue, considering that billions of such emails are sent. You may see examples which are hard to believe, but which are, nevertheless, successful, such as "You are arrested by the FBI. Click on the link for details of where to present yourself." The only advice I can give is to delete spam emails right away without opening them and without clicking on any link.

Email addresses must only be given to people you trust and should not be inserted on doubtful webpages. If you have built your own webpage and you want to receive feedback from the page's visitors, you can hide your address. (How this can be achieved is described in every reasonable good book about web design).

You might have asked yourself why spam is sometimes not recognized as such, or why regular mails are declared as spam. The answer to that question is that spam-filtering cannot be an exact science, because these systems have to analyze the contents of the email and then decide what the mail is about. This is quite hard because spammers design their emails to resemble regular emails. Example: if you requested to receive advertising material by email about a product you intend to buy, the filter cannot know if this email is unwanted or not. Spammers know how the filters work and react accordingly. It's like the game between the tortoise and the hare.

In the business

Before going into detail, something quite important about missing automation in the area of IT security must be reported. IT systems automate to diverse levels almost all areas of our daily business life. But IT departments were the last ones to be automated—comparable to the shoemaker's son going barefoot. When it all started around thirty years ago, the first applications were accounting systems, followed by applications covering the "front", and all the way to today's systems with extreme levels of complexity, interconnections over different time zones, and 24-hour availability.

Very late, about ten years ago, efforts were undertaken to automate IT processes. This subject is well-advanced, and in various parts of this book, you can find indications about what is already available (software lifecycle management, monitoring of applications, and much more). But there is one area left where very little effort has been undertaken, and this is the area of IT security. Now, don't misunderstand me: there are, of course, masses of software for all possible things—such as firewalls, intrusion detection systems, and so on. There is software for selective questions, such as controlling whether users have changed their passwords or whether employees who have left the company have had their access rights removed. But that is as far as it goes.

There is no software package on the market that would manage the agglomerated collection of all security rules defined in security concepts. Such a package should be able to prevent the breaking of a rule before it happens. In 2009, IT security is much more an audit subject than a management subject. It looks like we are ten years behind in this area.

The management of IT security processes works roughly in the following way: a specific question comes up (a new threat, a new system is introduced, etc.), and specific rules related to it are defined. Basically, this means that the wheel is reinvented each time. Paper documents are created to document how IT security is implemented for the relevant question. As far as technology exists, it is used (for example, defining specific rules in the firewall), but the majority of rules defined is monitored manually and, quite likely, only at the next audit.

Such a way of working often has severe consequences. The case of *Société Générale*, where a trader created a loss of more than four billion Euros is an excellent example to illustrate this. In this case, that person had access to two different systems (the one for the trading activity, and the one for the controlling of trading limits). Due to this dual access, it was possible for him to hide his actions by manipulating the controlling system. Could this have been avoided *automatically*? Not really. It could, of course, have been detected by an auditor in a yearly review, but there are no overall access rights monitoring mechanisms available from which all applications would derive the access rights for each user. (Ok, some experts may say now that *Active Directory* functionality can do this, but we are talking here about functional software, where this is inexistent.) In an ideal world, the different possible access rights would have been defined in a "meta" IT security system, and one rule would have specified that you can only be a trader or a controller, but never both. The underlying system would then have refused to give access to this trader.

Also, the case of bank LGT in Liechtenstein can be traced back to the fact that there isn't any possible automation of security rules. In this case, an external person was charged with the scanning of highly sensitive documents, and this person was taking home backups of this data which he later sold for several million Euros to fiscal authorities in Germany.

It is indeed worrying that IT security is more about forensics and audits than about prevention. What increases my worries is that customers are not demanding security solutions, but seem to be quite happy with the current situation. Consequently, I cannot see that the main software providers in this field would work for solutions into that direction. As far as I can see, this subject remains at the level of university research. It will take us quite a long time to automate IT security rules. I dream about a world where I would define a rule like this: "Sensitive data must be encrypted and cannot be forwarded into other systems." The "meta" system would know what to do in order to supervise this rule and would raise an alarm (or close the applications to prevent the break) if there would be an attempt to break that rule.

Therefore, for the rest of this chapter, you will find a description of the current situation—which is far from being ideal.

Governance

The problems begin with trying to decide to whom the IT security experts in a company should report. If it is to the CIO, then there is a risk that the CIO is more interested in completing his projects successfully and will turn a blind eye to security questions, as security slows down projects and makes them more expensive. A situation where the cat is trusted to keep the cream. If the security experts report outside of IT, they are too far away from what happens in IT, and they are perceived by IT staff more like policemen or controllers, rather than people adding value. Here, we face a classical dilemma for which there is no universally-accepted solution.

Risk analysis

To avoid a confusion of terminology, when I write about "risk" in this chapter, I mean only the aspects that fall under the category of IT "security." You need to know that there is a further subject called "risk management" which I will not cover in this book. This is an area that handles questions like: "What is our business risk if our main software providers go bankrupt?" or "What penalties do we have to pay if our network goes down beyond the agreed period?" or "What are our risks if more than ten percent of our staff resigns within the next twelve months?" Several hundreds of these kinds of questions need to be answered.

Not so long ago, the term "risk analysis" was foreign in IT. In the '80s, there was one big computer (mainframe), no network, and no PCs. The mainframe communicated via so-called terminals which didn't have any storage or processors. The introduction of software was rather straightforward, and there were only minor risks. This has changed dramatically today. The idea that the installation of a new printer (or a new driver for that printer) can lead to a breakdown of the network is only a slightly-exaggerated one. Our IT world is characterized by instability and incompatibility. Standards declare themselves as such and vanish as quickly as they came.

By principle, a risk analysis would need to be done for everything new you do. At every new project, assessments of the security requirements must be done and, according to the result, a security concept must be established in which all elements of each risk category must be reckoned. And there are many of these categories. Each must be evaluated for their probability (How often does a computer center catch fire? How robust are our systems? How often do hackers attack?) and how much damage they can create (financial loss, reputation loss, etc.). Such an analysis is not easy, requires very special know-how, and is therefore very often carried out by external companies. Each identified risk must be deemed "acceptable," or it must be addressed by special measures. At the end, a global evaluation is done, and the final decision makers must decide how much risk they want to accept (*risk appetite*). In any case, it can be said that there is no IT project or IT initiative without risks.

It is very often a question of budgets that determines to what extent specific risks will be managed.

But it can happen that there is no ideal solution for some questions. *Single-Sign-On* (a user has the same password for all applications and only needs to sign-on once) is such a topic that causes quite a stir. Every employee needs to remember a large amount of passwords, and, as this is not really possible, people write them down. It is, therefore, sometimes enough to look under the keyboard to find little notes with all the passwords. It didn't surprise me when, two years ago, I came across a situation where a lady at the Senior Management level had stuck a post-it with all passwords for remote access close to her laptop's keyboard. If it is decided to introduce *Single-Sign-On*, those little post-its will disappear, but consequently, it will be enough to look over the user's shoulder when he signs-on in order to get his password and, thus, access to all applications.

Every company that has sensitive data has one or more security officers. Their task includes monitoring permanently what happens in the cyber crime scene in order to identify new threats. It is possible to do so by subscribing to specialized services.

When a security incident (stolen data, hacker attack, etc.) has occurred, you can find plenty of forensic experts to carry out criminal investigations. There is so much invisible data in networks and applications (log files, audit traces, etc.) that can be used to retrace what has happened—not in all cases, but quite often. Even Microsoft's Word is a rich source of traces that are invisible to laymen.

Nobody needs to invent security standards. There are the ISO2700x (previously ISO17799) standards, from which individual security rules can be derived. These standards are described in quite bulky documents, but it is again possible to charge external experts to translate them into something more usable for internal purposes.

Where there is money, there is crime. Where there is crime, there is a need for security—IT security for that matter. IT security always puts the brakes on an IT project, and it always increases the costs of a project. IT security always reduces the user's comfort. It is not easy to find the right balance between security and service.

Let's look now at the various categories of IT security in a company:

Physical security

This is the classical area which has existed since the beginning of IT. You can protect yourself against water in a computer center by adding a drain. Against fire, you can use argon; in older times, halon was used (forbidden now, as it withdraws oxygen in the room and leads to death). Powerful air conditioners protect against the heat. A computer center is a high-security area with very restricted access; access protocols are regularly checked.

Network protection

Computer systems are attacked via their connections to the external world. Usually, there are plenty of these external connections (customers, providers, Internet, Disaster Recovery Center, etc.), and they require intensified attention. The network (and its external connections) is protected by firewalls. We have seen already what a firewall is; the principle in a company is not fundamentally different from the private usage. The only difference might be that companies protect themselves with several firewalls put in series behind each other. Should you break the first one, a new challenge awaits you with the following one.

Additionally, there are various encryption technologies which are, today, all quite easy to implement, and they guarantee that the data transfer with the external world cannot be accessed by an unauthorized person. Before we had the Internet, these connections were mostly point-to-point connections, and it was necessary to hack the physical line to get access to the data. Because this was quite difficult to achieve, the risk of being hacked was lower than today.

Because of the Internet, for the first time in history, we have private persons and companies operating in the same network, and this network is not under the control of the companies using it. This creates an intolerable situation for point-to-point communications (with a customer, for instance). But humans are ingenious, and we invented so-called tunnels (VPN); this means the Internet infrastructure is used, but it is hidden from other users in the Internet.

The area of network protection is a very dynamic one and requires highly-skilled experts.

Network monitoring

It is not enough to take the previously-described measures—it must also be made sure that security is monitored at all times and that all protection mechanisms operate as planned. One element which allows this is the usage of highly-complex *Intrusion Detection* software. It must raise an alarm if an intruder has succeeded in accessing the internal network.

When such an alarm happens, an emergency response team is called (on a 24-hour basis), and usually, all outside connections are cut immediately. The intruder is thrown out, and the problem is temporarily solved. The emergency response team must then analyze the situation and find means to avoid a continued attack as soon as the network is restarted.

Hackers in Hollywood movies are phenomenal.
All they need to do is "C:\hack into fbi"

(Unknown author)

This team can also play a more active role as it can build traps: the game can be reversed! A dedicated computer with a low level of security is added to the network, and to an external intruder, it will look as if it contains very interesting data to steal (*honey pot*). When the honey pot is successful, it is possible to trace the source of the attack. This makes legal action a possibility. In 2008, students from the German University in Mannheim created a honey pot to find out where hackers were hiding. They found masses of illegally-procured data, and they found that the hackers had highly-specialized tools for extracting the data they were looking for. It could be expected that these hackers are sensitive enough to protect their own data against unwanted access. But surprisingly, they don't seem to have an increased sensitivity for this: their data was almost not protected at all and could be counter-hacked relatively easily.

On a regular basis, specialized companies are asked to hack the security infrastructure on purpose (*penetration test*). The mission is to find out if the security mechanisms are still strong enough and to find any potential weaknesses.

Health checks are also an important element here. Once in a while, they are carried out to detect unusual activities. Special tools exist for this.

External network connection

Despite all security aspects, the network must be able to distinguish between authorized and non-authorized access. A user-id and password are not strong enough elements to do so: user-ids and passwords are easy to steal. There are specialized systems to add protection, and if you have electronic banking accounts, you will have seen some of them. Just to mention one as an illustration of what is required to implement this: there are small devices, called "tokens," on which a new number is displayed at regular intervals (like one minute). You are only allowed to login if the number on the token is identical to the one that you type in on the login screen. Maybe you asked yourself how the computer at the other end can know what the number on the token is? To make this work with absolute precision, it is necessary that the program at the back calculates the number in exactly the same manner as the token does; an absolutely reliable time stamp on both sides is required. If there's only a slight deviation in the calculation, the login will not work, and angry customers will flood the Help Desk. These systems cost a lot of money.

A network can become open by further unwanted security holes, namely when a foreign device connects to the physical network directly in the building where the network is. This is what happens when an employee brings his private laptop to work or a salesperson wants to do a demo. Potentially, every cleaning lady could do this with her laptop when she's alone overnight. If you have a network cable and a free network connector in an office, you are in the company's network. Quite a substantial risk that can be managed by dedicated software.

Theft of storage and processor power

Big companies and research centers have large computer centers with enormous storage space and processor power. This attracts criminals. There are plenty of criminal cases (like the offering of pedophilic material), where storage space is "stolen" for the purpose of illegal activity. Regular scans of the storage space should be done.

It also happens that processor power is "stolen" by criminals in order to save the expensive costs of an own computer infrastructure or to hide their identity. Over the Internet, they try to get access to an unsecured computer (there are plenty in the world) and let their programs run there. Spammers are very fond of this method and mail their dirt by the billions over foreign infrastructures. But this problem is not limited to large computer centers—it also happens with private PCs. If your PC is not sufficiently protected, it could very well be that it is a so-called *zombie* used for sending spam or virus-infected emails. These processes run in the background, and you don't even notice it. The number of *zombie* PCs worldwide is estimated to be several millions.

Malicious Code / Malware

Malicious code (or malware) is any piece of software doing harm to your computer or your data. A virus is malicious code. But there are also possible backdoors in software that would allow those who know about this backdoor to get access to all data by bypassing all usual access control mechanisms. When software is purchased, it is quite impossible to check this, because who could possibly say if a specific network controlling program wouldn't have a backdoor for the secret service?

Software received from a vendor can contain all possible functionality, and as the source code is not delivered, you can never have assurance about what you introduce into your IT biotope.

A famous example of malware became public in January 2009. A systems engineer with high access privileges was working for *Fannie Mae* through a service company. Between the time he was fired and his passwords were removed, he had enough time to connect remotely and install a program that, on Jan. 31, 2009, would have destroyed all data on 4,000 computers and led to a standstill for at least a week. It was detected by pure coincidence; it is not possible to detect malware automatically. There are no figures about how often companies get affected by this kind of problem.

Phishing

We handled this subject already, but from a business point of view, there's an additional aspect. If your company is doing business over the Internet, it needs to know constantly that its webpage hasn't become a victim of a phishing attack. Staff must be allocated to monitor the Internet for the detection of such activities. When it happens, a counter-attack can possibly be launched (there are anti-phishing companies which try to tie up the faked webpage) or legal action can be taken.

Software updates ("patching")

As already described for private users, software updates must be carried out in a firm as well in order to close security holes. The complexity is, however, substantially bigger as patching applies not only to the operating system, but to all possible systems. Due to the general instability of IT biotopes, it would be recommended to fully test each and every patch for compatibility with all other elements in the biotope. But as these patches are very often very urgent, and because of the overwhelming effort this represents, testing is rarely done. And to be honest, most patches work without too many problems. I wrote "most," not "all"!

"Always apply the latest updates" and
"If it ain't broken, don't fix it"
are the two rules of system updating.

(Unknown author)

There's a conflict between the employees in charge of security questions (who want to install patches immediately) and the system administrators (who fear the risk of instability). Discussions about how to handle this conflict is daily business.

Disaster recovery

This subject has been described in the chapter 11: *Damage in the millions.*

PC-Security

As PCs in a company don't work as standalones, but are connected to a network, it must be made sure they don't represent a contact surface for attacks to the company's security. This is not immediately realized, and it is an area which is directly visible to the users and where they experience a loss of comfort. CD/DVD-readers and USB connectors get disabled, software installation is inhibited, and much more. We call this area *"endpoint security."* The number of parameters that need to be decided and configured is large. It is not necessary to reinvent the wheel for this question, as the best practice guidelines can easily be found on the Internet.

To add one advice here: never store any data on the C: drive in office. The temptation to do so is surely high, as you do it on your private PC. But, should your PC in the office be replaced, your data will be lost forever, as it never gets backed up.

Encryption risk

To encrypt network traffic is very easy these days and does not represent a risk. Just as easy, but much more risky, is the encryption of data stored in databases. If the key is lost, then all data is lost! It becomes, therefore, necessary to have arrangements (like a master key stored in a central place) to avoid this risk.

Risk mobile devices

Mobile devices are laptops, mobile phones, organizers, digital cameras, MP3 players, memory sticks, and so on. The best security implementations are worthless if a user needs less than three seconds to photograph a screen with sensitive data by using the camera on his mobile phone. Recording a conversation without being noticed and transmitting it to the outside world in real-time is just as simple. Or using a service like *twitter* to secretly inform the whole world about what is presented in a secret meeting is no longer a fantasy. The technical progress has already bypassed the fantasy of James Bond movies. There is no protection against these scenarios.

A problem that needs to be addressed is stolen or lost mobile devices. Should there be sensitive data on them, the company has a serious problem A few figures: in the UK, dry cleaners find about 9,000 USB memory sticks annually in clothes. Every six months, taxi drivers in London find 6,200 laptops. (Source: *Conny Zuseh*)

We use encryption software here to make sure an unauthorized person cannot read the data. It is evident that laptops need to be kept at the same security level as PCs (anti-virus software, firewall, Windows updates, etc.). As laptops tramp outside the company, it is necessary to have specific technology and a dedicated process in place to manage this.

Protect documents with passwords?

As you know, any Word or Excel document can be password-protected. Quite a nice thing for private usage (as long as you don't forget your password!). But in a professional environment, this is not recommended. Every document created is owned by the company, not by the user who created it. If an employee leaves the firm without communicating the passwords for his documents, there can be serious problems for the daily operations of the company. This password protection feature should only be used if the password is known by the Line Manager or if a copy of the password is deposited in a safe.

It is not widely known that document passwords can be hacked under some circumstances. With every new Office release, however, this gets more complicated. Should your password be a dictionary word, hacking is relatively straightforward. Constructs like "r5Tg20" make the task much more difficult. The longer and more complex a password is, the smaller the chance it will be hacked. On the Internet, you can find specialized providers who will try, for only a few dollars, to hack the password with specialized programs. When they are successful, you will get access to your document again, but beware: they have been able to read the document's contents as well.

If you have forgotten your password, don't expect the IT department to be able to help you. Conclusion: use this possibility only with the support of your Line Manager.

Another aspect of password usage on the Internet should be considered. If you use services for your employer on the Internet, please give your login information to your Line Manager or store it in any other place foreseen for this purpose. If you leave the company one day, your employer can be assured that you will not be able to continue using this service without their knowledge. Such a situation could represent another substantial risk for the company.

Insider attacks

Some security experts like to pretend that the biggest IT risks come from internal staff. There would be many more incidents from internal employees than from external attacks. It could well be that this is correct. Occasionally, examples become public, and there is sufficient material to be found to substantiate this statement. I want to refer to a study done in 2008 by *Cyber Ark*. They found that 90% of IT administrators take home sensitive information as insurance in case they get fired. Very popular are critical passwords that would allow them to connect to the network even after they have left the company. Other sensitive data, like customer accounts or a list of salaries, is also copied frequently. Tom Wolfe's "Masters of the Universe" can no longer be found on Wall Street, but they are now the administrators of critical software applications. The only difference is that the IT version is much more discreet. Almost no CEO knows that his IT administrators have access to all critical company data with nearly no control. They take it very badly when they are laid off, and 90% react to this by taking home sensitive data. A study of the *US Secret Service* and *the CERT-team at Carnegie-Mellon-University* found out that 86% of all internal attacks are done by technical staff and 90% of attackers had administrator rights. These insiders don't necessarily have to do attacks themselves; they can sell this information to professional hackers. This kind of risk will immensely increase in these times of global recession.

Passwords in IT

There is an administrator for each system, and he has total control over it. He should either be obliged to have a copy of his administrator passwords deposited somewhere in the firm or it must be made sure that there is an alternative administration account defined for cases when he is absent. There is specific software on the market for managing this aspect of the job.

Backups validation

> *He who laughs last probably made a backup.*
> *He who laughs loudest probably hasn't checked his backups in a while.*

> (Unknown author)

At least once a year, it should be proven that data can be restored from the backup media. Usually, backups are done, but they are never used—except in case of severe problems. To make sure the restore will work, it is a good idea to test this.

It's some time ago now, but I came through a situation where a software error in an accounting program had deleted all loan records in the system. Quite worrying, but not yet a crisis. We took the backup tapes and tried to restore them, but the restore command ended in error. We escalated the issue with the hardware supplier, and there we learned that these tapes can be written in maximum density, but cannot be read! It didn't really help to hear apologies from the supplier for not having communicated this problem to the clients. Well, a few days after the incident, we received a letter sent to all customers explaining the issue. For us, it was too late: our backups were useless. All loans had to be put into the system again manually. It was the toughest crisis situation I have ever dealt with. As the whole action took several days, we had massive customer complaints, the loan administration department could not work properly, and the financial accounting books were all wrong. Since then, I am a big fan of backup validation—not only in the professional environment, but also at home.

More recently, I heard of an example at another company. For some technical reason, the system used for customer identification had to be rebuilt. The operation failed because of human error, and as a consequence, the database was empty. Such things happen frequently in IT departments everywhere around the world, and it is enough to take the last valid backup in order to restore the data. Users in business departments are almost never informed about those details. But in this case, the last available backup was four months old! The database administrator hadn't realized that the system had stopped sending confirmation messages about successfully executed backups. This situation triggered a massive crisis situation, and a company that specializes in forensics was enlisted to try to recover the data. At the start, nobody knew whether they would be successful or not. They finally succeeded after one week of intense efforts, and at the end, sent an invoice of about 100,000 dollars. The responsible database administrator had a very rough time following this event.

Social engineering

There's an alternative for external attackers to get access to sensitive data, and we observe a rise in using human weaknesses. This can happen through a person calling and pretending to do research for a poll institute. The questions are then: "What firewalls do you use?" or "Do you have an Intrusion Detection System?" and other questions of that kind. Quite strangely, when I tell the caller to send in his questions by email—which would give me the possibility to check if this is fake— I almost never get an email. The same approach happens with normal users, where someone phones them and asks for their passwords or wants to have some sensitive business information. This way of trying to get sensitive information is called *Social Engineering*. Staff needs to be sensitized not to participate in such requests. However, that's easier said than done. Human nature is very often helpful, and if the caller has a good story to tell, all doubts will vanish quickly.

A variant (called *Spear Phishing*) consists in sending emails to users which look exactly like those sent by the internal IT Help-Desk. The sender may have an email address like *servicedesk@myconpany.com*, and the user is accustomed to an address like *servicedesk@mycompany.com*, so he believes that this is an internal email and answers all questions about passwords, confidential data, or whatever question he gets. If you haven't understood, take a closer look at both email addresses.

The dangers of *Social Engineering* can be found in an unexpected area, namely in public transport. In a company I worked before, it was practice for almost all staff to come to the office by using the same tram. From 8-9 a.m. and 5-7 p.m., everybody else in the tram could hear staff discussing sensitive topics, such as the business strategy of the next twelve months.

Anonymous test data

A quite classical trap is the setup of a test system. The best security mechanisms are frequently bypassed due to this—and test systems are setup all the time! This can happen unintentionally, but also on purpose. In order to be able to execute tests in good quality and to make sure there won't be future performance problems, it is necessary to have test data which is as close as possible to real data, and only live data is as close as possible to real data! To note as well that in the case when software development is outsourced, there is the legitimate request from the insourcers to have access to meaningful test data. The easy way of doing this is to give them remote access to test data; this creates a gigantic security loophole.

When a test system is setup, a copy of the production environment is made, and it is copied to a test environment. Another risk linked to that is the usage of the copying media (like a DVD, for example) for transferring the data between the two environments. When the copying is finished, there is a straying media.

The security level in a test system is always significantly lower than in a production environment; it just doesn't matter as much—it's only test data. When organizing tests, it is quite usual that all involved persons get all possible access rights. Therefore, at every setup of a test system, extra care should be taken that sensitive data is removed. If this is forgotten (unintentionally or not), it becomes possible that highly sensitive data (like VIP accounts) become visible to unauthorized staff.

Many times, we have also seen a system administrator getting confused about test and live environments. This is quite a disaster in the case of Internet applications. With a simple, erroneous copy/paste, highly sensitive data will be visible to the whole world. The malediction of copy/paste delivers enough material for filling books.

Sometimes, using real data is the only way to test a new program. If you have written a new program that is checking your customer base against a database containing the names of all known crooks in the world, well, you can't really create significant test data. In this case, the new program will have to run on the live data to find out whether it produces meaningful data.

To avoid the problems around test data, specific procedures and guidelines must exist. It is necessary to have a company's compliance officer involved in this. A study from *Freeform Dynamics* in 2008 showed, however, that more than 70% of all companies use live data as test data, and that 40% of the compliance officers couldn't answer the question how their company's IT department handled this question.

Access rights

Access rights for users must be documented precisely and be controlled regularly. Especially for administrators with maximum rights, a permanent control must be implemented. But treacherous pitfalls lurk here. It is of no use to have correct access rights in one system if that precise system is also sending data to another system (for archiving purposes, for example) and if the access rights are not absolutely identical in both. Staff members with a "researcher" mentality will find this out very quickly, and the initial setup of access rights in the first system becomes maculation.

Data and documents must be classified in categories such as "public," "confidential," or "secret." All relevant documents must then be labeled accordingly, and access rights must follow.

Data loss or theft

On the day of President Obama's inauguration, the payments settlement company *Heartland* announced that data concerning 100 million credit cards was stolen—the financial damage could reach 500 million dollars. In February 2008, the White House reported a loss of several million emails due to a migration of the email system. In the UK at the end of 2008, a USB memory stick with the data of more than 84,000 prisoners was lost. In autumn 2008, the German *Telekom* announced that the mobile phone numbers of their 30 million customers were directly accessible over Internet; the passwords to access this data were known by hackers. Vanished laptops containing names of customers and their credit card numbers are quite frequent events. The number of cases of call centers selling customer data illegally is rising quickly. The occurrences of data loss or theft get more and more frequent from year to year.

In the US, it is the law to report about data loss or theft, but in Europe, this is not the case. It is believed that, in total, only 5 to 10% of all cases get public. And when a case is reported, the details remain rather unclear.

For many companies, the data is its most important asset—for banks, always. In fact, the word "stolen" is totally misleading. You cannot "steal" data—you only copy it illegally. The consequences for the owners are devastating.

To some extent, one can manage this risk, but one can never fully cover it even when comprehensive security concepts have been established and appropriate measures have been taken. There are plenty of specialized firms offering services in this area, and it is a fast growing market. This problem is closely linked to the insider attacks we have seen above and are often addressed together. Without going into details, I can list some of the questions that need to be answered: "Who is allowed to view, copy, or print this data, and how can I make sure that this is technically enforced?" "Is the transport of data between the main computer and the PC encrypted?" "Can the copy/paste function be disabled, and can a download to Excel be inhibited?" "Are there weaknesses in the program which open a backdoor to the data?" and "Is there a log-file showing all access to the data?" It seems to reflect human nature to simplify arguments with rising complexity. It sounds funny, but I've come across it: a compliance officer with limited IT understanding might face you with the request to put the computer into a dedicated and locked cage so the data cannot be stolen.

Operating error

There's a further source for data leakage which is so extraordinarily trivial and, at the same time, so totally impossible to avoid. I would bet that everyone of us has already come across the situation described below. We are all very much pleased with the functionality offered by email systems to propose names from the contact list (including all names to whom you have ever once sent an email in the past) when you start typing the recipient's name in the "To" field. Suppose that your CEO's name is "Smith, John" and the CEO of your company's worst competitor is "Smith, Mike." You start typing in "Sm," and the program offers you the two "Smith" addresses to choose from. It is so easy to select the wrong one from the list and to send your highly sensitive business strategy paper to your competitor instead of your boss.

Security awareness

Most aspects of IT security are unknown to the employees in a firm. It is of major importance to inform them on a regular basis and to sensitize them. Non-respect of security rules can lead to disciplinary measures.

The subject of IT security is, without a doubt, one of the most fascinating of all IT subjects. It operates in the background, and only when there is a security problem does it get into the limelight.

As you know from reading this chapter, despite all security measures, the general level of security in the computer industry is too low. And we discover new security loopholes constantly. The higher the security measures are, the higher the sportsmanship for some people to find a way to circumvent them. I heard of a case (okay, it is not a very fresh example, as it is twenty years old, but it illustrates what I want to say) in the processing of salary printouts. This process was considered as being very sensitive and had special security mechanisms implemented. The Head of Human Resources went in person with his magnetic tape to the computer center, chased away the IT staff, and started the printing program on the big mainframe computer. He then planted himself right in front of the printer to avoid the possibility that anyone would see the salary slips. He even handled paper jams. When finished, he took his tape and all the printouts and went away. This irritated the IT staff in the computer center—they saw themselves as "Masters of the IT

Universe," and in this case, they were out? They brooded over finding a way to get access to this data. And, of course, they found the security loophole. At that time, printers were comparable to typewriters because they had a typewriter ribbon. At the next occasion, these smart guys put in a new ribbon and removed it immediately after the printout was done. You can imagine what this meant: by simply rewinding the ribbon and holding it against a light source, they were able to read everything the printer had generated. They now knew the salaries of all employees in the company! Too bad one of them couldn't keep his mouth shut. One guy was so angry about his alleged low salary in comparison to his colleagues that he publicly complained about it. The security loophole was then closed, and the next time, the Head of HR took the ribbon away with him.

Conclusion

The difficulty in IT security is that new technology gets launched on the market relentlessly. And every time, the new functionality is the focus, and security limps behind. As a consequence, any company operating with high security requirements must renounce new technology and wait until it becomes mature. This is definitely true in banking, where new technology is always only introduced prudently. This means, then, that many business requests to IT cannot be done as quickly as the business expects. Due to this, disappointing the users becomes one of the tasks of an IT security officer.

The other problem is the impossibility of automatically monitoring security rules and managing the situation before the problems occur. IT security is much more about forensics and audits than about management.

We will see an explosion of security issues in the months and years to come. While this is dramatic for the victims, it is—on the other hand—necessary to have major problems in order to terminate the step-motherly treatment of IT security questions by the computer industry.

For the immediate future, I see no light at the end of the tunnel, and my outlook is pessimistic.

The most deplorable jobs in an IT department are those of the IT security officers; they have all my sympathy.

Real managers have a solution for every problem;
real lawyers have a problem for every solution.

Jean Paul

Worst Case

About legal aspects and the cooperation between IT and its supervisors

As with the introduction of new technology or new products, where functionality is the driver and security is only addressed much later, we observe the same phenomena when it comes to the question of the legal framework.

Indeed, it takes a lot of time for the legislator to realize that there is new technology that requires a legal framework. We see this clearly with the Internet (as we have seen in the previous chapter) with its fast-growing number of new applications and services made available to the entire world. In addition, there is the difficulty of making laws in one specific country for a technology that doesn't know country borders.

Email is an excellent example: even though email has existed for many years now, it is still not clear in most countries around the world what the legal obligations of a company are in that matter. It is still unclear whether emails need to be archived or if employees are allowed to delete archived mails. Do emails have the same enforcement power than contracts, or are only signed documents legally binding? Additional difficulty is added by the fact that emails may be falsified quite easily by any Internet Service Provider the email passes through. Emails do get lost sometimes in the data Orcus; they may have been sent to the wrong recipient, and they can't include signatures like contracts. Most countries don't regulate whether an employee has the right to send private emails over a company's infrastructure; if yes, will the employer be allowed to read it? This kind of question even stumped the security experts at the White House when the new President announced that he wanted to continue using his Blackberry. There's a law specifying that all written communication by the President must be recorded, but when this law was enacted, Mr. Nixon was President, and something like the Blackberry was decades away.

It has always been a constant in IT to have this lagging-behind of the legal framework. Bit by bit, the necessary laws and regulations are decided by legislators, and every company is obliged to implement them into working solutions and processes. This means that, almost constantly, every IT department has some projects running which are mandatory and encounter the same types of problems described in previous chapters. The only difference here is that those projects are not allowed to fail.

On top of that, like any other department, it is necessary for an IT department to comply with the internal control and supervision mechanisms in the company. This human interface to lawyers, compliance officers, and auditors is never free of problems; it crunches sometimes, and has some particularities of its own.

IT staff is paid to find solutions to a given problem and implement change; their outlook is always future-oriented. Over time, the pressure exercised by the business to implement decisions even faster has never stopped growing.

Auditors, compliance officers, and lawyers have different tasks. They'll have to excuse me for putting these varying responsibilities into one basket, but looking at it from an IT point of view, they act like brakes on a car, bringing additional elements which can lengthen projects.

Lawyers also look ahead, but with a different mindset. They focus on the worst case scenario. They must do everything they can to make sure nothing happens that makes the company look bad in front of a judge.

Auditors and compliance officers have the obligation to find the difference between "what is" and "what should be." Their view is rather backwards-looking because they need to find out what went wrong in the past. The way these colleagues think is definitely foreign to IT experts (and vice versa), and therefore, the cooperation is sometimes difficult and occasionally catastrophic.

I learned years ago that they feel much more at home in texts, even when they're boring and bulky. Graphical figures (showing IT solutions) are something they often can't read, to the point that they hate them and don't make the extra effort to understand them. Interpersonal trouble easily arises from this incompatibility, and it requires intensive work at the psychological front. Both sides need to do earnest effort to understand the other side and should be prepared to cut back—at a minimum.

Personally, I was mostly lucky to have a good relationship with these people, and my problems with them were few and far between. But I was surely much luckier than many of my colleagues.

At this point, I want to take the opportunity to show sympathy for this professional category. The job they have to do—when it comes to IT matters—is anything but simple. We have seen today's IT complexity and the problems we face. Even the CIO cannot know everything that happens in his area. Alone, the technical questions are so complex that many things need to be managed on an exclusive basis of mutual trust. And how should an outsider bring light into the jungle when he has only a very small time period to do so? His only chance is to focus on some points, even if this will not expose any major problems. Documents swarming with *https, VPN-tunnels, strong authentication, certificates,* or *demilitarized zones* are tough to digest. But, at the end of the day, an auditor, a lawyer, or a compliance officer has no choice and must dig into the material; they can ask help from external experts, or they must remain silent. If IT says: "The data is encrypted," the lawyer must not answer: "Great!" Instead, he must ask the question: "Who possesses the decryption key?" and "Is there a master-key?"

> *Programming can be fun, so can cryptography;*
> *however they should not be combined.*

> Kreitzberg and Shneiderman

No doubt, it is easier for an IT expert to understand laws and regulations than it is for lawyers to understand IT technology.

Technical documents are often only understood by their author. His colleague next door will already find it difficult to follow the thoughts in that document. This is the real challenge for auditors, lawyers, and compliance officers.

With this in mind, it's understandable that the same focal points are always audited. Every CIO notices this after some time and adapts to it. With everything that can go wrong in IT (and that's really a lot, as you know now after having read so far), it is not realistic to expect having an empty audit report. And even if the perfect world existed, we should not be fools: auditors have objectives set by their bosses, and they are obliged to criticize a minimum number of issues in their audit reports.

Knowing this, it is easily possible to elegantly throw out some appetizers in order to get some issues included in the final report. On that basis, it then becomes easy later on to have budgets approved for that subject.

It's not enough that audit companies are outsiders; the people sent are also often newcomers. Those guys surely have a very good education, but they are totally lacking in practical experience. In the worst case I experienced so far, I had an auditor who had finished his degree just three months before! Situations like these are anything but sane and aren't helpful to anybody. In the same way, as I wrote about project managers many pages ago, it should be made sure that only experienced people are allocated to this task. When we look at all the scandals related to audit companies in the last few years, where it was proved that, in fact, there hadn't been any real audit, my statement doesn't seem to be true only for IT, but for all areas. Without experienced staff, any audit is just an alibi performance.

IT contracts get increasingly complex and should be taken care of by experts. Therefore, by principle, they must be legally checked. It is surely anything but trivial to understand the technical and functional details included in these contracts. Even if a lawyer understands what a "7*24*2" service condition is (7 days by 24 hours with 2 hours of maximum response time), he cannot make a judgment if this is an acceptable risk or not. With the wide-spread outsourcing and the increase of legal complexity, business risks have also further increased. Lawyers must be integrated in the elaboration process of such contracts right from the start; the complexity exceeds the legal know-how of any IT expert.

Quite a special set of problems has to be faced in the Internet, where the provider of a webpage cannot know in what country its website visitors are located. Some things are allowed in one country and forbidden in others. A web designer, with the support of legal advice, needs to consider this fact. This is the reason why you are asked so many times on webpages in which country you reside. Lawyers not only need to know their country's laws, but must also stay up-to-date with international law.

There has been a flood of new regulations for computer systems, and their monitoring is an ever-increasing challenge. Audit-safe software development, documentation standards, Sarbanes-Oxley, archiving requirements, traceability, and much more are an increasingly-constrictive corset. Until the financial crisis started at the end of 2008, I thought we had too much regulation—now, I realize we didn't have enough, and on top of that, we had regulation in the wrong places. At the origin of the crash—in Investment Banking—there wasn't any regulation at all. Considering the (existing and upcoming) regulations in the banking business, which have a direct influence on IT, it's a foregone conclusion that the execution of projects will continue to become more and more complex. We expect a massive increase in new regulations to make sure that such a crisis will not be repeated.

But interestingly, software companies are by no means controlled as intensively as the average IT department. There is no mandatory external control at all for a new piece of software. A person can put out on the market whatever he develops—just like that. Considering the damage that can be created by software, this is surprising. Yet another sign of the immaturity of the industry. This will remain unchanged for a long time. Is there any other industry allowed to launch products without independent control authorities?

Legal obligations can be pretty tricky to follow. Let's take the archiving requirements as an example. Specialized systems are used for archiving documents, such as statements of accounts, and it must be made sure that there is no possibility to erase a document once it is archived. To be sure there isn't any backdoor to this request is almost impossible. But the essence of the problem lies in the fact that nobody can guarantee that the system will survive the legal minimum archiving period (ten years or more). Should the provider go bankrupt, or should he give up the product, the legal obligation to archive the documents is imminently in danger. It does not help to "freeze" the system (no more new data) and start implementing a new one. It will only be a question of time until the old system will no longer be compliant with a new Windows version; or the day will come when it will be impossible to get repairs for broken hardware pieces. The migration from an old archiving system to a new one is a Herculean task. The task of converting millions of documents can keep a complete team busy for weeks, if not months.

Another problem in this respect is the impossibility of fixing an error, because you are not allowed to delete an already-archived document. If there are many erroneous documents (a faulty program, for example), the situation is such that the archive will always be wrong, and the legal obligations will have been broken.

A quite similar set of problems exists with old data backups. It is a legal obligation in some countries to keep data backups for ten years. Should there be a customer complaint, the data would still be there, and investigations could be undertaken. France goes one step further: they require not only the data to be kept, but also the whole technical environment (programs, operating system, and databases). It is always difficult to explain to a user that we still have the backups from 2000, but they are useless. Due to technical progress, there isn't any hard- or software anymore that would be able to read that old data. The French requirement was intended to fix that problem, but they forgot to think about the hardware aspect of things. A floppy-disk (a predecessor of the diskette), that was created on a Commodore-64 back in 1982 cannot be read by your PC, as there is no floppy-disk reader available anymore. This kind of problem is something every company experiences once in a while. Even the renowned NASA made public in 2008 that they were unable to read data that was stored on tapes some 40 years ago in order to analyze moon dust; the necessary devices for reading those tapes were, of course, no longer operational and could only be found in museums. At the end, they found one in a museum in Australia that they hope to have it operational again within a few months. If they are unsuccessful, all data on those tapes will be lost forever.

Hardware: a product that if you play with it long enough, breaks.
Software: a product that if you play with it long enough, works.

(Unknown author)

Christmas

There's one more reason why computers crash. Computers have mechanical parts (like the reading arm in a harddisk), and when running 24/7, the mechanics run in. When they are switched off after a long period of usage, this becomes an unexpected disturbance with unforeseeable results. This problem has been around since the beginning of computers and is still not fixed today. With your PC at home, this is less dramatic because it is switched on and off all the time, and the mechanics don't run in.

Louis, one of my past experts and a luminary in his area of responsibility, did not know about this, quite strangely. It was on Dec. 24, sometime in the middle of the '90s. As usual on that day, all staff left around noon to start the Christmas holiday. Louis decided to be nice to his computer and offer it a quiet holiday season as well. Mistakenly, *but Thank you, God!*, he carried out the system command in such a way that the computer had to restart after being powered down. He noticed his mistake immediately and decided to wait until the computer rebooted. But all of a sudden, all the control buttons turned red. It was no longer possible to restart the system: both storage units were broken! The system was designed in a way that one broken unit would not have been a problem, but in this case, both said "goodbye" forever at the same time.

Pandemonium broke out. When he called the Help-Desk of the hardware company, he was told that there was only a minimum service available during the holidays. Christmas is the only time of the year which is always a bit quieter, and out of respect for this very important celebration, there's usually no project-related activity. The hardware company tried to find a technician who would sacrifice his Christmas Eve to spend it in the basement of the bank. Well, there are always lonely bachelors in IT, and by late afternoon, a guy was on site.

He tried to order replacement material through his usual supply channels. But there, it was holiday season as well. Shortly before midnight, he got the answer that a taxi would come down from Brussels with replacement material the next day at six o'clock.

Louis drove home in order to sleep for five hours. The lights on the Christmas tree had been extinguished, and his family had gone to bed.

The next morning, Dec. 25, the taxi arrived late at around 10 o'clock. The installation took until late afternoon. By late evening, the storage devices were up and running again, but before the data could be reloaded, it was necessary to first load the operating system (like Windows on your PC) and the programs (like Excel and Word). This again lasted until midnight. Louis went home for a few hours of sleep. His family had gone to bed already.

The next day, Dec. 26, he was there again at six o'clock, together with the bachelor technician in order to carry out some final tests.

The loading of the database took until the afternoon. Louis carried out some further tests, which lasted until midnight and were successful. For a few hours of sleep, Louis went home. His family had already gone to bed.

Dec. 27 was a normal working day. No staff member in the bank noticed that the computer had crashed, been repaired, and had all its data restored. Louis, husband and father of two daughters, had spent Christmas in the basement without a Christmas tree, jingle bells, or gifts, but with a bachelor technician.

Of course, his wife was pissed off, and the bank offered her some flowers as an apology. I am not so sure if this calmed her down.

We paid a fortune for the technician.

Louis had learned the hard way that it is not a good idea to switch off computers, and the bank paid him an overtime premium of 350%.

Though it wasn't his intention, it was at least a good affair from a financial point of view.

It's a little-known fact that the Y1K problem caused the Dark Ages.

(Unknown author)

One hundred years of waiting loop

About IT and the media.

Considering the incredible impact of computers on our daily lives, it is indeed very surprising to find so little about IT in the media. Furthermore, considering the computer industry's immaturity and the damage created by faulty software or security breaches, the lack of media coverage is totally incomprehensible. IT deserves to have a solid slice of every newspaper or TV magazine. But, only extremely rarely does an IT subject make it to the headlines. You may find small articles about disasters in some hidden "bits and bytes" corner of a newspaper. The few exceptions where IT is in the headlines are more-or-less found in the following categories:

Data leakage

At the time of this writing, data leakage is a hot topic. Around the world, the number of cases in which data gets "lost" or "stolen" is rising sharply. The problem worries normal users, because information like a credit card number is very interesting to criminals. Similar cases which get a lot of attention in the media are incidents like the data theft which happened at the Liechtenstein Bank LGT, where the names and portfolio holdings of customers were purchased by German fiscal authorities.

Stock exchange

Technology shares were very much in the public eye at some time in the past. The bubble related to the "new market," where tiny Internet startup companies had higher stock market values than Chrysler or Bank of America was largely covered in the press. Everyone wanted to get rich very fast, but at the end, plenty of people lost plenty of money. What is really striking is that there was almost nobody who was interested in the products developed by these companies or who understood them.

Fancy new products

Whenever fancy, new, electronic consumer products are launched, there is a big echo in the press. The latest *iPhone* model gets more attention than any other new, revolutionary technological evolution. The newest Windows version can drive the world crazy, although it's only an operating system for the PC.

Functional software gets no attention at all in the press. This helps explain why consumer software is less faulty than functional software. When nobody looks at you and you have no risk of being publicly exposed, well, then you make less of an effort.

Computer crashes

Computer crashes happen by the thousands every day around the world. But almost none become public. The only occasional exceptions are when the train network collapses, flights are cancelled, or if there is a breakdown of the power supply.

Projects

Public reports about crashing projects are as rare as a snowstorm in the Sahara. It only happens when the impact on the public is very visible or if the amount of money lost will shock the public.

It is easy to "sell" to the public anything which may lead to an immediate end-of-the-world, and where the cause can be understood easily by everyone. The migration to the year 2000 (Y2K) was such a project. Many books were written about it, special broadcasts were done, and horror scenarios were developed in numbers. It was the biggest public interest in the work of IT experts ever! But strangely, the technical difficulty of this question was very straightforward. In those days, many systems only used two digits for recording the year in a date. Therefore, from Jan. 1, 2000, the computer programs would not have been able to handle the transition from the year 1999 (stored as 99 in the database) to 2000 (stored as 00), because 2000 would be interpreted as 1900. Computers would crash, and the world would fall into pieces. There were predictions that people would become 100 years younger from one day to the next, and that old persons would get a call to register for kindergarten. Banks would calculate negative interest or, alternatively, interest for 100 years. Criminals would have to stay in prison 100 years longer than sentenced. An incident in a nuclear plant would only be recognized as such with a delay of 100 years. You probably remember similar scenarios that have been developed publicly.

It was a nice-and-easy subject for the press. Everything was easy to understand, and it was so terrifying that it sold well. The whole agitation was, however, incomprehensible for IT experts. The fact that the two last digits would change on Jan. 1, 2000, had been known for many years, and there was plenty of time to prepare. For software that had been purchased and for which a valid maintenance contract existed, the provider was expected to deliver a solution on time. For internally-developed software, the problem was just a little bit trickier and required more effort: it was the time when already-retired *COBOL* programmers got their second professional wind.

It was also a nice, commercial opportunity for software-developing companies, as they could sell new and compliant solutions. Billions of dollars were earned in the process. Anyway, the project management around this subject was easy to overlook. IT experts were not very successful in communicating this situation to the CEOs. Well, maybe they didn't really try either, because it was an excellent occasion to get their budgets approved.

Senior Management in every company was driven by panic and spent fortunes with external consultants who were charged to verify whether the migration was running well. I remember that every company was obliged by its auditors to send letters to every single business partner to inform him about the state of progress of work and ask for a confirmation that the partner would be ready in time as well. The fear behind it was that, due to global interdependencies, a disaster was still possible when the external partner wasn't compliant. Lunacy! Madness! Nonsense!

The postal service sold millions of stamps (or was it billions?). External consultants made fortunes.

It was easy to drive everyone crazy with all possible scenarios. One of my colleagues from New York even tested the following one: an email which is sent on Jan 1, 2000, from Luxembourg to New York at a time when New York was still in the year 1999—would it work correctly?

We all know that nothing happened at all: power supplies didn't fail, no planes crashed, and no nuclear plants exploded.

One bank in Luxembourg was so relieved about this that the Senior Management sent a big "thank you" to all its IT staff by publishing a full-page advertisement in the most important local newspaper.

Such a "thank you" would have been much more welcome one year before.

On Jan. 1, 1999, the European Union introduced the Euro, the new, common, accounting currency—cash came only in 2002. This project bore significantly higher risks than the Y2K migration. But, as it was difficult to communicate the related risks to the public, the media didn't talk about the IT-related problems at all. But the risks were much higher. A money transfer of, let's say, one billion Italian Lira, executed incorrectly as one billion Euros could have killed the bank.

But back to the Y2K topic. One of my acquaintances had squeezed out the whole Y2K foofaraw. I met him by coincidence on the street on Dec. 22. He wished me a Merry Christmas, and by the way, he told me that he had booked a flight to Jamaica to spend the holiday there with his wife. I was quite surprised he got a flight on such short notice.

"Yes, me too. Getting there was a bit more difficult, but for the return flight on Jan. 1, there were plenty of free seats." I thought about it for a short moment and said, "Jan. 1, flying back from Jamaica? Aren't you afraid?" He was surprised and said, "Why should I be afraid. I even got 50% discount for flying back on that day!"

"But what happens if the computers crash because of Y2K? Maybe your plane must fly waiting loops for one hundred years before you are allowed to land!" He got as pale as clay and said: "Damn it. Now I understand why I got the discount. Nobody wants to fly on that day." All of a sudden, he was in a hurry to rush to his travel agency. But he couldn't change the ticket; all other days were booked. Finally, he returned on Jan. 1, and it turned out that his plane didn't crash—and it's not still flying waiting loops, either.

It works at home!

Why there shouldn't be any user-developed software.

If you have stayed with me so far and understood everything, you are now aware of the complexity of an IT biotope.

As if the tasks weren't already complex enough, IT is regularly confronted by business users who want to install privately-developed software or software which has been downloaded from the Internet. This question is categorized under the term *end-user-computing* (EUC).

Before we explore the problems this generates, I will say a few words about why this situation arises at all.

When PCs became largely available to the public at the end of the '80s, there were many people in IT who believed that personal computers would make IT departments obsolete. It was broadly accepted that IT departments would substantially shrink or even vanish. Now, we know this did not happen. It is quite the opposite: the PC world has created plenty of new possibilities and led to countless new applications, but it also led to an explosion of complexity and it created instability.

Because most of the public had PCs at home, IT departments were faced with a large number of employees who had cultivated half-knowledge about IT subjects, especially in purely technical questions.

Every time a specific topic is not of substantial importance in a firm, management finds business users who have a "better understanding" of it than the other IT experts.

But being a *PC freak* doesn't mean knowing what is required to develop software.

Today, it is a very straightforward process to load the required tools on a PC for the development of software (Java, Visual Basic, etc.) or to install a database (MS-Access or MySQL). These tools are, in most cases, even free of charge or they are copied illegally from a friend. The PC user can then develop, in his spare time, some programs and databases of whatever complexity he is able to handle.

Currently, we are experiencing the quite interesting, but also worrying, phenomena of the *EUC-comeback*, which is due to increased outsourcing. Every time areas of core importance (like the main accounting system in a bank), with permanent adaptation needs, have been outsourced, the inevitable happens: the whole cycle of business request, analysis, specifications definition, negotiation, implementation, and tests have to be completed with the insourcer—even for the smallest of all requests. This takes too long for the users, and it is probably also too expensive. There are good chances then that the request will not be approved. The user is left alone with his problem, and he starts looking for alternatives.

But also in the case that the specific area is run by the internal IT department, the same phenomena may happen. IT often answers with, "It will take one year," or "It will cost one million," or "This is not a priority." And one day, the user comes in joyfully with a CD and asks to install the program on the firm's network.

The dialogue somewhat resembles the following:

"Can you please install this program for me?" The user continues with pride, "I have developed it myself. It works at home!"

The alarm bells start ringing for the CIO and the responsible system administrator. "We can't install invalidated, foreign software just like that."

"Why not?"

"We need to check first to see if our standards have been followed."

"What standards? I developed this quite normally in Java, and you are using Java as well, aren't you?"

"It's not that simple. There are plenty of other things to consider. First, we need to understand how it can be integrated into our IT landscape, and there's much more. But right now, we have no time, as we have other priorities."

The business user goes away deeply frustrated and rails against his IT. ("They act like they were born yesterday. What is so difficult about installing such a little program?") Depending on the user's character, he either gives up, or he installs it without IT knowing. To note here, the computer industry is very inventive about creating ways to circumvent the will of an IT department; I don't want to list these possibilities here, but it is definitely true to say that if an IT department wants to avoid such a scenario fully, it requires substantial effort to close all possible doors to non-approved software.

The IT guys shake their heads over these eternal hobby programmers who believe that professional software development is a leisure activity. Would this be the case, we surely wouldn't be talking so much about outsourcing software development to India.

Whenever I talk to colleagues in other companies about this subject, I notice a certain resignation. They all fight with this problem—nobody has found the *panacea* as far as I can see. Most of the time, EUC is accepted tacitly, and some basic rules are defined as to what is allowed and what is not. Controlling these rules is, however, very difficult. Another possible approach to this is that IT hires staff that is in charge of accompanying the hobby programmers in their work and supporting them when they have difficulties. A further possibility consists in obliging the end user programmers to report to IT about all self-developed software. However, such reporting never works too efficiently.

A definition of where a user-development starts is necessary. Is an Excel macro already an EUC? Hard to say.

Usually, no CIO is happy with this subject.

In principle, the CIO is right to forbid or strongly constrict EUC. However, the communication around this problem is not handled well; the reasons are not sufficiently explained, and they are not sufficiently understood by the business users. In the following lines, I will list the main requirements that a software development must fulfill, and I invite my CIO colleagues to use the following in their discussions with their users.

Here, now, the reasons against EUC:

Maintenance

The one who has written the program is the only one who knows it well and can correct upcoming errors. Just like in any software, it must be expected that user-developed programs contain errors. And it is rather clear that the error density is even higher than in professional software systems. When professional software is purchased, there is usually a maintenance contract in place, and the provider will correct the errors. It goes without saying that this is not the case with EUC, and the firm becomes dependent on a particular hobby programmer. During holidays or illness, there is no maintenance. If this employee leaves, the problem gets even worse. Even when he is in the office, he most likely doesn't have the time to work on software problems as his first priority. It could well be that he is sitting in a meeting with a customer, and the wheels stand still for the part that his program covers. In such situation, the same thing always happens: the business department asks IT for help. But IT can't deliver that easily, at least not with its usual speed and quality. First, it could be that the chosen programming language is not used by IT, and, therefore, there is no expert around to help. Second, IT doesn't know what the program is supposed to do and has no knowledge about its internal mechanics.

Analysis

It can be taken for granted that, in the case of an EUC development, there hasn't been any analysis in terms of functionality, size, and required effort. Why should there be? The analyst and the programmer are the same person, and why should someone analyze something that he already has in his head? A substantial mistake. Experience shows that appetite comes while eating, and a software development is never really complete. It is easy to catch something that will never stop.

Multi-User

Software that has been developed at home has always only been tested by one user at a time. Professional software, however, must be able to handle multiple users at the same time. This is a different kettle of fish. To illustrate this: when a user retrieves information from a database in order to change it, this information must be locked for a second user, and the program must wait until the change is completed. Let's take the following example: user John wants to add the order of 1 case of a specific wine in his system. User Frank wants to add an order of 2 cases of the same wine for another customer. There are a total of 10 cases in stock. John's program reads out the information: 10. Frank reads out the information: 10. John places the order and updates the stock: 10-1=9. Frank updates the database now: 10-2=8 cases left. This is wrong, of course. The total number of cases left is 7, not 8. The correct procedure would be that Frank finds the program locked while John is in the process of updating it. As soon as John has completed his update, Frank's program gets unlocked, and the second update can be done.

Things like that are only known by experienced programmers.

Commit

Commit means the ability of a program to group updates in a database that logically belong together. To stay with the previous example: as the stock is updated, an update of the customer order file must be executed. Should the program crash between those two updates, we would have quite a mess in our database: the stock would be correct, but no invoice would be created. There's an obvious consequence for the business, but also for the technical part: it could be that the database stops working with the message *"corrupted."* The *commit* instruction will tell the database that the two updates must be done together, meaning either both are carried out, or in case of a program failure, all updates done so far must be *rolled back*. Again, this is something that only an experienced programmer will know.

Auditing acceptability

Every change in a database must be logged (before and after image) in order to be able to retrace later who did what and when. Which programs were used (and who has used them) must also be logged. In recent times, we observe that there are requests to even log pure read accesses to a database.

Should the company you work for have to comply with SOX regulation, it is a good idea to totally restrict EUC, as SOX imposes strict rules in this regard. It stipulates that business decisions cannot be made on the basis of a document when it cannot be proved who made changes in that document. Basically, this means that a program like Excel cannot be used for critical decision-making. Auditors like to take a close look at EUC developments, as it is very easy to find misconduct there.

Access rights

Software must be capable of allocating different access rights (input, change, delete, authorization, controlling, etc.) to different (groups of) users. According to the importance of the data managed, a four-eyes principle must be implemented. Developing access rights functionality can be quite a nightmare, and it is impossible to find any software one can integrate into other software which would allow spending only a minimum of effort on this question.

Tests

EUC developments have only been tested by the person who wrote them. Truly not a good idea! It is important to have a neutral view on a new program. If you are busy with something for a long time, you somehow become blind to things that strike others immediately. Third parties can recognize strengths and weaknesses much better. Maybe some important things have been overlooked? And the question of how user-friendly a program is can only be answered by someone who doesn't know it too well.

Life cycle

As described in the chapter *Change is the only constant*, software has a life cycle. How can someone outside IT know when the support for a specific product will be terminated? In the case that IT doesn't know about a program installed by the user, it neither manages this nor searches for alternatives in time. As a consequence, some things might no longer work from one day to the next and panic rises.

A similar question is whether a used program will be compliant with the next Windows version. Whatever the answer is, there is endless effort. "Yes" would mean testing, and "No" would mean rewriting.

Creating a test environment for the validation of a new program version presents nasty pitfalls. An inexperienced programmer tends to hard-code the names of needed files directly in the program, like *X:\mylivesystem\myfile.txt*. When a test version of the program runs, it uses the files from the live system and not the ones from the test environment, for example: *X:\mytestsystem\myfile.txt*. It is not difficult to avoid such pitfalls; one only has to be aware of it.

Documentation

IT has standards on how it documents programs in relation to its internal mechanics and its interconnection with other components. Outside IT, this is not known. Furthermore, it is necessary to write a user-guide; the history of program changes must be maintained, and much more.

Version management

Every piece of software is alive and undergoes continued development. Is it known that old versions need to be archived for the purpose of future audits? It could become important to have an old version still available in order to find out why an error occurred.

Communication

Another major risk with EUC consists in considering that external factors in the IT biotope remain immobile. It's already quite complex for IT to manage all the dependencies between all known components. It needs to be known with what other components the EUC program communicates. Can you know for sure that it will work in all constellations? If not, what error management does it have? It must be documented where the data comes from and where it goes. A permanent monitoring of things that can have an impact on EUC must be done.

An employee outside IT has no way of knowing about all this. When IT changes one of the countless components in the biotope which has a link to the EUC program, a crash is close-by.

An example to illustrate this? A system which has a data element in its database to represent profit-and-loss information is using the value "0" for loss and "1" for profit. A user who writes a program to exploit this data will have a nasty surprise on the day IT extends the definition of that data element, perhaps by adding the value "2" meaning "not yet calculated." If the EUC program is designed in the way that any value different from "0" is being considered as profit, this will lead to totally wrong numbers. Using these wrong numbers as a preparation for a management decision can quickly become disastrous.

Furthermore, there might be internal company requirements that the software needs to fulfill: electronic confirmations sent to customers, for instance, could be required to be archived centrally, and therefore, the program must be interfaced with the company's archiving system.

Help-Desk

How are reported errors managed, and how are they prioritized? Can users of an EUC program be supported correctly? Is a hobby programmer good at this? Very unlikely indeed.

Technical finesse

Does an Excel-macro programmer know that his program is stored along with the Excel document? Yes, most likely, but does he know what problems this creates? Most likely not. Well, with every *Save as*…in Excel, a new copy of this macro-program is saved. If the macro needs to be changed later, there will be plenty of Excel-documents that need to be changed. This is an unpleasant side-effect. The separation between data and programs should be guaranteed—both have diverging lifecycles. The same is true for the EUC database MS-Access. Separating the database and its logic is not easy for a non-expert to achieve. And separating "test" and "live" in a database like MS-Access is difficult to guarantee: it is so easy to add a field into the live database quickly, but rolling this back is much trickier.

Performance

Will the program succeed in mastering the expected data volumes? Has this been analyzed and controlled? Let's take an example: an Excel document is loaded with all customer positions, and for each position, the current market price is requested from a market prices provider. If we have 10 price requests, then it is not a problem. With 100, it is already becoming a bit tough. With 1,000, it's impossible. Excel is a spreadsheet program, not a database. This is a structure composed of rows and columns which looks a bit like a professional database and which can be handled as such for many of its embedded functions. This simplicity of usage seduces inexperienced programmers and users to flood it with data. But it is not meant for that. This is like organizing heavy loads on a van. The many embedded functions, however, which allow data analysis (something which is not offered to the same extent in database systems), remain mostly unused. Many companies do buy expensive programs for charts and statistics without considering that Excel already includes these functions. An experienced programmer would build a database, enquire the database, and load the result into Excel. A nice output can then be done by Excel. A user would have trouble going that route because he wouldn't understand the database structure.

As mentioned before, SOX might completely inhibit this way of doing.

Backups

Where are the data and programs stored, and how should they be backed up? A question that is not always easy to answer. If the data storage is on the C: drive, you will experience data loss in the case of a complete PC crash. This is surprising, as "at home," the C: drive is the preferred place for data storage. A data backup concept is something each software developer needs to define.

Confidentiality

Is the data managed by the EUC program classified as "confidential" or even "secret"? Is it, therefore, a requirement that the database be encrypted? Is it made sure that there isn't a possibility to make illegal copies of the database? Having salary data on a publicly-available network drive is not a good idea. Are there specific data protection laws in the country that need to be considered by the software? Hands-off from EUC when confidential data needs to be managed.

Functional enhancements

For future functional enhancements of the EUC program, it is necessary to create a test system where the new version will be validated before its move into production. Is it clear how this can be achieved? Does the hobby programmer know how to migrate from a test database to the live one? Does he know about the risks linked to this exercise? I guess that the answers to these questions would be "no."

Emergency planning

How are things when it comes to an emergency situation? In the case that the EUC program has been installed without involving IT, it is certain that this program will not be available in the Disaster Recovery Centre, and the impact on processes will be rather unpredictable.

Conclusion

Leave software development to the experts. An accounting clerk is not a programmer, in the same way as a programmer is not an accounting clerk. A business user is not supposed to know about the things written in the lines above—and therefore, he should keep his fingers out of the pot.

IT is a jungle, and it doesn't make sense to have an additional herb garden beneath the jungle.

Users may now argue that these are nice and wise explanations, but they haven't helped make any progress with their problems. Here is my advice: if you need a solution to a problem, talk to your IT department, and insist on urgency. In cases of really risk-free programs, your IT will most likely be prepared to accept your EUC program, but allow IT the necessary time to investigate first. If IT refuses your program, you should believe that there are good reasons. If you think you really need a solution, you still have the option to take the matter to your CEO and to ask for a re-prioritization. An additional budget for the development of a professional solution might help; it could well be that there is already a solution on the market that could be purchased.

If you can't talk with IT about your request openly, the company has a totally different problem that needs to be fixed at a higher level.

But in any case, don't make the mistake of ignoring your IT's opinion. Settling for a short-term solution will generate a lot of mid-term problems.

Normally, the described aspects above are applicable to software development. But there are cases where the dialogue between IT and the business is so massively bad that extensive and expensive software packages are bought directly by the business. In this case, the CIO must ask himself crucial questions about his role in the company and should start looking for a new job.

It gets particularly bad when the business has its own opinion about the hardware that should be used (PCs, printers, modems, servers, etc.) and starts to purchase them and administrate them on their own behalf. Should this happen, Senior Management needs to do something very urgently.

There are cases where Senior Management orders hardware without asking IT; once the boxes have arrived, IT is commanded to implement the equipment. This is the precise moment when the CIO has no other choice than to resign.

I had a battle of that nature to fight many years ago. At our Christmas party, it must have been 1992 or 1993, I had a member of the Board sitting next to me. We started talking, and as we discussed introducing PCs, I told him about the kind of problems we experienced. He listened carefully and proposed a solution: we should buy *Atari* computers, because the one he had at home didn't cause him any problems at all. Nothing wrong with *Atari*, but these computers were very focused on gaming and not suitable for a professional environment. In the following days, he called me several times and tried to convince me. It took substantial effort to prevent the introduction of gaming computers in the bank.

It will be much quieter next year

An outlook into the future

Around Christmas, people everywhere around the globe like to look back at the year that has passed by, and they try to take a look into the future. This is no different in IT.

Every year, and this has been true for more than 20 years, IT staff dreams that next year will be much quieter than the year before. A year of consolidation would be great, and honestly, do we need all this stress? No matter what IT position you hold, the job is challenging and exciting, and there's a legitimate wish to slow down a bit.

For decades, this wishful thinking has remained every year, without exception, even while there has been an increase in work complexity, the number of challenges, and the volume of work. It could well be, however, that due to the worldwide recession, for the first time, we will experience a slowdown from the furious pace of the past. I don't think, however, that complexity will decrease—quite the contrary. But we might see a reduction in the number of projects that need to be run. Another thing that won't change is that technology in 2009 and 2010 will continue in its storm-and-stress phase. And I am not so certain if IT experts around the world would welcome a decrease of their stress levels or a decrease of the complexity; they are quite a specific population.

In October 2005 (but it could as well be in June 2009), IBM produced this ad: "How do we succeed in adding value without creating complexity?" Almost four years later, the answer to that question can only be that nobody has an answer: complexity continues to explode. Recently, I read another ad that said: "Solutions that work" and "Stress-free IT." I wish we would someday get there! These ads are a good summary of where we should go, but there isn't any convincing proposal of how to reach these goals.

What will be the new challenges we will face in the future, and where will technology lead? I don't know, and nobody else does either, in spite of the many prophets announcing how the world will look like.

If there had been computers in 1879, they would have forecasted that,
due to the increase of horse carriages, by 1979,
one would be suffocating in horse dung.

John C. Edwards

Some 25 years ago, nobody was using a PC; 15 years ago, nobody could imagine how the Internet or mobile communication would change our world. How should we be able now to imagine what will be in ten or only three years?

Certainly, there won't be anything like "Beam me up, Scotty," as computers will not be able to move material over telecommunication lines. But apart from that, any guess about the future is welcome. It's not even possible to make a reliable forecast for the next 12 months.

I will not participate in reading tea leaves the way financial experts do who tell you in the morning— "We have a strong Euro, this will put down the stock exchange prices." —only to explain in the evening why it came totally differently: "The rise of the consumer confidence index in the US has surprised everyone. This is good for the economy." By the way, these days, who would believe anything a financial expert tells us? If somebody were able to predict the future, he wouldn't have to work anymore.

IT is not free of vogues; one hype chases the next. These days, it is very popular to stick a "green" label on new IT products—this helps sales. But IT products are not "green," and they will not be "green" for a long time. This is just another hype. I sometimes get the impression that the climate will be saved if just enough "green" computers are bought. Similar selling arguments can be observed in the automobile industry, where the ads make you think that driving a car is saving the world. So, at the end, it looks as if the IT industry would be learning from the automobile industry, which, in many respects, would be a massive improvement.

There are a few things, however, which are easy to predict:

- Technical possibilities will continue to explode, and new wishes will be created in business. The economic downturn will, however, reduce the number of approved projects around these technologies.

- We will see more regulatory pressure as a consequence of the financial crisis, and they will have an impact on projects that need to be realized by IT.

- The data cemeteries will continue to grow. The requirements to archive everything you can imagine will increase, and masses of unused data in gigantic dimensions will be created.

I have tried to describe in this book the current challenges and tasks of a company's IT department. I have documented the most urgent and important problems we are facing. And even if I can't predict the future, I can, nevertheless, express some wishes:

- Improved software quality.
  The comparison with the automobile industry has been made at various places in this book, and many IT experts argue the same. The user's expectations for software are comparable to the ones they have when buying a car. We are, however, very far away from that, and we cannot see that the computer industry has even started moving into that direction. We are, more or less, in the same state the automobile industry was 100 years ago—with the difference that computer systems have decisively more impact on our lives than automobiles did 100 years ago. Software development continues to be a manual process: computers are not able to do that for us. We continue our storm-and-stress phase, if not our infantile period, and we don't see a trend towards maturity. The little standardization efforts we observe are not successful: they become obsolete as quickly as they are created. The foundations (technology, methods, processes, etc.) are on moving ground, and therefore, we cannot have stability in the foreseeable future. We need to

forget about this because every few months a new version of each and every piece of software needs to be installed and tested. The introduction of a quality label for software seems like a fantasy. But as long as software development remains bricolage, the introduction of such a label would ease the crisis. It would facilitate IT's work significantly. Such a label should evaluate the stability and the easiness of integration into unknown IT biotopes; the window-dressing of new functionality in software would be left to the software provider's marketing departments.

- The providers should warrant their products—this is not a revolutionary claim; however, it is still a total fantasy.

> *That's the thing about people who think they hate computers.*
> *What they really hate is lousy programmers.*

> Larry Niven and Jerry Pournelle

- More general IT understanding in the public and from business users.
  To know that an IT department is operating in a difficult, and sometimes even uncontrollable, environment should be in the consciousness of all computer users. This is not a cheap justification for possible problems, but an accurate description of the current situation. The main tasks of IT experts can be summarized by saying that they are managing "change." And change means instability; this is a general rule for all areas of life. Mr. Resch, whom I cited at some places in this book, formulated this even more drastically: "IT manages dependencies," and he was talking about the dependency toward the software industry. Let's tell our users that, on a worldwide basis, the majority of IT projects fail, and let's tell them the reasons why. But let's talk in a language they can understand, a language which is not technical and overblown. Let's tell them that the introduction of a new system generates costs that cannot be measured simply by its purchase price, but that they need to be calculated by multiplying the purchase price by up to ten. Let's tell them that the introduction of software must be compared to the building of a house. As we, the IT managers of this world, leave this field of communication vacant to the largest possible extent, we create the possibility for consultancy firms to present themselves with all-embracing concepts. In management magazines, they

promise to solve all IT problems (too slow, too inflexible, too expensive, too instable, and too insecure) in one go. External consultants seem to be more trustworthy than the company's own staff, and these messages find an excessively receptive audience at the Senior Management level. I hear many times that some of my colleagues in other companies are appalled by the fact that they don't get the necessary attention from their CEO when they argue that these all-embracing concepts, which swallow tremendous amounts of money, will not work because IT is simply much more complex than what they can see on a PowerPoint presentation. A consultancy company will never mention the problems listed in this book. We also know that external consultants pursue their own goals, which are predominantly to sell many consultancy days. A CIO knows that IT means mental work in an open pit, but we don't communicate that sufficiently.

- Security.
  The exasperating phenomena that the computer industry is not sufficiently interested in security questions should become a thing of the past. There's so much damage due to insufficient security levels that it's hard to believe nothing is being done about it. To stay with the automobile industry: no car producer waits to build brakes until after the accidents start. Missing security is definitely another annoying sign of industry immaturity.

- Speech Recognition.
  Someday, in the not-so-distant future, computers will understand human language, and the dialogue with machines will get easier. This would be the end of the endless swapping through the menus and the *where-was-that-function-again?* searching. I am looking forward to seeing high-class, automatic text translations. But this will only be the case when we have:

- Faster Computers.
  Of course, computers get quicker every year, and this is a good thing. The industry is making tremendous progress in the area of having multiple processors in one PC. But this will make software development more complicated, which, I fear, will not improve its quality... For many tasks, computers are still too slow today. We won't reach the limit of possibilities for a long time. However, I don't think I will see the day when a computer will have calculated if there is a winning strategy in chess.

Working in IT remains an exciting adventure, and IT jobs will not become boring for a long time. In spite of all the problems we face every day, it remains true that we are permanently amazed about new technologies and new software solutions. Permanent variety remains a constant of our job. If I am fortunate enough, I will have another ten years or so to spend in the IT world. And with a lot of luck, I could live to see the shortcomings listed in this book become obsolete. I remain optimistic.

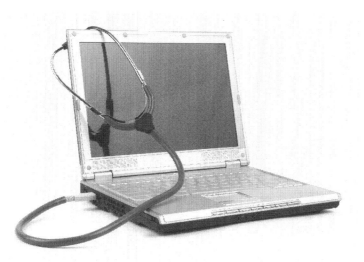

Appendix 1 - Press Reviews of the German edition

manager-magazin.de

Industry sector criticism

"The IT Industry is immature"

by Anja Tiedge

Crashed computers, lost documents: the IT world is considered by many as being confusing or even dangerous. But it's not the users being the problem, says Claude Roeltgen. The Head of IT of Banque LBLux looks behind the scenes of his industry and reveals how IT professionals really work.

mm.de: Mr. Roeltgen, you surely know this: you want to start a computer program and an error message appears on the screen. In these moments, do you blame the producer of the program? Or do you search for the error with yourself?

Roeltgen: I have to face such programs every day. Therefore I don't look for the error with myself. I rather think of Bill Gates and his friends and at the fact that something must have gone wrong in their company. However, someone who doesn't work in IT immediately thinks: "What wrong button did I push? What did I do wrongly?"

mm.de: The users shouldn't look for the problem with themselves?

Roeltgen: No. Software must be written in such a way that it doesn't crash. But this is the weakness of many programs: they are not sufficiently tested. The producers simply take it for granted that the user will restart the program, or even his computer, and that he hopes that it will work better next time. And indeed, this really helps in most cases.

mm.de: Can the producer avoid this frustration?

Roeltgen: Yes, but that's exactly the problem. The IT industry is immature. The aspect of quality plays a secondary role in software development. It is mainly about launching new functionality quickly onto the market and to sell it quickly. When there are errors happening, then the producers only profit from it: on top they cash-in from their customers 20 percent of maintenance fees—for errors which they have produced themselves.

Concerning private users, the producers imagine that every customer always finds someone who can help. And indeed, this is true in most cases. Therefore, the pressure for taking more care about quality is not there for the industry. To my opinion this will unfortunately not change over the next years. We all do accept this because we are quasi addicted to new applications—be it privately or in the job. Due to this push for new things we accept that the products are immature.

mm.de: Are immature programs also the reason why IT projects often take longer and are substantially more expensive than planned?

Roeltgen: This is an important reason, yes. One need to know: programming software is handicrafts. Applications are not produced industrially, but to some extent the wheel is reinvented each time.

mm.de: Are there further reasons why IT projects are often delayed or even fail?

Roeltgen: I call this the IT biotope: companies have so many diverse and specific requirements to IT that a large number of different systems are being used. But software providers are not interested in the biotope in which their products are integrated. They develop a product which is working well left alone. But as soon as it is used in a different biotope, situations arise for which it had not been tested—and the program doesn't work. As soon as one adjusts a small screw in the program, everything crashes. In IT projects this often leads to enormous delays or even to a failing. A simple example for this is that software from the USA doesn't immediately run on European computers because possibly umlauts haven't been considered.

mm.de: This is creating frustration on both sides: the producers and the users. What can they do against it?
Roeltgen: The users must be prepared to wait once a bit longer for a solution. We don't really want to leave the time to the producers that they need for testing. We prefer to have a solution which changes the world within three weeks. It is necessary to be realistic and to see that it cannot work like that.
And the one who buys software must be aware that an IT project is not like buying a car: that you make your choice, then it is delivered and it works immediately. An IT project is much more comparable to building a house.

mm.de: To what extent can IT projects be compared with the building of a house?
Roeltgen: When building a house the structural engineering must be calculated and it must be taken care of for the installation of external connections. And then continuously new problems come up, which however can be solved somehow. At the beginning you do know about the target, but the way to get there is not totally clear. This is the same with a system implementation, however somewhat more complex. The reason is that there is much less standardization in IT.
Partially it is also the producer's fault because they simply don't care enough about the quality of their products. Being an IT customer, you are almost always in a weaker position, but CIOs should nevertheless try to conclude warranties in their contracts. Also they shouldn't always accept the usual 20% of maintenance fees, but this is an almost utopistic request.

mm.de: According to your description, an IT project will never run according to plan. Should enterprises plan from the beginning across-the-board costs surcharges?

Roeltgen: This would surely be a measure to take. On top of the purchase price one should, according to the complexity of the project, add a double, five or ten times multiple amount. What needs to be considered as well: also in the day-to-day operations immense costs arise after the introduction of the system; be it due to maintenance, new versions and much more.

mm.de: You have written a book about your experiences in the IT sector with the title "Eine Million oder ein Jahr" *(One million or one year)*. How did you get to this title?

Roeltgen: This is a phrase which I often hear at day-to-day work. When IT projects get started, the employees in the business sit together and they develop a new idea. When they present it to the IT department, the first reaction is most of the time: "But this will cost one million". Or even two or three. The first disappointed faces are already there. When it comes to the time frame, it doesn't look much differently: "Therefore we need to foresee at least one year", can be heard then.

This is always the same scenario: the optimism in the business departments is huge when an IT project gets kicked-off—and the disappointment as well when it is explained what will be really needed in terms of time and money.

mm.de: Are you then pleading for companies to approach IT projects in a more pessimistic manner?

Roeltgen: I am in favor of more realism. Many problems in our sector arise from being too optimistic in the beginning. But the truth that problems will come up is as sure as death and taxes. And when you can't keep what you have promised, the situation is highly frustrating for everybody.

mm.de: In the IT sector there are currently intense discussions about IT security. The case of *Société Générale* was spectacular, where a treasurer created damage in the height of several billion Euros with unauthorized trades. A failure of IT security?

Roeltgen: Yes, clearly. When you take a closer look at the case you get dizzy. The treasurer had changed the department. In this process it had quite simply been forgotten to revoke his access rights for the IT system. A downright bagatelle—but with lunatic consequences.

There are many similar examples, every day. Most of them have substantial fewer consequences and don't make it to the media like with *Société Générale*. But when you are an IT security officer and you are making yourself aware which small details can become threatening for the existence of your company, then you can really get sleepless. A job from hell.

mm.de: Would the Head of IT in the bank have been able to prevent the damage according to your opinion?

Roeltgen: Someone has missed removing the access rights of the treasurer. So it was a case of human error. You can have the best IT processes in the world—if an employee doesn't follow them or just simply forgets something, then you cannot do anything against that.

It is like driving a car: actually you know that you must stop at the stop sign. But in one case out of thousand it will nevertheless happen to you that you are unwary and you don't stop. There is no such thing as one hundred percent of safety—neither in IT.

(September 1, 2008)

How does this actually work? IT is like a biotope

Claude Roeltgen, CIO at Credit Suisse in Luxemburg, has written a book. For his father who has drudged his whole life in the steel industry and simply didn't understand what Claude was actually doing in the bank.

Claude Roeltgen is tapping with the finger on an ad from Hewlett Packard (HP), which he has just teared off from a business magazine: "Configure 64 servers in 15 minutes" is written there in cold print. "Do you know what happens when a CEO reads this?" asks Roeltgen, who doesn't wait at all for an answer to his question, but immediately adds to it: "He calls the hotline and informs himself before he confronts the CIO with it and asks why everything is so complicated in our own company".

With his book "Eine Million oder ein Jahr" Claude Roeltgen picks up the usual reservations of IT being too expensive and taking endless time.

His message: IT is not a car where you sit, turn the ignition key and accelerate. IT would not be a landscape either, even less a blooming one, but rather a biotope composed of diverse IT systems and one which is always good for a surprise. Especially the interfaces between different systems would be an exasperating subject, something which is first and foremost tedious and requires a lot of maintenance.

These are understandable words—in the first place addressed to his father, who had only to deal marginally with computers. "What precisely do you do?" asked the man. In a bank, something with computers: that much was clear. "I'll write it down for you", said the Luxembourgish CIO upon that. One of his most important messages: "Nothing is working at the push of a button," does know Roeltgen after 18 years of experience as bank-CIO. This is also new to many employees of the bank.

The reasons for this are so manifold, like the relationship between reed, algae, toad, dragonfly and water strider in a tarn. Nobody knows whether added value will be created by adding a new species or if the balance will be destroyed, writes the business data processing specialist. To be added that service providers present their software in their own biotope; however the main biotope in the company being substantially larger and considerably more complex.

Roeltgen knows about this latest after the introduction of a portfolio-management-software for the private customer business: "It had nearly killed us", says the Head of the IT department with a staff strength of 18 persons in Luxembourg. The presentation of the renowned provider was convincing. But then it got clear that the tool was "developed miserably" and the "support was bad", comments Roeltgen. After crisis meetings, retained payments and much seesaw there was finally a version for the 25 relationship managers after two years of dogged development work; after that they had to wait 20 to 30 minutes every morning before getting access to their customers' data because the system almost paralyzed the network. Today the program runs. Following that, the idea of signing a new contract was abandoned. And Roeltgen's hope that the prototype would become a group-wide solution seemed to become a distant prospect. But a few days ago the provider sold its software. "This could change the situation abruptly," says Roeltgen.

During the crisis the CEO of the Luxembourgish bank with 240 employees always held fast to Roeltgen. The reason: Roeltgen deals openly with problems, he even regularly sends newsletters, in which for instance he gets to the grounds of software problems and explains to all employees why there isn't a solution.

By this Roeltgen chooses an offensive direction which other IT managers in a senior position don't dare doing yet. Especially in the non-IT management the opinion that there must be no errors is too widely spread. One reader got downright into conflict with his conscience when he held Roeltgen's book in hands. "I can't give this to my boss for reading," so the IT manager, "for him the IT is perfectly controllable—and I prefer keep him believing this."

This does not change anything about a problem which has a high weight in Roeltgen's book—badly developed software. Why, asks Roeltgen, isn't there any neutral quality check for software—somehow comparable to clinical studies of new medicine in the pharmaceutical industry? Programs are released for companies that really aren't free of risks and side effects. Roeltgen likes such provocative theses. With 23 years of experience as IT man for banks, thereof 18 years as CIO, barely can someone fool him about something.

Talking Turkey ABOUT SOX, ITIL and similar

Why not tell the truth at the end? For example about the Sarbanes-Oxley Act ("The idea behind this was that controls do exist, but these controls are not controlled"). "Auditors control things which are very often outside of reality and some IT staff participate, this is simply hair-raising.", adds the bank-CIO. As a next example serves the Information Technology Infrastructure Library ITIL: "It is often forgotten that ITIL is extremely voracious in terms of human resources needed," moreover some companies apply ITIL "dogmatically," which again frustrates the users to the highest degree.

Also outsourcing may become a problem. Especially in cases when the administration of applications is carried out by an external service provider. He calls this phenomena "End-User-Computing-Comeback" and means that users start programming themselves because the service provider is often more sluggish than an internal IT service and the solution must be there faster.

Daring (but wise) is his appreciation about the subject centralizing or decentralizing. Roeltgen has gained some imperturbability here over the years: "when you don't like a strategy, you only need to wait until it is recognized that it didn't stand the test and yet it goes into the other direction."

But this doesn't mean that he leaves his own processes to chance. In a customer satisfaction survey last year the CIO realized that the services were rather well rated, but there were surprises. Upon this he initiated workshops in which he wanted to go to the bottom of things. "The employees didn't have any overview at all about the IT framework"

Roeltgen realized in the process. Also here many employees started from the point that IT works like a car.

CEO OFFERS BOOK TO ALL STAFF

To help them to finally understand what the company-IT can do and what not, the CEO of the Luxembourg dependence has offered the biotope-book to all 240 employees. For marketing slogans à la HP he is anyhow not receptive.

This is not everywhere like this: too many times there is still a communication gap between the business and IT. And then it is said again: *"Why is everything so complicated for us? All this can be done in an easier way.* Phone calls like these from the CEO are no longer to be expected after having read *Eine Million oder ein Jahr."* Alike, no longer with the usual nerved comments from employees about a lame Internet, non-working mail-servers or a porous spam-filter. Although there isn't an explanation for everything (key-learning: there isn't always one), instead there is now a new general culprit—the IT biotope. And this one is jolly complex.

Andreas Schmitz

(September 2006)

An unusual book, not (only) because the foreword was written by Luxembourg's Prime Minister, but because a professionally substantiated book is presented about IT as it can be found in larger companies and administrations—without using any kind of subject-specific terminology. It can be read like a thriller.

What is it that makes the book so worth reading for administrators, but even more importantly for the PC user?

It is a fact that there is a deep canyon between PC users and IT experts. The normal PC users in general don't have a conception of how IT really works, and how the experts work behind the scenes. Why is IT so expensive? What do the IT experts do in fact the whole day? Why does it take so long to bring a new IT project to an end? Questions like these are on everybody's mind who deals with information technology on a daily basis, but who knows IT only from the outside. On these issues the author makes clearly understandable statements. He is a real insider and he reports about how in his workaday life IT professionals are making efforts to offer an IT system, preferably failure-free, on 365 days per year. With elementary examples, he explains to the users how the professionals are left out in the rain by software developers, and after the reading of the 236 pages it should achieve more understanding between both sides.

But the author is not only criticizing, he is also giving precise suggestions on how the software industry could offer more customer-oriented products instead of letting the users, respectively the IT experts, search for errors in the software.

Claude Roeltgen is building a bridge between laymen and experts and by this he makes the grey IT monster transparent; this is the key to this worth reading book.

(September 21, 2008)

Why is it possible to buy easily even the most complex and sophisticated products on the market, but one has then to initiate with the IT in every case multi-million, year-long, and most of all, risky projects? To make it short: Why is everything so complicated in IT?

This question is addressed by the longtime bank-CIO Claude Roeltgen in his first book and he knowingly sends his answer not to colleagues, but to all of us, the users in the companies—and with that to all sufferers.

The result is a colorful potpourri of explanations, recommendations and anecdotes about the subject of IT in a firm. In brief and easy-to-read chapters, the reader gets an understanding for the diverse areas in the day-to-day IT business, like projects, training, disaster recovery planning, IT security and IT compliance.

The ensemble is aerated with entertaining inserts of true events which Roeltgen (had to) experience(d) during his 25 years long career.

All in all "Eine Million oder ein Jahr" is an unusual book in the positive sense of the word, a frontier crossing between seemingly incompatible worlds and a courting for more mutual understanding. This book should be handed out to every new PC user together with the Support-Hotline.
Target audience: All those, who want to understand what a CIO does exactly, why everything is so complicated in IT and how users and IT staff can understand each other better in the future.
(March 2007)

der EDV-Leiter

Understanding for the CIO

Claude Roeltgen, Head IT of a bank in Luxembourg, builds with his new book "Eine Million oder ein Jahr" a bridge of understanding between laymen and experts from the IT world. With irony and humor he depicts situations and interdependencies, in which every IT responsible recognizes his personal *Déja vu*.

Why do IT projects take so long, are so expensive and so complicated? How can users be introduced best to the usage of new software? Why is it so complex to establish a complete IT emergency plan? Claude Roeltgen has the experience of 25 years in IT jobs, starting from programmer to IT project manager and Head IT of a bank. He knows as well punchcard sorters as the current situation.

The perception that IT in an enterprise resembles a biotope—sometimes even a jungle, sounds simplified maybe. But whoever has already begun to integrate new components or to remove them in an IT biotope understands that here is being reported from real life.

"Eine Million oder ein Jahr" is not a reference book in which the IT responsible can hope to find solutions to his professional tasks. But it is a humorous, also often an ironic view on systems and interdependencies which sometimes have quite few connections with the hard facts of technology. We recommend the book as bedtime reading in the hotel, for an average long train ride or the next "superfluous" project meeting.

(December 12 , 2006)

"IT in the year 2006 is an organized jungle"; that simply or still that complex describes Claude Roeltgen the world of information technology. "IT experts are not doing enough (or better: not at all) marketing for their own sake" he believes and tries to push the missing dialogue between users and producers with his casually and airily written work…He compares the purchase of a new computer system or the installation of new software with the exposure of species in an unknown biotope: problems arise from the incompatibility of different systems in the frame of special fields of activity. This applies most of all to enterprise strategies, the processing of data and its security, the system administration, the management and the control. A large field where users, programmers and IT experts can get their wires crossed. Roeltgen analyzes these problem fields, gives suggestions for improvements or ticks them off with a light ironical touch. Most of all, he doesn't blame the user for the ubiquitous problems when using computers, but the industry which unscrupulously throws faulty products at the market.

The book offers fun, insights at every level and clearly formulated factual information. It is written mainly for all those contemporaries who feel at home in the IT domain—and who still are not permitted or don't want to despair.

Horst-Joachim Hoffmann/fm
c't Magazin 15/2006

lëtzebuerger
Journal
Politik, Finanzen a Gesellschaft

"The sector is not adult yet"

LJ: Mr. Roeltgen, what gave you in fact the idea to put your experiences as an IT insider on paper?

In a press review it was written that this book builds a bridge between laymen and experts and makes so the grey IT monster transparent. I had planned to explain to laymen what the IT world is about without using gobbledygook. And then there was as well my father, who had worked his whole life in the steel industry and asked me all the time: "What in fact are you doing the whole day long?" I realized quickly then that there was no book at all which explains the computer world and the people who work in it every day in a form which would be easy to read for a layman. Besides all the problems which bring us to furor again and again, we also experience a lot of very funny and interesting things. Barely any job is as fascinating as those in IT and as there is no day like the other we have a lot to tell.

LJ: "Eine Million oder ein Jahr" — what does the title mean?

We exasperate our "customers," meaning the users in a company, again and again. When they want to have something, we reply with "but this costs one million," or "you need to wait one year for it." The title shall point to the big misunderstanding between experts and users. As the users envisage the introduction of a program like the purchase of a car, we reply like a building company which wants to build a house. This misunderstanding produces many victims—on both sides!

LJ: Some months ago was released "Version 2.0" of your work. Why? And what is new about it?

The feedback to the first edition was markedly positive, as well from the readers as from the press. For example: "The book closes an important gap in the communication between users and providers in the professional IT environment," or "This book should be handed out to every new PC user together with the Support-Hotline." One CIO-colleague of mine testified about the first edition: "…a really excellent description of the real challenges of IT." Well, there was also here and there some criticism for excursions into topics which did not belong to the book and because of the too big part allocated to anecdotes. Furthermore, two years had passed and our world develops itself so terribly fast that some things in the first edition were no longer correct and some new things had to be added. The subtitle "Everything you were always supposed to know about IT" matches now the contents much better. I am currently working on the English translation and a few passages need to be adapted to new evolutions again.

LJ: How will the IT landscape look like in, let's say, ten years, when you will publish the third edition of your book? What do you think?

Our guild struggles with predicting the future, because we are too much busy with fighting against the daily disasters. Everything moves sensationally fast. Therefore I can only express some wishes; however I think that ten years will not be enough.

Firstly, I wish that the computer industry gets mature: it is in a storm-and-stress phase and it refuses to get mature. It has most massive problems with software quality, where we see much more bricolage that professional processes.

Then there is the subject of security, which is a very serious and unsolved problem: here the customers stumble from one disaster into the next and the industry from one embarrassment into the next. Unbelievably fierce efforts need to be undertaken to get this under control. From the already originated damage (in the height of billions per year, with a rapidly increasing tendency), the IT industry hasn't learned yet.

Thirdly: nothing matches with nothing; there are no standards of how things fit together. Every provider cooks his own soup, reinvents the wheel each time and seals off jealously towards the others. It will surely take at least ten years until we will have a world where all things match together: one buys for example an accounting program from SAP and an interest calculation module from a competitor and everything will work straightaway without too many efforts.

It will remain a rather rough and exciting world out there for many years. Enough material then for many new versions.

(February 9, 2009)

"It is definitely a clear and exceedingly practical signpost which should not be missing in IT interested people's library."
(July 5, 2006 — for the first edition)

d'Wort

An IT expert explains his job

"What in fact are you doing the whole day long?"
by Arne Langner

IT experts are doing things that others cannot always comprehend. After 20 years in the IT business in banks in Luxembourg, the business IT expert is blowing the whistle now. In his book "Eine Million oder ein Jahr" he raises the curtain of Information Technology a bit for John Doe.

By principle: an IT project lasts one year or it costs one million. Both are possible as well. Should it cost less, the company management is happy and also accepts that it might take even longer than one year. The Luxembourger Claude Roeltgen has included findings like these in his first book.

"What in fact are you doing the whole day long?" has asked his father once. In spite of numerous attempts to explain it to his father, Claude Roeltgen didn't succeed to make it clear with what he earned his money. Today Roeltgen junior is Head of IT at Credit Suisse. There he takes care of IT projects around security, software and system administration. The author tells in his book about his early experiences with punchcards up to working with operating systems like Windows XP.

The IT world in understandable words.

Prime Minister Jean-Claude Juncker continues to fell more comfortable when the writing is accompanied by the "scraping of a pen," he writes in his foreword. Nevertheless he sums up about Roeltgen's first work: "With his book, Claude Roeltgen has succeeded in depicting the IT world in understandable words—both for non-IT experts and those for whom IT is their daily business."

The IT expert succeeds indeed to present an entertaining book about the perils and mysteries of the computer world in an understandable language. He combines there personal anecdotes from his yearlong career in the IT sector with the offering to the readers to increase their basic knowledge in a casual manner.

He chats informally about the planning difficulties of large IT projects and asks for more mutual understanding between experts and managers.

"There are simply no criteria based on which one can test software reliably before it is used in a company," says Roeltgen. Each computer system in a company differs from the next: "They function like biotopes. Delicate and unique." IT experts know about this; business users often lack understanding. Although marketing ads promise that a specific software will ease the work, will be easy to use and will of course function flawlessly. Roeltgen: "but it is not that simple." On top, the purchase price for new programs is not the only cost factor. Roeltgen knows that the software must be implemented; something that sometimes may take several months.

Not least, company managers always also need to clarify the question: "Do we need at all a new program?" The cost-benefit-relation is there a decisive factor. And on top, the information technology is still in its storm-and-stress phase, thinks the man who is already in the business since 20 years and who knows how things are: "IT refuses to get adult." This may explain beautiful, but superfluous programs as much as software errors and longsome projects that require a lot of money and time. The author is courting in his book for understanding for the useful inventions of IT.

Jean-Claude Juncker
Luxembourg Prime Minister

Appendix 2 - Foreword by Jean-Claude Juncker (German edition)

Plug it in, switch it on, and then it has to work! The email comes in, the webpage builds up, and the printer prints. I don't see myself being a particularly demanding computer user. But it cannot be excluded that especially those ones are a mere nightmare.

I confess: I still feel more comfortable when writing is accompanied by the scraping of a pen and not the rattle of a keyboard. As a Prime Minister, you also enjoy some privileges. So I am sufficiently being taken care of so I don't have to wait for a free line at the "Helpdesk."

Nonetheless, there is no escaping.

Be it as Head of Administration or as an economics politician, be it about tax reform or the settling of new enterprises, after 30 minutes (and often earlier), every discussion comes to the unavoidable subject of Information Technology.

And when the legal objection against a planned reform can be overcome with a "then we just change the law," one often feels at the mercy of the computer experts. For the rest, the fact that, to all appearances, they speak a different language is also of no help.

So, there is no escaping: interface, public key infrastructure, data warehouse, convergence, updates and migrations, IP-telephony, and Internet-backbones are just a few of the new terms not even the Prime Minister can elude.

This a fortiori as the Luxembourg government wants more than just incur the entrance to the knowledge society or simply accompany it.

We are strongly determined—true to the longstanding experiences of our country in the radio and satellite business—to ease, accelerate, and systematically encourage the introduction of new technologies, new services, and new business models.

As the last 40 years have shown, Luxembourg is an ideal location in order to approach the European market, due to its central position in Europe, its economic openness, and its linguistic and cultural diversity, accompanied by a stable, serious, and competitive legal framework. Certainly, there is no other domain more attractive for a European portal than for electronic trade and electronic services.

The government is strongly determined to make Luxembourg one of the best epicenters of information and telecommunication technologies in Europe and in the world. Some big names in e-commerce have already made their way to Luxembourg and have positioned themselves strongly with finances and operations in the Grand-Duchy. Others even have their origin here. Therefore, in the future, we will continue to invest in infrastructure, made out of steel or fiber optics. Therefore, we will continue to pursue a modern and appropriate legal framework. And therefore, we will continue to react quickly and flexibly to new situations. Due to this, Luxembourg will continue to attract more and more IT experts. Their language will, nevertheless, remain strange to many people, and the problem of "It will take one year" or "It will cost one million" will continue to generate frustration.

With his book, Claude Roeltgen has succeeded in depicting the IT world in understandable words—both for non-IT experts and those for whom IT is their daily business. Hence, he has chosen possibly the most intelligent form of courting for understanding: to help laymen understand better.

As he succeeds in doing this also in an amusing way, his book is much more than only a compulsory reading for concerned persons.

Appendix 3 - Interview Computerwoche 29/2007 with Dr. Resch

COMPUTERWOCHE

"Software as a product is extremely immature."

CW-editor Christoph Witte talked to Andreas Resch, CIO at Bayer, about his expectations towards the software industry. Resch criticizes strongly.

CW: Do the software providers fulfill your product expectations, or are they usually far behind?
RESCH: Let me begin by saying that I talk from the perspective of the users and I don't criticize a single software provider, but I rather comment on the state of a sector or, better, the services this sector represents. Having said this, I need however to state that users do buy catastrophic software. There's probably no other industry where companies cooperate with providers over such a long period of time

and still see such a bundling of imponderability, quality problems, unwanted performance consequences and erratic financial conditions than the software industry.

On the other hand we, the users, depend extremely upon those same providers. To illustrate this: there's probably no other sector where a company couldn't break with an important supplier within a time period of one or two years. When it comes to software, this is different. Looked at it empirically, companies rarely succeed in doing this faster than every ten years. They are stronger tightened to software providers than to any other supplier.

Software as a product is still extremely immature; it has however a very innovative image – everything is possible with software! On the other hand it hasn't had nearly the same explosion in performance as we have seen with hardware in the last few decades. In the companies, software continues to be shipped to us with unexpected deficiencies.

Even with reputed standardized software suppliers we experience serious deficiencies in the process of technical updates which we are unprepared to handle. By no means does software fulfill the expectations that purchased products in other areas, like in the industrial environment, do.

This is also one of the reasons why the IT-management in the user companies is constantly on the defensive; The IT is essentially pinched in a bench vise between the glossy promises of the software providers – everything is possible – and the as much illusory and disappointed expectations of the users.

CW: How do you proceed when there are technical deficiencies? Can you claim damages against the providers or impose penalties?

RESCH: This needs to be looked at pragmatically. Because of the tight bond between provider and user, conflict management happens differently than in normal customer-provider relationships, where a change of the supplying source is at stake. For software we have relatively well established escalation techniques in place; both sides know that they want to work together for a longer period of time.

When it is proven that the provider is the cause for the bottleneck, then he is almost always prepared to solve the problem at his own expense. It is of course different when the detected deficiencies aren't errors but the result of user expectations being too high, or when the source of the problem is a user error.

CW: Do you consider that the product's immaturity is a consequence of the dependency?

RESCH: Of course I do. Anyone who doesn't recognize that his interaction with large suppliers is in fact only a management of dependency doesn't quite understand his part correctly.

The software industry is a very peculiar sector. It is characterized by an extremely low-key force, yet we see very strong monopolistic tendencies. Trends comparable to that of the aviation or arms industry. What are your choices in the ERP-area – or in groupware – when you are middle-sized or a large company? To dare choosing besides Exchange or Notes requires a quite high readiness to assume risk.

Therefore, where enterprises choose their software, the situation is often characterized by monopolies. The user, who pretends to be acting in a buyer's market, is naïve. Fundamentally, we manage dependencies.

CW: Would the products be better if it were a buyer's market?

RESCH: I don't think so. You can think what you want about Microsoft what you want, but the fact that these monopolistic structures allow the providers to create standards is also something quite positive. These standards also allow for further modularity, exchangeability of components and services; all of which are aimed at with concepts like SOA. And I am convinced that the software industry develops itself into that direction. A stronger fractionation in the provider's scene wouldn't necessarily ease the finding of agreements on interfaces and standards.

CW: But would the quality of the individual products be better if there was more concurrence?

RESCH: I am very uncertain about this. The actionism of announcements is always the bigger the announcement, the stronger the competition is. The resulting consequence is that companies want to launch their products at an earlier target date. This doesn't necessarily raise the quality. Luckily, there seem to be some companies shifting their focus again to Quality First. They prefer this long-term principle to the quick-and-dirty solutions, which of course have a substantial advantage from a sales perspective: installed software binds know-how and resources at the user's side in a much stronger way than license costs burden him. As a consequence, these license costs cause users to swap software rarely, even if he has invested in faulty software; the costs are just too high. The secondary dependency derived from a software purchase has to be rated much higher than the initial purchase price that we pay to those companies. Despite of the turnover margins being indecently high, they would be exceeded manifold by the costs of a change. This is obviously a precarious situation. It is in any case better for an IT-manager to be aware of this dependency than to negate it.

CW: What should providers urgently change in order to support the users in a better way?

RESCH: The interface is for us users the fundamental evil par excellence. We are doing quite well with individual software modules but the integration of different components with different update cycles from different providers makes our life extremely complicated. In German we call these interfaces "Schnittstellen". Translated literally the term means "cut surfaces" and rather calls for a sticking-plaster or a visit at the doctor. The word "interfaces" reveals that we in the IT-departments are barely able to satisfy the user's wish for more flexibility and compatibility. That's why the SOA-concept is so largely attractive for us. It promises to be able to win the interface-battle.

We need the providers to make easier the possibility to combine elements, a better handling of interfaces and everything related to this. We need to realize that we haven't yet developed a spontaneous feeling or an intuition for the statics of our systems. With cars or building construction, this is the case. Everybody knows that one cannot remove the supporting walls of a house without having it collapse. We know that we can't drive with a racing car over an acre. With software this is different. Sometimes even experts have big difficulties evaluating how changes will affect the functioning of a system. Here we often believe that a racing car, just because it has a powerful engine, can perfectly drive cross-country. So, what is so difficult about changing a system with numeric customer numbers into one with alphanumeric ones? After all this can be done very easily on a manually maintained file card. There one realizes that the statics of an IT-system has totally different strengths, but also more weaknesses than one would expect.

These user misjudgments lead to disappointment, as expectations regarding flexibility, convenience and ability to change software are often let down. The statics of our systems today simply doesn't allow this. The users don't understand why something can be easily changed in Excel, but the applications can't just be rewritten or the structure of the database can't be completely changed. At the same time we have very high expectations in terms of integration. This makes the systems even more complex and more inflexible.

CW: Compared to other industries, where is the software sector in terms of development?

RESCH: In its infantile stage. Compared to the life cycle of other sectors, the software industry stands at its very beginning. This is true for development and production, but also for the business market. Just take as an example the absence of a second-hand market. Find me another industry where no used products are traded.

CW: Who has to be made responsible for failing projects more often: the user or the provider?

RESCH: The largest risk factor for a software project must be identified in the project management, followed by training and organization; only after them comes faulty software. It would be totally one-sided to declare the provider as the only responsible party. In the triangle of humans, organization and technology, the latter is only one third of the whole.

CW: Can the software industry produce more flexible and better-integrated products and still operate in the same way as today?

RESCH: I am uncertain about this. It is of course conceivable that the provider landscape develops itself along the same lines as the automobile industry: a few worldwide operating providers dominating a host of sub-contractors. I can imagine this in the area of operating systems and middleware, but I have difficulties envisaging this with core applications. If ever, this could only happen in the lee of a broadly organized modularization. These days, I see more of a vertical integration. The big providers are trying to expand their operating sphere. For example SAP is trying to establish itself stronger as a leader in the area of manufacturing execution systems. The classical providers in this area strive for their place at the top of the software-stack. I believe that in the market the concepts of vertical integration are superior to the modular ones.

CW: Wouldn't a far-reaching modularization presuppose the dominance of a few providers, having the power to impose industry standards that would be mandatory for all the others if they wanted to continue to play the game?

RESCH: Concerning industry standards you address an area in which users should exert much more influence. A bundling of forces would make us, the users, much more assertive. However it would be naïve to think that such dominant providers would set standards for users without pressure. I am very skeptical whether we will ever see plug-and-play logic in our software that would allow a far-reaching compatibility of modules from different provides.

CW: Why don't the users coordinate themselves better? If large companies got together and made common requests towards the software industry, it would be possible to exercise much more influence.

RESCH: I am hurt that disgruntled users do not get organized (outside of the user groups organized by the providers). In principle, the know-how is there and the power to influence standards as well. We should do more here, especially in Germany. You may say that at this point we are just as immature as the products that we use.

CW: How long will users allow the software producers to have such high profitability margins? Is this something that will only become more bearable once there is less dependency?

RESCH: The difference between the margins of the software industry and margins in other sectors is unbelievably high. Of course, this is not the case for all providers; there are many, especially smaller providers, who can only survive at the costs of extreme self-exploitation. But it is true for the big players. If you take a look at the profitability margins of the big players like Microsoft, Oracle, Adobe, SAP, Symantec, you see that they range between 30 and 40 percent. Even when compared to my current sector of activity, the chemical/pharmaceutical industry, this seems indecently high; not to talk about the automotive industry. In the core area of Microsoft, concerning Windows and Office, the operational profitability margin is 70 percent and more. A conclusive explanation as to why software providers should continue to be allowed to keep their margins that high does not exist.

CW: Is it simply because the users put up with it?

RESCH: This is expressed too simplistically, but of course the technical dependency makes it more difficult to exercise pressure in the pure commercial sense. To put it somewhat bluntly: slaves are not so versed in bargaining.

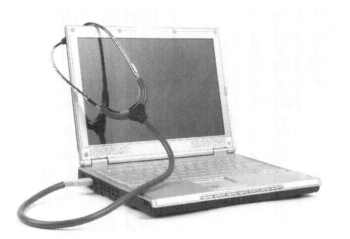

Made in the USA
Lexington, KY
18 August 2018